Please
return
materials
on time

HIGHLINE COLLEGE LIBRARY
P.O. BOX 98000
DES MOINES, WA 98198-9800

DEMCO

ISSEI WOMEN

ISSEI WOMEN

ECHOES FROM ANOTHER FRONTIER

BY EILEEN SUNADA SARASOHN

Pacific Books, Publishers
Palo Alto, California

Frontispiece: Photo of the author's grandmother,
Koriyo Takenaka Ishida, as a picture bride.

Library of Congress Cataloging-in-Publication Data

Sarasohn, Eileen Sunada, 1943-
      Issei women: echoes from another frontier / by Eileen
  Sunada Sarasohn.
          p.   cm.
      Includes index.
      ISBN 0-87015-266-1
      1. Japanese American women — West (U.S.)
  Interviews. 2. Women immigrants — West (U.S.) —
  Interviews. 3. Women — Japan — Biography.
  4. West (U.S.) — Biography. 5. Japan — Biography.
  I. Title.
  F596.3.J3S27   1997
  920.72'089'956073 — dc21
  [B]   97-24194
                                                            CIP

PACIFIC BOOKS, PUBLISHERS
P.O. Box 558, Palo Alto, California 94302-0558, U.S.A.

Contents

Foreword

The Board of Governors of the Issei Oral History Project was formed in 1973 to record histories of the Japanese immigrants who came to America between 1898 and 1924. The members of the board believed that these histories needed to be recorded as soon as possible since most of the immigrants were in their seventies and eighties. Many social scientists had ignored the issei or been frustrated by the language and cultural problems involved in interviewing them, but they all agreed that somehow their histories needed to be preserved. Fortunately, the close communal life-story of the Japanese immigrants provided a rich untapped source of information for scholars, ethnic study programs, and future generations of Americans of Japanese ancestry who needed to know of their ethnic roots.

The task of the Issei Oral History Project was to interview the Issei in their native language, translate their stories into English, and to disseminate this information. The early years of our project were financially difficult. Although the project was endorsed by the Japanese Presbyterian Conference, funding was a constant problem. Grant proposals were made to various organizations with limited success. Donations from Japanese American churches, businesses, organizations, and individuals enabled us to continue our work. The project was also able to progress because of the volunteer assistance of many dedicated persons and because of the minimal remuneration accepted by those involved in the monumental task of conducting and translating the interviews. Ours was a labor of love motivated by a keen sense of appreciation for the contributions of the issei pioneers to our lives.

Since May 18, 1973, when the Board of Governors held its first meeting, much has been accomplished. The original goal of taping one hundred interviews was doubled; all two hundred have been translated into English, and the valuable tapes have been properly stored in the Sacramento History Center Archives. To the best of our knowledge, our collection of issei interviews is the largest in existence in the Japanese language. The project has also supported the publication of three books, produced an exhibit, participated in workshops to share interviewing techniques with other ethnic communities, and had members lecture not only to the Japanese American community but also to academic organizations and the general public. The board is especially indebted to its editor, Eileen Sunada Sarashon, for her work in producing two volumes for the project: *The Issei: Portrait of a Pioneer* and *Issei Women: Echoes from Another Frontier*; the latter being the Issei Oral History Project's final publication.

Having worked together toward a common goal for more than twenty years, members of the board have formed lasting friendships. We appreciate the dedication, talents, and contributions that each has made to the overall success of our project. We also acknowledge that our success would not have been possible without the support and assistance of others. We are proud of our accomplishments and grateful that we had the opportunity to contribute to the preservations of the issei legacy and its role in American history.

OSAMU MIYAMOTO, D.D.S., M.S., F.A.C.D.
Chairperson, Issei Oral History Project, Inc.

Author Notes and Acknowledgments

The eleven life stories used in *Issei Women: Echoes from Another Frontier* were selected from the Issei Oral History Project's library of over 200 interviews. These eleven interviews were chosen because they reflect the broad range of experiences and attitudes common to most issei women, and because they contain the detailed recollections that personalize and enhance a story. Varied geographical distribution and urban/rural location were also among the criteria of choice, since employment opportunities and life-style are influenced to some degree by those factors.

Although most issei are minimally conversant in English, all of the interviews were first conducted in Japanese and then translated into English. The use of translations in any work poses specialized problems, especially when the work proposes to study subtle changes in cultural determinants over a period of time.

In conversations among Meiji-era Japanese immigrants, a speaker may make a statement and then wait for a response. Instead of a flow of words and the offer of a similar incident from a listener, there is instead a knowing nod, or a slight inhalation of breath and an "Oh, yes, so that was what happened." This common response indicates that the listener has remembered a similar personal experience, empathizes, and acknowledges that he/she has embellished the speaker's words with a personal experience. It is only because Japanese culture was so homogeneous and the code of morals and ethics so thoroughly understood that this development in language was possible.

To the Western observer, Japanese speakers seem to understate their experiences, and their conversations are sprinkled with rhetorical idioms that are the products of a unique Japanese cultural consensus. Many of these idioms require lengthy explanations, as opposed to word-for-word translations, for two reasons.

First, there are no English equivalents; and second, in addition to translation of the spoken words, a translation of what is not said is necessary. The surface simplicity of the Japanese language and its use of rhetorical idioms are indicators of the use of omission as a means of communication. English is a language of overt expression with very little use of negative space, silence, or omission, as a language tool. In Japanese, the spacing of omissions and recognition of what is omitted is extremely important.

Whenever possible in the text of *Issei Women*, the idioms and the expressive omissions have been filled in with commentary; but in order to retain the flavor of the language and the personality of the speaker, the author has attempted to simplify the commentary as much as possible. Some of the more common Japanese phrases are transliterated and a limited translation is included. It is beyond the scope of this work to provide detailed explanations, but the transliterations may help those readers who wish to explore the fascinating differences between English and Japanese.

The Issei Oral History Project, Inc., is a nonprofit organization whose major goal has been to record the personal histories of the issei before they were lost to time. The Project's library of issei interviews is the largest collection of its kind in existence. In 1969, Heihachiro Takarabe, the Project's director, Dr. Thomas Swift of California State University, Sacramento, and Dennis O'Brien prepared a structure and outlined a set of goals for the Project. O'Brien, previously an interviewer for the foreign affairs section of the Kennedy Library, also provided professional advice for the Project's questionnaire and for processing the tapes.

The academic community had made several attempts to organize oral history projects in Japanese communities, but none produced interviews with the depth and candor of those completed by the Issei Oral History Project. Between 1969 and 1979, the Project, with meager funding but with enormous reserves of dedication and commitment, interviewed West Coast issei in California, Oregon, Washington, and Nevada.

Initially, the Project used a team of bilingual interviewers, but after reviewing the first tapes, several important decisions were made to improve the quality of the interviews. First, Takarabe recommended that the issei be approached through a local community representative, in particular, a clergyman or relative rather than by an unknown Project interviewer.

As a bilingual immigrant himself, Takarabe, though several generations younger than the issei, was sensitive to the concept of *tanin* or outsider. The Japanese classify everyone as an insider or an outsider, depending on the situation. Even members of the same family may be outsiders in some circumstances. Most of the interviewers would never be classified as insiders. Consequently only those views and attitudes considered "community accept-able" would be shared, and the interviews would be of minimal value.

The interviews conducted by Takarabe were the most success-ful by far. Because of his respected position as a clergyman in a Japanese American church, Takarabe was accepted as an insider by the issei. Aside from his excellent objective qualifications, Takarabe was simply a gifted interviewer, whose careful and patient observance of form and customs allowed his entrance into an issei household, earned him acceptance as a trusted family friend or relative, and eased anxieties and concerns about shared confidences. The Issei Oral History Project's Board of Governors asked that Takarabe personally conduct as many of the interviews as possible.

The Project's board also decided that control of the Project must remain with the Japanese community. In the process of seeking funding, it became obvious that affiliation with an academic insti-tution would be a distinct advantage. The issei, however, needed a personal point of reference to accept an institution as an insid-er, and there was none. It was decided that no amount of funding could match the loss of candor.

Translations of the interviews for work sponsored by the Issei Oral History Project continued for several years after the inter-viewing had been completed. Japanese is the native language of the translators, who are bilingual and have lived in both Japan and the United States.

I am deeply indebted to the Issei Oral History Project's Board of Governors for their continued support while I worked on the man-uscript for *Issei Women*. Osamu Miyamoto, who has served for several years as the Board's president, was responsible for solicit-ing much of the funding for the Project's work on *Issei Women*. Asako Tokuno, president in the Project's formative years, helped maintain the Project's focus through the years, a most difficult task that she managed with intelligence and care; and Saburo Masuda's advice and perspective have been of great value. Joyce Honda lent her secretarial and organizational skills, and Michiyo Laing offered her financial expertise to complete the many busi-ness-oriented tasks.

Heihachiro Takarabe, the Project's director, leaves his indelible imprint on any work that uses the Issei Oral History Project's collection of interviews. His foresight, energy, and commitment were responsible for the Project's modest beginnings in 1969. When the manuscript for *Issei Women* began to take shape, Hei kindly read it in its various forms and offered invaluable advice, as well as constant encouragement.

My thanks go also to Howard Sarasohn, Sara Keiko Sarasohn, David Sunada, and Dr. Kenneth Owens, who read the manuscript at various stages and provided excellent critical comments.

My deepest gratitude is extended to the issei women whose life work provides my life and the lives of so many others with a strong, secure foundation. The life stories of these remarkable women reveal their role in the continuous building of American life.

EILEEN SUNADA SARASOHN

ISSEI WOMEN

Prologue: The Setting

Although they traveled across the Pacific Ocean to their destination and were born and raised during the Meiji Era (1869-1911) in Japan, issei women consider themselves pioneers of the American West. In its original context "issei" meant first-generation immigrant, but as these Japanese immigrants lived their lives, "issei" has garnered the important addition of "pioneer" to its meaning.

Raised to be demure, submissive, feminine, and even coquettish, totally dedicated to family and children, issei women lived in a Japan that confined them to a domestic world with no status, little power, and few opportunities. As adults they seem to have functioned with an extreme sexual dichotomy. The elderly issei woman seemed subdued, extremely polite, soft-spoken, acquiescent, tidy, hard-working, and modest. Years of childhood training, though tempered by emigration and other circumstances, preserved these characteristics; yet the same issei woman whose first instinct was still to bow rather than shake hands in greeting and whose words of praise were rarely self-directed, declared with confidence and pride gained over decades of hard work, persistence, and sometime simple endurance, that she was an American pioneer. Issei women saw themselves as pioneers who carved new lives for themselves in the American West in a very different but no less important context than those who crossed the Great Plains in covered wagons.

Who was this woman who declared herself a pioneer despite the dichotomy between her strict, disciplined rearing circumscribed by the Meiji code of conduct and her success as a pioneer woman?

The historical setting provides some clues to direct this identity search for the issei woman, but it is the personal recollections of these women that are the most revealing. Their life stories, offered after age provided the leisure and perspective, as well as the freedom, to express emotions, reveal that as children they were adept students of Japan's Meiji Restoration.

The Restoration began in 1867 when Emperor Meiji took back the traditional powers of the emperor after his armies defeated the last of the Tokugawa shoguns. The Restoration was initiated by the disruptions caused by Commodore Matthew Perry's opening of Japanese trade to the West in 1853 and involved rapid, massive changes in the economic and political structure of Japan. Although these changes were significant, it was the Japanese commitment to a spiritual and moral rejuvenation that was the primary focus of the Restoration. As a result, the monumental changes of this period were classified as the Meiji Restoration rather than the Meiji Reformation, because its primary objective was to maintain centuries-old Japanese integrity against the influence of Western nations.

A new Japanese leadership, mainly the younger samurai (warrior class with specific code of ethical conduct), believed that Western civilization was superior in technology, science, and trade, and consequently established Japan on a course of modernization in those areas; but they concluded that Japanese culture and ethical values were superior to anything offered by Western civilizations and launched reforms to reeducate the Japanese in the old values.

The new leadership abolished the old feudal structure by dismantling its foundation, the samurai or military class, and by instituting sweeping financial reforms. The newly established goal of universal education took longer to accomplish, but because it included the education of girls, the impact on issei women was enormous. Universal education was considered an important reform for its teaching of Western rationalism and pragmatism and for its teaching of the Meiji Restoration's value system.

Values were taught and preserved by encouraging *all* Japanese to adopt the basic samurai code of conduct, which reflected the spirit of the old Japanese moral code. The official dissolution of the samurai class allowed peasants and commoners readily to absorb samurai attributes and standards. In effect, the class-conscious Japanese all became samurai in spirit and action, though ancient class stratifications were maintained in the social realm.

Commoners were quick to adopt that which seemed to elevate their status. Accessibility to learning the tea ceremony, flower arranging, playing musical instruments, and enjoying the *no* drama – all prerogatives of the samurai class – served to inculcate samurai values as well. After 1870, commoners were allowed to assume family names, a privilege previously reserved for the nobility and samurai.

In Meiji Japan, the smallest unit of society was the family, not the individual. In 1871, the Meiji Restoration required all families to register according to the custom of the privileged classes, and in so doing reinforced family bonds and encouraged the individual's acquiesence to family will. Because individuals were legally registered by household, the existence of an individual was based on his place in a family – eldest son and heir, youngest daughter, eldest sister, et cetera. The Meiji woman, as caregiver of the Japanese family, supervised the family's adherence to the value system and became the physical embodiment of those spiritual values. The emphasis on revitalizing the samurai code of values had such an impact on Japanese women that even today the reference to someone being "like a Meiji woman" evokes powerful impressions of extreme dedication, enormous strength of will, patient self-sacrifice, and duty to family.

The samurai code stressed work with diligence and patience. The commoner adapted this ethic to accept years of apprenticeship and internship to learn a skill or trade. Frugality was another tenet of the samurai code that was adopted as a universal value in Japan. Accepting the values of hard work, patience, and frugality, the Japanese became a nation of people who could postpone, for a lifetime if necessary, personal comfort for the gain of future generations.

A belief in and acceptance of a "natural social order" are difficult tenets of the samurai code for Western minds to grasp. Why would any person work skillfully, diligently, and even artistically when personal advancement was not an immediate possibility?

Schooled in Confucian thought, the samurai adopted the idea of a harmonious society that emphasized a natural hierarchy of classes in which each individual occupied an allotted place and worked industriously to fulfill a mission in life. If a person worked with diligence, patience, and honesty, the earthly reward might be the immense satisfaction of doing one's best; for a Japanese this would often be reward enough. The recollections of a Japanese emigrant illustrate how well these samurai tenets were accepted and valued even by the ordinary laborer.

I once knew a workman – one who was paid by the job, not by the hour – to voluntarily undo half a day's work, at the cost of much heavy lifting, just to alter, by a few inches, the position of a stepping stone in a garden. After it was placed to his satisfaction, he wiped the perspiration from his face, then took out his tiny pipe and squatted down, nearby, to waste still more un-paid-for-time in gazing at the reset stone, with pleasure and satisfaction in every line of his kindly old face.

As I thought of the old man, I wondered if it was worthwhile to exchange the delight of heart pride in one's work for *anything*. My mind mounted from the gardener to workman, teacher, statesman. It is the same with all. To degrade one's pride – to loose one's hold on the best, after having had it – is death to the soul growth of man or nation.[1]

To relate one's daily work, one's smallest task to the growth of "soul" and ultimately to the welfare of an entire nation – this belief in a natural hierarchy and the ability to see oneself in a total continuum provided a spiritual mission for every Japanese. That mission of excellence may have produced progress and even upward mobility as by-products, but they were not considered inherent results.

Japan had embraced Buddhism centuries earlier, and the Buddhist belief in reincarnation was easily juxtaposed to the idea of a natural hierarchy. Christianity received more attention during the Meiji period, as the government encouraged mission schools temporarily to supplement the small but growing number of public schools. These mission schools and colleges were used as models for the new government schools. Accepting Western rationalism and pragmatism, but maintaining the Confucian emphasis on moral education, the public schools became purveyors of spiritual and cultural attitudes, as well as secular knowledge.

Still, Christianity was not acceptable to the general population, who displayed harsh prejudice toward those who converted. Many Christian converts continued to revere the memories of their ancestors with visits to Buddhist temples and Shinto shrines. It was not their lack of dedication to Christianity that is evident here but the continuing need of the Japanese to integrate their lives with the past and the future to ensure a meaningful continuum.

Almost every Japanese household maintained a small shrine where daily prayers were recited to one's ancestors. In a society where each individual act was measured by whether it added to or detracted from family honor, these daily rituals were a constant reminder that one's duty to the family came before personal need, and that personal need must always be placed within the context of a collective, even historic, good.

[1]Etsu Inagaki Sugimoto, *A Daughter of the Samurai* (Garden City, NY: Doubleday, Doran & Company, Inc., 1928), p.195.

Above all, the samurai code was based on complete loyalty to the overlord and bravery in defense of honor. The commoner had lived for centuries under the sword of a feudal lord and had little difficulty transferring that loyalty to the emperor, Meiji. Service and homage to the spiritual patriarch of the nation were as imperative in the lives of the Japanese as homage to one's personal ancestors.

While promoting massive modernization in the economic and political spheres, the Meiji Restoration also successfully wove the tenets of the seemingly ancient samurai code into the daily lives of the people. Besides *shinsu*, or moral lessons, in school, the study of music, the tea ceremony, dance, calligraphy, gardening, fencing, almost anything was never an end in itself, but a means to teach values – patience, diligence, economy of money, motion, and time, filial obligation, modesty, endurance. Every facet of life seemed to reinforce the moral values of the Meiji Restoration. The recollections of issei pioneer women provide specific testimony to the pervasive influence of those teachings. Their voices echo through the years to explain how they laid a secure foundation for successive generations.

CHAPTER ONE

Reaching Back

IYO TSUTSUI

"'You must behave in a way appropriate for a woman!' my father would scold whenever I took off my geta [wooden slippers elevated on two horizontal slats] and did not put them away neatly. Since my father was a teacher," issei Iyo Tsutsui explained, "family rules were strict. What I mean is that we were raised to be disciplined."

At the age of eighty, Iyo Tsutsui vividly recalled instances in which lessons of what was appropriate, "especially for a woman," were drilled into her by both parents. Personal tidiness was among traits of female propriety to be practiced. All Japanese girls were taught to place their geta neatly and to be careful that their clothing was never loose. "If my tasuki [a sash to tuck up kimono sleeves] was on the floor," Iyo said, "Father would comment sternly, 'What is this?'" The virtue of tidiness was extended to the entire household. Sliding doors were closed immediately after opening, and all utensils and objects were replaced immediately after use. Although boys were taught to be orderly, it was the girls who would as women be ultimately responsible for order within the home. As a result, household tasks were assigned only to girls, never to boys.

"Father was a very precise, orderly person," Iyo explained. "If he read newspapers, he would fold them neatly. I was taught how to arrange things in an orderly manner, so I am very good at that.

"Even now I teach my children. I say, 'If you keep throwing things in the closet, you will not have enough space. If you arrange things neatly, then you can put a lot of things in there.' I live with my children and grandchildren, and I know that they don't like to have their mistakes pointed out and corrected. They say, 'There goes Grandma again!' However, I care for them. That's why I say these things. This is what my father taught me." Iyo considered discipline so important that she declared, "This is [part of] the legacy [of discipline] which I want to leave for my children and grandchildren."

Another aspect of Iyo's pervasive discipline included economy of time and materials, which was an extension of the samurai tenet of frugality. "I learned about economy of time and materials from my mother," Iyo declared. "Mother, the daughter of a farmer, was most careful about economy because she had many daughters. If I made a mistake on a sheet of writing paper and threw it away, my mother would scold me severely and point out, 'There is more space on it for you to write.'

"If I was sent on an errand, I was not to come back empty-handed. There had to be something that I could bring back. We lived in the countryside and had to burn wood, so I could come back with a piece of firewood if I was alert, or bring some water from the well. This is the way I was raised." So ingrained were these lessons of frugality that Iyo added, with feeling, "When I see my own children wasting things, my heart aches."

Although every aspect of life was prescribed, none of the rules were arbitrary. Their purpose was to produce the Meiji woman, a woman who embodied the essence of the Japanese spirit.

Proper behavior for a Japanese woman included a sense of modesty, which was reflected in body language and speech. Her voice was soft, her manner reticent, never aggressive.

Courtesy was a trait taught to both boys and girls, but for girls, courtesy also meant deference to men and male siblings. Girls were taught to bow lower to men and boys who might be their social equals, and proper body movement was also a measure of courtesy. A Japanese girl learned to complete many tasks in a sitting position because it was discourteous to rise above a guest. A Japanese girl was not allowed to be outspoken. "If I talked back to my father," Iyo said, "he would throw a piece of firewood at me. I suppose my parents wanted us to form good habits; that's why they were so strict," she explained. Yet Iyo also discovered that her father admired her outspoken tendencies. "Still, when my mother complained to him that I had a temper, he told her, 'A person without a temper will not succeed! Children who are quiet and don't bother their parents cannot get ahead in society.' I overheard this and thought, 'Well, it's all right to have a temper.'" And with this unexpected approval, Iyo maintained a spirited sense of self throughout her life.

"Papa once said, 'You don't need to be timid if you are right and speak the truth.' If you are wrong, then you should be ashamed. I believe that. Sometimes I might sound very arrogant, but when I feel I'm right, I will argue with anybody."

Iyo recalled the difficulty she had with certain household tasks, but she knew the fact that a chore was distasteful was not an excuse to avoid it. Such self-indulgence was not tolerated. A girl was taught that household tasks must be completed before she could retire for the evening. "I really disliked sewing," she said. "One evening I was reading a book and I became very sleepy. My mother said to me, 'Girls should not be like that. Tonight you should remove the stitching from your father's kimono. You may go to sleep as soon as you finish.'

"I had been feeling very badly about my poor habits, so I said to myself, 'Tonight I'll keep myself wide awake and finish this task!' I started to remove the stitching from the kimono, but I became sleepy right away. I went to the back of the house and drank some cold water. I was wide awake for a while, but soon I became very sleepy again. I smeared mint juice over my eyes and tried to stay awake. Even then I must have fallen asleep. My mother and sisters started laughing at me and woke me up. My mother felt so sorry for me that she finally gave in and told me to go to bed.

"I had lots of sisters, you see," Iyo continued, "and [Japanese] girls had to live with their husband's families when they married. They needed to have good habits so that they would not be embarrassed." Harsh criticism, part of a new bride's life, was also a reflection of her past family training. A new bride worked hard to keep from shaming her natal family. "That's why," Iyo explained, "parents were so strict with girls."

As Japanese girls moved into adulthood, sewing lessons, music lessons, and instruction in the tea ceremony and flower arranging were taught to crystallize the emphasis on proper behavior and to add the final lesson, elegance. Flowing movements tempered by modesty and economy produced a restrained and simple elegance that was more difficult to achieve than any casual observer might realize. "My mother sincerely tried to raise me to form good habits and become a refined woman," Iyo continued. "She sent me to learn flower arranging, the tea ceremony, and other arts," but Iyo chafed under the yoke of so much formality and restraint. "She [my mother] really tried to guide me without scolding me.

However," Iyo lamented, "I just could not accommodate her wishes, even when I tried very hard.

"I was left with the impression that fathers are very strict. As I grew up, I came to understand that it was necessary for my father to be that way; otherwise we wouldn't have listened to him. My mother, however," Iyo said pointing out the contrast, "spoke to us gently. She was a very clever woman," Iyo added, indicating that she realized how important it was for a Japanese woman to maneuver discreetly to attain her objectives.

With the perspective offered by her years and experiences as a mother, Iyo quietly added, "I understand my mother's love for us, and I am truly grateful."

Though her parents were strict, Iyo had many pleasant memories of her childhood. "Every year my mother used to take us by train to swim at a beach called Agisu. We passed through three small depots, got off, and took a ricksha to the beach." Recalling the happiness these outings generated, she said, "We made friends there; it was such a pleasure.

"My mother used to take me there often. Even though I had two older sisters, my mother chose me to visit places with her because I was the tomboy and could help her out." Apparently Iyo's older sisters were too concerned about deportment to be of help on an outing to the beach. Echoing the Japanese belief that fate compensates to produce a balanced life, Iyo offered, "Helen [Iyo's daughter-in-law] used to say that it was because I had to leave my mother [to go to the United States], so instinctively, she wanted to be with me as long as she could and make me feel happy. It must have been true. She must have had a premonition.

"I had a very happy home life," Iyo continued, "and had fun with my sisters. As I was the third child, I didn't have as many chores at home because my older sisters did most of the household work." Iyo felt that she never measured up to her mother's expectations or her older sisters' examples, but she obviously assumed a share of the household chores. "I had to go to sleep early," she said, "and get up at 5:00 A.M. every morning. Before I went to school, I opened the door and cleaned up my room and did some weeding. My father used to designate how much to do. He'd say, 'Today you do up to here. Tomorrow up to there.' Because of the physical work, I was in good condition. I still work very hard.

"My father's discipline was a part of my spiritual and psychological training. *Gaman* [physical and emotional endurance] is a very important learned value," Iyo explained. "Without this, one cannot handle responsibility. When I think of these things, I understand now how much I learned from my parents." *Gaman*, especially emphasized in the rearing of girls, became a hallmark of the Meiji woman.

Though family units were the primary source of instilling values, the schools were also exacting and echoed the teaching of samurai/Meiji ethics. "I recall that the teachers were strict, too. We couldn't even go to shows. I mean movies, acrobatics, circuses, and the rest." Decrying frivolity and extravagance, Iyo recalled, "On rainy days, teachers didn't let us use nice, silk umbrellas. We had to use cloth ones, and they made us dress in cotton clothes. That's all we were allowed. It was sixty years ago," she added in explanation.

Still, children were provided with "wholesome" fun, and Iyo recalled with pleasure, "We had some happy occasions, though. School excursions, playing with friends, playing *karuta* [a card game]–those were the only things we could do. Picking *warabi* [young, edible bracken] was also fun. But that was the extent of it. Oh, yes, and clam digging, too.

"The best years of my life were those twelve years in school," Iyo declared, "but I didn't like the examinations. They were bothersome! My father used to say, 'Things enter one's brain easily, but they also leave easily, too.' Well, that's true with me. I was very quick to learn, but I also forgot quickly, especially after an examination. This was my weak point."

In school, as in other phases of life, a child was encouraged to do well, but because humility and modesty were also important qualities to internalize, ambition needed to be tempered. "My father never encouraged us to be greedy about getting good grades on our assignments. However, he said that we must do well in math, reading, composition, and geography. Music and physical education were important, but not as much as the other subjects.

"I would say," Iyo declared, "that the most important inheritance that children can receive is parental discipline to form good manners and good habits. [Years ago] when I went back to Japan for a visit, I told my sister, 'Our father was a very strict person. I don't approve of that much discipline.' Then she said, 'Well, it was good for us.' I guess I'd have to agree, because I was a spoiled child. I realize now that behind that stern manner there was love and concern. Father wanted to raise us to be good people."

Though Iyo valued the discipline ingrained in her, she realized her inherent nature moved her in other directions. She referred to

herself as "boisterous, a tomboy," and said she had constantly
sought outlets for her independence. As she continued her commentary, Iyo indicated that whatever was different had great
appeal to her. Even her ultimate religious commitment began
with an affinity for the unusual.

"Our family religion was Buddhist, Shinsu," she stated. "During
certain seasons, merchants gathered around the temple [to sell
their goods]. If I went with my mother, I knew she would buy me
something. That is the only memory I have of going to the temple, but it was when I was very young.

"Oddly enough, I was drawn to Christianity when I was quite
young. There was a Methodist church near [our house]. It had an
A-frame roof," Iyo explained to mark its unusual shape in comparison with the other village structures. "Whenever I passed by, I
heard very nice music. I wanted to visit the church, but I was
bashful. Besides, my family religion was Buddhist. After I left
Japan," she commented, "I attended church."

For Iyo and other Japanese women who valued their Meiji discipline but also needed to fulfill their more independent nature,
their education, another prod toward independence, revealed new
possibilties. A particular geography lesson had enormous appeal
to Iyo's bolder nature. "One day in class," Iyo recalled, "my teacher
said, 'Japan is a small island country with too many people. The
main industry is agriculture. If Japan does not change its course,
she will not develop. Look at England. It is a small country, but it
has many colonies and it is an industrialized nation. That's why
England is said to be the most powerful country in the world.
Young people must go abroad and develop themselves.'

"Well, even though I was a girl," Iyo stated, well aware of sexual limitations in Japan, "I was very much impressed and the words
stuck in my mind." Of the more adventuresome Japanese, Iyo
observed, "Most of the people were going to Manchuria,[1] and I
thought of going there to find a job. I didn't want to stay in a
small, crowded Japan," Iyo explained. "Within a half year after I
graduated from high school, I was asked to come to the United
States."

[1]Japan had acquired the Liaotung Peninsula in southern Manchuria in 1905
after the Russo-Japanese War.

SATSUYO HIRONAKA

Satsuyo Hironaka's life was almost completely circumscribed by early lessons of filial duty on which she continued to focus throughout her long life. "When I was a child," Satsuyo recalled with an amused chuckle, "I liked nothing better than to listen to folktales or retell them. The stories were simple but taught us to be dutiful to our parents. There was one about crows whose children let the parents perch on a tree branch first, then the children followed. There was another about bees which gathered honey to bring home to the parents.

"I was a great talker and storyteller. I even made up some stories. There was one I remember about the great, wise Washington in America who was obedient to his parents when he was a young boy. I had only four years of schooling, so [for lessons] I just have these stories of obligation to my parents."

Every Japanese child like Satsuyo was continually taught these lessons of filial duty and obligation through folktales, songs, etiquette lessons, and formal lectures in school.

KO HAJI

Issei Ko Haji also recalled learning traditional lessons of filial piety at home and throughout her lengthy formal education. In Japan, moral lessons emphasizing family obligations were considered so important that they were a central focus of the school curriculum. Ko attended elementary school in a small country village, Ashimori, in Okayama Prefecture. She completed junior high school, attended a year of girls' high school, and then entered and graduated from a school of midwifery. Most Japanese girls received only minimal schooling, but Ko, like many issei women, was better educated than the average Japanese woman.

Besides her education, Ko added, "I think I was influenced by my grandfather greatly. Both he and my father were *yoshi* or adopted sons-in-law," she revealed. Continuation of the family name through successive generations was of primary importance to a Japanese family. A family with no sons resorted to the practice of adopting a son-in-law. These adoption arrangements were usually included during negotiations for a marriage. The new bridegroom was received into his wife's family, took the family name, assumed the filial obligations in the new family, and also inherited all family property. It was virtually impossible for a Japanese woman to inherit property or accumulate personal wealth in her own name.

A Japanese marriage was not the union of two individuals, but a means to perpetuate a family's lineage. The placement of family before self was a lesson Ko lived each day. Two generations of *yoshi* was an added reminder to Ko of the importance of family lineage and filial obligations.

"My grandfather," Ko continued, "was a reputable man, and people would ask him to come into their homes as a peacemaker when they had troubles. He did not have much education, but he was a gentleman. Grandfather made me sit beside him while he made ropes and slippers during the winter months. Many times he repeated the life story of Nichiren Shonin (a Buddhist saint, founder of the Nichiren sect) and told me to believe in him. He also gave me a lot of advice. I never slept late in the mornings, because he taught me that one loses a lot if one is a late riser. He also taught me to polish the pots and pans before I powdered my nose." But Ko's grandfather was no tyrant. "He always thanked his wife for a meal, even if the menu was very simple," she explained. Believing that these early lessons were of great value to her, Ko added, "My grandfather left so much for me. I hope I leave something worthwhile for my grandchildren."

HISAYO HANATO

Hisayo Hanato was born in Hiroshima Province on April 5, 1899. Of her father, Hisayo remembered very little. "My father was a farmer," she stated. "He was not particularly strict, just an average father." It was Hisayo's mother who filled her memories and became a lifelong role model.

"My mother was a traditional woman of the old school. She had no education, but she was a very tender, loving person. When we were young children, many people used to come and confide in my mother. After their talk, my mother would often take some small token and give it to the troubled person as a remembrance. As a child, I used to wonder why the people who came to talk to mother would cry and carry on. I thought it was strange. Many were young married women who did not get along with their mothers-in-law."

As a child, Hisayo was unaware of the dynamics in a relationship between a daughter-in-law and mother-in-law. In Japan a newly married couple did not set up housekeeping themselves but went to live in the husband's family household. Traditionally the mother-in-law was a tyrant, and the young bride, often treated worse than a valued servant, could only look forward to a time years in the future when she could rule over her daughters-in-law in a similar manner.

"They [the young married women] talked to my mother about their problems," Hisayo continued, "and stayed with us overnight. When I became a young woman, I asked my mother, 'Why do those people who come to see you cry?' She answered, 'I cannot tell you because much trouble might be created if these things are repeated. There are many people who are very poor and miserable.' That's all she would tell me. As I think back on it now, I realize that my mother was a very wise and admirable person.

"Mother had experienced troubles in her own family. After her father died, the oldest brother acted irresponsibly and accumulated huge debts. Everything had to be sold to pay off the creditors. Then this brother died, leaving four children and a wife behind. They were forced to auction off everything they had.

"Well, in times like these, relatives are supposed to come around and help; however, as the family auctioned off their possessions, the bids did not go up as expected. They even served more *sake* [rice wine] to the bidders, but the bidding remained low. Later on they found out that the relatives had conspired against my mother's family so that the prices would not go higher.

"When I learned of this, I was really angry," Hisayo recalled. "I asked my mother which families were involved." Proud of her mother's attitude, Hisayo added, "My mother refused to give names. She was right about not telling. Otherwise my relationship with my cousins would be affected. After all, they were not responsible for this act."

With recollections of the Russo-Japanese War, Hisayo related another example of her mother's compassion. "I must have been six or seven years old at the time of *Nichiro Senso* [Russo-Japanese War]. The headquarters of the Fifth Division of the Imperial Army was in Hiroshima, and my hometown was only two *ri* (2.5 miles) from Hiroshima. Soldiers from all over Japan were gathered there. They had to find lodging and stayed with families nearby. Our parents also housed a few soldiers.

"It might sound as if I'm bragging about my mother again, but she took really good care of those soldiers. If they left for active duty at night, we stood by the roadside with *chochin* [paper lanterns] to see them off. One of the soldiers who stayed with us used to call my mother *okasan* [mother]." Hisayo revealed that when he left, he performed one of those simple acts that the Japanese reserve for extraordinary personal respect. "He stepped out of line, bowed his head to my mother and said, '*Okasan*, I must be going now. Thank you for taking care of me.' Unfortunately," Hisayo added, "he died in action."

"As I think about all these things, I'm very impressed by my mother's character and her wisdom. She was such an outstanding person, even though I am such a foolish and limited person."

Hisayo's childhood memories, like Iyo Tsutsui's, were filled with happy recollections of festivals, picnics and school field trips. "I went through *koto shogako* [the eighth grade]. I didn't like arithmetic but enjoyed reading and composition. I particularly liked history. I liked *shushin* [moral lessons] very much. *Oyakoko* [filial piety] was the most important lesson taught in school," she affirmed. "Later I went to a sewing school and learned many things there. I also learned the tea ceremony and flower arranging. These were all considered necessary in a young woman's education," Hisayo explained, because they instilled further the lessons of orderliness, importance of place, and self-discipline, as well as grace and beauty.

The emphasis on moral lessons and the constant example of living with such a compassionate mother affected Hisayo, who internalized these influences at an early age. "There was a student in my class," she recalled, "who was a member of the *shin heimin*. *Shin heimin* are considered the lowest class of people in Japanese society," Hisayo explained. They worked at the most menial of jobs, killing animals or working with hides for a living. The designation is a remnant of the feudal caste system in Japan. These persons and their families, like the Untouchables of India, were generally shunned by the rest of Japanese society. "In those days," she continued, "we thought that we were supposed to be discourteous to a *shin heimin*. I did all kinds of mean things without thinking. When I saw my *geta* placed next to those belonging to a *shin heimin*, I used to say, 'Get them away from mine. They're dirty!' I didn't realize how much it could hurt the person.

"There was a holiday called *Chikyo Setsu* [Empress's Birthday], which we celebrated at school. We cooked rice, bought vegetables and meat, and ate together. We also had a talent show. It was such an enjoyable party that I remember it to this day. Well, the next day I said to this student, 'Yesterday, it was such fun, wasn't it!' She answered, 'Was it so?' I was very surprised and asked, 'You mean you didn't come to the celebration yesterday?' She replied, 'No, I didn't.' 'Why didn't you come? It was such fun!' She simply said, 'If I came, others would not like it.' When I heard those words, my heart sank. The lesson really struck home. I felt so badly about what I had been doing. After that day, I was never discourteous to any *shin heimin* again."

After relating her great admiration and devotion to her mother, who was a compassionate, giving person, it is difficult to imagine why a young woman so attached to her mother and enjoying her life would consider emigrating. "Japan is a small country," Hisayo explained, "even so, I had never traveled except to Shimane Ken [Province]. It was such a period, you see [when women traveled very little]. All of the photographs of America that people sent back to Japan were very beautiful. In the pictures people wore their best clothes, and there was beautiful scenery and houses in the background. I thought America was like the pictures, that everybody wore beautiful dresses. I think everybody thought as I did.

"Our town had no industries at all, so many of our villagers went to Hawaii and to the United States to work. The main reason I came to America? I don't know exactly. Many of my friends had gone, and one of my older brothers was in America. The other was in Hawaii. Also, I was a tall girl and thought America was for tall people. I did not have any great hopes or dreams of emigrating, but," she recalled, "I did want to come here."

KATSUNO FUJIMOTO

"In those days it was jinrikshas and trains," Katsuno Fujimoto began, as she recollected her happy, secure childhood in a transitional Japan, which combined the old ways with an often abrupt jump into the modern world. "We had not heard of automobiles. Once in a while I'd see a motorcycle. I guess you'd say it was uncivilized. Not much electricity, just one light bulb to a room; and we'd pull it all over the room wherever we needed it. It was so dark! And we loved to read. I used to go to the library and bring back lots of books. No wonder the Japanese have to wear glasses.

"I attended *jinjoka* [elementary school] for four years, and then I went to *kotoka* [the equivalent of a junior high school] for four years. After that I went to *hosuka* for two years. It's something like a finishing school for girls, where I learned manners, sewing, and floral arrangement." Attending *hosuka* was also a signal to families with sons that a young woman was being properly groomed for marriage. No matter what level of education a Japanese woman attained, marriage and child-rearing were considered the fulfillment of her life.

Katsuno lingered on her memories of school days. "I will never forget those happy days," she declared with renewed vigor derived from her happy memories. "I always looked forward to *kengaku ryoko* when the whole classroom went on one-day trips. We would rise early in the morning to make *onigiri* [rice balls] for lunch, and my mother would see me off. I also liked to play tennis. I played in my *geta* and my mother used to get so exasperated with me, because I would wear out a pair in a week. My mother would say, 'There must be *nata* [hatchet] under your foot.' I was a tomboy," Katsuno explained with some pleasure at the admission. It was only in these early years of childhood that Japanese girls enjoyed the freedom to play with so few restrictions. By the time Katsuno had finished elementary school, she would be expected to conform to a rigid code of conduct that was formalized in etiquette and morals classes. "I had few difficulties as a child, although my father was a terrible drinker. You see, father was a good businessman, but in Japan the transaction of business is always done over *sake* [rice wine]. When he'd come home at night, he would be in such a state of drunkenness that my mother would be in tears as she cared for him. She would tell me to pick a husband that didn't drink, gamble, or smoke. But my parents were both good people who loved children dearly. They gave me everything I needed."

Katsuno recognized that though her father had caused his wife much grief, he was not only a loving parent but also one whose ideas were an enormous influence on the unusual direction her life would take. "My father was *shinpoteki* [a progressive, modern person]. He did a lot of business traveling and wanted to learn about new things. He believed in new ideas and in going to foreign countries and breathing new air. He was way ahead of his times. He believed that even a woman must study hard to be successful in the world, although my mother said a girl didn't need much education. Father kept saying that times were changing and that I should get all the education I could."

Excited by the prospects of a changing Japan, Katsuno's father foresaw a dramatic difference in the future of Japanese women and conveyed these ideas to Katsuno.

SETSU YOSHIHASHI

Setsu Yoshihashi had no strong parental influences or forceful role models in her childhood to guide her, but unusual customs and circumstances molded in her a fierce determination to maintain her sense of self and later to support and sustain her own family, even under the most severe and arduous life situations. Setsu's early life was marked by what the Japanese call *kuro*, severe physical, or, as in Setsu's case, emotional hardship.

"I was born in Akita Prefecture in the twenty-eighth year of Meiji, 1895. My father was the only child of an aristocratic family and was very spoiled," Setsu began. "He loved to drink. Yes, he loved his liquor. But as I look back," she continued and attempted to clear the dust off old memories, "I believe he was a very clever man. He worked at the local district government office in Akita."

Setsu could add no more detail about her father, but she unfolded a life story that explained why she knew so little about her parents. It was a tale so unusual that it could be constructed only from real-life circumstances.

"It is a tradition in Akita, an old Akita custom, to keep just the eldest son and one daughter at home--to raise them lovingly," Setsu explained in halting phrases, as though the years had not erased old feelings of rejection. "The rest of the children are sent away. It was not just my family that did this; all our neighbors did. The wealthier families would keep their oldest son and the prettiest daughter. The rest of the children had to leave the family home. Some families had as many as ten, even fourteen, children. Akita is such a place. A child was sent from home sometime between the ages of one and five years." But understanding that this custom was common practice among the wealthy families of Akita did nothing to mitigate her pain.

"I was with my mother and father for only three years after I was born, so I don't know what it's like to be loved by my own parents," Setsu continued. "I don't know too much about parental love. It was my fate in life. It's a strange fate, indeed. I seldom saw my brothers and sisters and always wanted to return to my hometown.

"I was not the only child to be sent away in my family. A younger sister and some elder sisters were sent away, too. Only the one daughter," Setsu repeated, "was raised by my parents with much love, and also, of course, my eldest brother was too." Although she remembered her surrogate mother as a loving, caring person, Setsu could not contain the painful rejection she still felt eighty years later as she repeated again and again, "Only those two were raised so lovingly and warmly. The rest of us children were sent away. I never knew my parents' love for me. And," she confided, "it was painful. So," she added earnestly, "I was determined never to be separated from my children.

"I remember vividly the place where I was sent when I left home. I even dream about it. It wasn't a prosperous family that I lived with; it was a farm family. I loved them the most of all the people I have known in my life.

"I called the head of the house 'Aba.' Aba used to carry me on her back and take me to visit my real family in town. We left my parents' hometown when I was five years old. We lived out in the country, and Aba had to go into town through the snow, mind you. I still remember those trips—the scenery and all, the snow. Aba was so kind to me." Clinging to warm memories to assuage the emotional pain, the young Setsu was already learning one of the most important lessons of the Meiji Restoration. Every Japanese girl was taught that *kuro*, or hardship, whether physical or emotional, was an integral part of life and that one must endure it with strength, dignity, and grace. The reward for enduring *kuro* might not be immediate but often would skip a generation when good fortune might grace one's children.

"When I was about six years old," Setsu continued, "I became seriously ill, so ill that no one knew if I would live or die. We used to have a statue of Kannon [Goddess of Mercy]. My natural mother went out at night to pray to this goddess and vowed that if I was allowed to live, she would give up chicken and eggs. She prayed for my recovery and made an offering. I'm very grateful to my mother for this," she avowed. "I got well after that. This is the only thing I remember about my mother's love.

"Aba had three children of her own. One was a year younger than I. They were my brothers and sisters, really, and I enjoyed my stay with them so much. I wanted to stay with them always. My elder sister had lived with them for two years before I was sent there. Later on, after we no longer lived in Aba's house, we just couldn't wait until Saturdays, when we were allowed to visit Aba and her family."

Despite Aba's kindness, the feelings of rejection remained with Setsu, feelings that were reinforced as she was placed in households that lacked nurturing and warmth.

"When I was about eight years old, I went to live with my mother's eighty-year-old aunt. She didn't have any children, took a liking to me, and so asked my parents to let me live with her. There was another elderly person living with her, but they were very lonely and wanted a child for company. I stayed with her for three years."

"None of the other children ever listened to her, but I never complained or talked back. If she said to wear this or that, I'd wear it, even if it was all worn out. She said I was so obedient that she kept me for three years." Eight-year-old Setsu had already learned to be graciously compliant and had also learned to blend into a household without asserting her presence.

At the end of those three years with her great-aunt, Setsu was sent away again. "I had an aunt and uncle who lived in Tokyo. They were childless and wanted someone to live with them. They had heard how I never complained and was so very obedient that they sent for me when I was thirteen years old." Setsu may have been hesitant to go to her aunt and uncle's home, but she was extraordinarily obliging and respectful of decisions made for her. Besides, in those days Akita was somewhat isolated and considered backward, and the invitation to live in Tokyo was viewed as an opportunity.

"No one from Akita had ever left for Tokyo to go to a girls' high school," Setsu stated. "My, that was very extraordinary in those days! The most a girl could do was to attend a prefectural high school. That was in itself a great feat. I was the envy of many people. Remember the times," she reiterated as she continued her narrative. "When I went to Tokyo, I was a third-year student in [junior high] school."

As Setsu outlined her life in Tokyo, she said of her uncle, "He was a military man," and to another Japanese, the statement explained his exacting attitudes and life-style as well. "His wife, my aunt, was notorious for her personality. She was a very stubborn, neurotic woman, shrewish and nagging as well, and no one could work for her. But, since I was patient and tolerant, everyone thought I would work out there. She never had any experience raising children and was short-tempered with us," Setsu recalled, but she continued to be respectful and as objective as possible in her assessment of her elders. "I guess a lot of it had to do with my aunt's complicated background," Setsu generously rationalized. "She was the daughter of a very much respected upper-class family. Her father was an army surgeon inspector," Setsu said in an attempt to explain her aunt, but as the memory of this moody, shrewish woman prevailed, Setsu's understanding nature was set aside and the feelings of a younger Setsu tumbled out. "She was such a cold, cold woman. And I had to stay in that household for seven long years."

The value of compliance was taught to every Meiji girl, and Setsu Yoshihashi embodied the trait to near perfection. Compliance was reflected in the physical ability to be present but appear not to exist, to blend into a room rather than to assert a presence. Girls were also taught to comply to brothers and future husbands. This ability enabled a Meiji woman to survive distasteful situations or complete arduous physical labor with emotional detachment. That detachment allowed for a conservation of emotional and physical energy; later its value to the issei woman was immeasurable.

"I had a very hard life with the Matsui family," she continued. "My aunt was so neurotic that when she didn't want to talk, she would be silent for a whole week. I would say, 'Good morning, aunt,' and she wouldn't say a word. I'd come home from school, and she wouldn't give me a snack or anything. She was that kind of woman. My elder brother lived in the Matsui household also and attended Seicho Junior High School. When I returned to Japan in 1961 for a visit, my younger sister said, 'Whenever our big brother gets drunk, he always talks about you with tears in his eyes.' My brother went through hard times with me in that house, and he saw how difficult my life was. Yet, when I came to America, I had an even harder time. My brother knew that, too, and so my sister told me, 'Yes, he always cried about you whenever he got drunk.'"

Reminiscing about her school days in Tokyo, Setsu said, "I didn't particularly like or dislike school, but because I came from Akabane, in Akita, I had a Tohoku dialect, what people call a 'zuzu' dialect; so the children used to laugh at me all the time. At first I was embarrassed and scared to go to school. The *betto* [military aide's] wife had to take me to school every day. It took a long time and much effort to correct my Tohoku dialect into standard Japanese. My aunt would not allow me to go home to Akita Prefecture, because she said she didn't want me to revert to my

Tohoku dialect and forget my etiquette." A lonely, affection-starved child must have yearned to return, but Setsu simply said without assigning blame, "I didn't go home once in seven years.

"I attended Ushigome High School in Tokyo. It's still in existence. Now it's called Seijo Koto Jogakko. It was fun going to school in Tokyo. That was all the fun I had. I remember that we weren't allowed to play any sports in those days, but we used to get very dirty playing other games. My uncle would get so angry at me because I would come home with soiled clothes," and soiled clothing, Setsu explained, was offensive to a disciplined military man.

"My uncle was a very strict man. He wouldn't let me go to the theater or the movies. One night he had a meeting and was to have been gone for the evening, so my aunt let me go to the movies with the *betto*'s wife. Unfortunately, my uncle returned early from his meeting and was waiting for us. I got called into the room and he was absolutely furious with me. I still remember that incident.

"I did not have to work after I came home from school because we had two maids who took care of the household. I had no specific chores around the house," Setsu explained. Her work was of a different nature than that of a common maid. She and her aunt worked as hostesses for the men. This was very taxing service which often involved long hours and careful attention to minute details of Japanese etiquette.

"My uncle's military friends would come over and drink and drink and drink. Since the maids had to get up early in the morning, they couldn't be kept up until all hours of the night, so my aunt and I had to keep the *sake* warm and serve my uncle's friends. Whenever he called, we had to serve." Compliant and unobtrusive but attentive to her uncle and his guests, Setsu was becoming the model Meiji woman.

Unfortunately for Setsu, the educational advantages of living in Tokyo escaped her. "Even though I completed high school, I don't have any real abilities, mainly," she explained, "because I never had the time to study. The maids would start fixing the master's dinner at three o'clock in the afternoon. His dinner took two hours to serve because he drank as he ate his dinner. Then he would go for a walk, have a beer, and his friends would start coming to visit. They knew if they went to the master's home, they could always get Japanese *sake*, or beer. They came every single night, and they drank so much!

"After all these years, I think of his revelry as a waste of money and time, but in those days, I believed my uncle was still quite honorable and intelligent." Expressing the Japanese belief that all good or bad behavior is eventually reflected in the family's fortunes, Setsu said, "In the end the Matsuis had nothing left except their ancestral tomb. They sold it to buy a 500-*tsubo* [a space six feet by six feet, the area covered by two straw mats] mansion in Tokyo. The mansion was an extravagance. But then the war demolished their possessions. They weren't able to hold on to their home, and another family took it over. I returned to Japan in 1961 and cried when I saw what had happened. The Matsui family line had collapsed.

"My aunt's mother was very kind to me. She would rub my shoulders at the end of a hard day, tell me to be patient, to take life in stride, and said that some day good things would happen to me. 'I know life is very hard for you,' she would say, 'but just have patience and endure this for now.' Imagine, my aunt's mother would try to console me. You can imagine how difficult it must have been."

During the seven long years of what amounted almost to servitude in a demanding household dominated by a moody termagant, Setsu's single act of defiance indicated that her outward manner belied a strength of character–an incredible strength of will–that was to serve her well in years to come.

"Well, when the present emperor was the crown prince, he opened a newly built palace in Akasaka. The leaders and the families of Akabane were invited to view the palace," Setsu stated. Because of her uncle's esteemed position, the Matsuis received an invitation, which was considered a great honor. Of course, formal dress, a long-sleeved kimono, was required. "My aunt and the rest of the ladies wore black kimono with white emblems, and even young children had to wear a long sleeved kimono or they wouldn't be allowed into the Akasaka Palace. My aunt said she wanted me to go and ordered a formal kimono for me from Kyoto." But Setsu adamantly refused this most prestigious opportunity.

"Every time my aunt bought me anything," Setsu explained, "she would always remind me that it was she who made the purchase. I really hated that, and she was always that way towards me. (Whenever a Japanese person does something for someone, he continually reminds you of the kindness. I think that's a bad practice. If you are kind to someone, you shouldn't have to keep reminding a person to be grateful.) I refused to go with her," Setsu declared, "because I knew she would forever remind me about a kimono that she bought especially for me." Setsu's aunt and the rest of the household must have given her several opportunities to reconsider, because she said, "I continued to refuse to go to the ceremony, and in the end I did not go. I'm surprised that I had such courage in those days. It still amazes me to know that I had such unusual characteristics.

"My aunt was indeed a difficult lady, and she was like that when I prepared to come to America as a bride. Though I told my Matsui aunt that I didn't need any kimono in America, she insisted that I take at least one and said, 'I can't send you off naked when you are about to marry.' So, she gave me a set of beautiful kimono." This custom, the gift of a trousseau from a mother or close female relative to a young woman, was usually treasured by a young bride. But Setsu needed to feel free of her aunt, who had bound her by custom for so many years. To be rid of any obligation to her aunt by keeping the clothing, Setsu said with finality, "I donated all those clothes to the Ladies' Association in Hollywood when I lived in Los Angeles.

"I lived in that household from the time I was thirteen until I was twenty. I'm glad that I didn't end up with a chip on my shoulder or a callous view of the world," Setsu stated. With the dignity that comes from inner strength she declared, "I survived living with that difficult lady without becoming bitter."

KIYO MIYAKE

Kiyo Miyake's childhood contrasted sharply with the rejection and criticism that Setsu Yoshihashi experienced. Born in Hokkaido in 1898, Kiyo Miyake was favored with a stable family life and supportive parents. "Mine is a lengthy story," she began with confidence, "because I have been in this country over sixty years." Kiyo's commentary includes a lengthy description of her father, a Christian minister, whose dedication to a Western religion prescribed a life that combined both Japanese and Western cultures.

"My father was a very quiet person. He did not talk much, but he loved young people. Because he was a person of dignity, you could not intrude on his feelings. When I brought home a report card, he'd say, 'Well, your teacher was very generous.' He was never one to say, 'Do this!' or 'Do that!' And he never criticized me about anything. However, he must have thought I was a little hasty, because I remember that as I was leaving for college, he said to me, 'Kiyoko, you are entering the dormitory now. When you carry your *chawan* [rice bowl] back to the kitchen, be careful not to break it.'

"My father wanted to create a Christian model farm in Hokkaido by the Ishikawa River," Kiyo explained. Hokkaido, the northernmost province of Japan, is harsh in climate and lacks good, tillable soil. The Japanese government, though definitely anti-Christian at that time, was anxious to encourage population growth in the area. The young, ambitious Japanese considered moving to Hokkaido or emigrating to the United States for better economic opportunities.

"A Mr. Takechi from Stockton [California]," Kiyo continued, "had a relative who donated a large sum of money for this project; therefore, he [father] was able to buy a piece of land in Hokkaido and invited newly converted Christians to the land. The farm seemed like a Puritan colony. My mother taught English to the young people, and during the winter when we couldn't work much outside, lecturers came and mother and father held various classes.

"Unfortunately the benefactor died, and my father could not continue the farm because he lacked funds." Settling in Yamada for a time, Kiyo's father increased church membership to over 100, built a church, and inspired several young men to join the ministry.

"I was attending Osaka Jogakuin [Osaka Women's College] at that time," Kiyo continued. "It was called Wilhelmina Jogakuin in those days and was one of three women's colleges in Osaka. The others were Ferris and Reiker.

"I was not that smart," Kiyo stated, demonstrating she had learned the value that Japanese place on modesty, "but," she added, "I was there on a scholarship and had to study hard.

"I remember clearly those four years that I spent living in the dormitory. It was a world of women. I studied English, music, and some other subjects. It was a mission school, so it was administered and taught by white people and was built with American funds. In any case, there were four or five American teachers. Other teachers were those who graduated from *koto shihan* [a higher normal or a teachers' college]. English translation was taught by a graduate of Aoyama Gakuin. I learned math and other subjects, but I've forgotten everything. I don't know how I ever received a diploma.

"There were a lot of pleasurable times that I remember. I participated in the school drama and I remember singing in a big choir.

"I also had a job that I liked very much. After the morning assembly, we gathered for worship, and I took care of all the details for these services. When I was a freshman, I worked with one other person. Later I worked by myself moderating meetings, helping to write speeches, and completing all the other details."

As she recalled her life while at Wilhelmina Jogakuin, Kiyo revealed what a strong and influential role model her mother was. "While I was in college, I experienced some inner struggles. My parents had moved to Kobe because my father became seriously ill. I wrote to my mother and said that I wanted to move to Kobe Jogakuin [to be near the family], even if I had to work. But I also wrote to her about my other reason for wanting to move to Kobe. I wrote about problems I had [with certain individuals]. Mother did not reply for a long time, and I grew anxious. I even thought my letter might not have reached her. Letters came to us through the dormitory mistress, who would hand them to us in the dining room. One day the mistress finally called my name, and I went up to receive a postcard from my mother. In large letters it simply said, 'Thou shalt love thy enemies!' The message was loud and clear to me.

"My mother was a very gentle, quiet person. She was the first graduate of Kyoritsu Women's High School," Kiyo added with quiet pride. At a time when educating women was not considered an advantage in Japanese society, Kiyo's mother taught her daughter the value of juxtaposing intellectual learning with the problems of daily living. "My mother was well versed in literature, and her father had a degree in literature from Waseda University. She used to tell us stories about Tolstoy and other writers as we warmed ourselves around the *hibachi* [charcoal brazier]. Mother was an idealist, and in some ways it became my handicap. She cared for my father after he became ill and also took care of many other sick people, too. Although she was a very busy person, she studied hard all the time. Whenever she had a few minutes to herself, she took out a book to read. She read all the books my father had. She also knew English, so she also read new things in English and helped my father in his work.

"One day I asked her, 'What are you going to do with your learning? You are an old woman now.' Her reply was, 'Many people have all kinds of pain in their heart [and lives]. They want to talk it out. I study all kinds of things to become a good listener.' I thought it was a very strange answer. I would have understood if she had wanted to know as many things as possible, so that she could discuss any subject with a person. But to become a good listener? Sixty years later I began to understand."

Like Hisayo Hanato, Kiyo admired her mother's facility as an informal family counselor who gave advice to young adults and even took in troubled people on the verge of nervous breakdowns. "People came to her and consulted her about many problems. When a college student came to talk with her because he was tormented by different political thoughts and did not know which way to go, my mother was able to listen to him and understand. It was at a time when communism was introduced in Japan. Some young people who came from good families were affected and that caused many heartaches. People who had nervous breakdowns came to stay with my family because my mother could handle them.

"Mother said that in order for her to be a good listener and let others speak, she had to be knowledgeable about many things. For instance, if a stockbroker came to talk with her, she could not begin by talking to him about God. That would end any possibility of conversation. She would begin with stocks in order for him to start talking. Mother met with highly educated people, as well as with the wife of my father's ricksha man or the wife of a grocery store owner who lived with a very difficult father-in-law. She also had to learn the kinds of things that could not be learned from the wives of rich men or highly educated people.

"Years later, when I was leaving for America, she said to me, 'Please become the kind of person who learns things from the people you come in contact with.'" Assessing these precious recollections of her mother as she spoke, Kiyo added, "My mother was more than a mother. She was also my teacher and my confidante." In a relocation camp some twenty years later, Kiyo emulated her mother's work when she became a case worker for the camp's social services section.

Another major influence in Kiyo's life was her advanced education. It reinforced her Christian, and therefore Western, religious training and introduced her to other aspects of Western culture. "When I was a student, I liked Millet's painting, *The Angelus*," Kiyo stated. This painting by Jean Francois Millet depicts a farmer and his wife stopping work to pray in the fields as the six o'clock bells toll. "My dream was to live like the picture, to work and be able to return thanks at the end of each day. I thought that this was the most beautiful life that I could ever have." Though Kiyo's image of the ideal marriage was one that shared work and spiritual values, she added, "However, you can't hope to match your dreams with reality. Anyway, I thought marriage in Japan was not quite right for me. I had been associating with teachers who came from America and I wanted to continue my studies even after graduating from college. I also taught Japanese to an American who was a teaching assistant and who knew a little Japanese. Because of these experiences, my thinking became very Westernized."

Kiyo's assessment of her situation was precise and correct. Being better educated than the vast majority of Japanese women in a country that did not value educated women was already, by Japanese standards, a liability. That she was a Christian set her apart even more, and then to admit that she embraced Western values meant that her prospects for the kind of life she envisioned were nonexistent in Japan. Yet Kiyo was a Meiji woman, and her only vehicle for a future was marriage.

TEIKO TOMITA

Teiko Tomita's earliest recollections of her youth are memories that also reflect the importance of filial devotion, that primary constant in Japanese family life and in the character of a Meiji woman. "My father," she began matter-of-factly, "was drafted to fight in the Sino-Japanese War and in the Russo-Japanese War. I was not born at the time of the Sino-Japanese War, but I was six years old and had begun the first grade when my father went to fight in the Russo-Japanese War; so I do remember that very well.

"In those days we had a custom called *oyakudo mairi* [saying one hundred prayers]. A member of our household went to the shrine every day and prayed to have our father come back safely. Even though I was a very small child, I also went to the shrine, and as I prayed, I walked around the shrine one hundred times. It was very difficult for me to keep count of the prayers, so my family put one hundred dry beans in a bag. Each time I walked around the shrine and offered the prayer, I took one bean out of the bag and placed it on the floor. I repeated this until all the beans were taken out of the bag.

"My father came home safely," Teiko stated, believing that her devotion was rewarded, "and we were overjoyed at his return. Even though ours was a small country village, we celebrated the war's end for several days. People sang songs and marched round the village.

"Father was a farmer. He had a lot of acreage, and many share-croppers worked for him. He tilled only a small piece of land around the house to raise vegetables for his own enjoyment and kept a hillside tangerine orchard. He also operated a *shi chiya* [pawnshop], and as I grew older, I helped him with the bookkeeping."

Teiko remembered her father, Mr. Matsui, as a typical domineering Japanese father figure who controlled the major events in her youth. "He was a man of very few words who frightened us with his stern looks. When he came into the house, we stopped everything we were doing. If we children were fighting among ourselves and were scolded by our mother, she would ask him, 'Papa, would you please scold them?' 'Don't fight!' was all he'd say. He never uttered an unnecessary word. Years later, when I got together with my sisters, we talked about my father and recalled that even though he never raised his voice against us, we were very fearful of him."

"Perhaps," Teiko speculated, "because my father was a man of few words, my mother was very talkative. Even though she scolded us a lot, we were not afraid of her."

As Teiko continued to describe the particulars of the Matsui family, her commentary, like issei Ko Haji's, once again underscored a social structure that emphasized male dominance and filial duty. "Because my grandparents didn't have any children," she explained, "they adopted both my mother and my father. My mother was a *yojyo* [adopted daughter], and my father was a *yoshi*." Teiko's parents dutifully fulfilled expectations. "I had eight brothers and sisters," she revealed.

Teiko's grandparents did not live in the same house as their children, but they lived nearby and were cared for by their children and grandchildren. "My grandparents retired before they were sixty years old, giving all family responsibilities to their son and daughter. My grandparents lived in a small house made especially for them. The kitchen was on the side of the house, so we had to carry meals to them three times a day on an *ozen* [a small dining table]. When they finished eating, they would leave the *ozen* out on the *engawa* [veranda]. They clapped their hands to let us know when they had finished, and we would go to clean up.

"They indulged us [grandchildren] and gave us spending money. They used to tell us, 'If you want some money, ask any time. We'll give it to you.' I was in school then, so when I needed something, I asked them to buy it for me. My grandparents died after I came to the United States."

Nurtured in a large, busy household and indulged by grandparents whose lives underscored the importance of filial devotion, Teiko gradually became a strong, self-directed person. Intense and intelligent, she was allowed to devote all her youthful energy toward the goal of becoming a high school teacher. Achievement and respect, which all Japanese parents coveted for their children, were to be her rewards.

After four years of elementary school and another four years of junior high, Teiko declared, "I wanted to become a respected person, a teacher, and for that I had to go to a high school and then to a normal school. In Nara Ken," she explained, "there was a prefectural high school called Sakurai Koto Jogakko and the Nara Municipal Normal School, which prepared students to be teachers. These two schools had good reputations and high standards, and I decided to apply first to Sakurai Koto Jogakko [and later to the normal school].

Because she was a young woman instilled with the attributes of a Meiji woman, Kiyo knew that it would be impossible to leave her home village without proper supervision. As she explained, "Both my mother and father came from Nara Ken, so I also had many relatives there." An ocean and many decades later could not erase her need to convey assurance that proper supervision had been present.

"The entrance examination was very difficult," Teiko said. "They took only one hundred students out of seven hundred applicants. Now, it's even more difficult to be accepted there. I worried a lot, but fortunately I was accepted.

"It's really odd to think that grades were the most important thing in my life then. Having good grades is not that important in real life, but at that time, getting one more point on my exam was a very serious matter. I was an honor student in school. The only recognition I received was a certificate each year, but if I could graduate with the highest honors, I would receive a beautiful prize from the school and also a remembrance from the governor of

Nara Ken. I really wanted this distinction, so I prayed that I would be the recipient."

Despite the personal humility taught to every well-bred Japanese, Teiko revealed, though with hesitation, "It's rather embarrassing to speak of it now, but I did become the top student and received those honors. The governor gave me a very good book, the biography of Ninomiya Kinkiro [a folk hero who was a self-made man]; I also received a gold lacquer inkstone case. In those days we used an inkstone box all the time. The material prize itself wasn't valuable, but I put it in a trunk and brought it with me to America when I got married." The book and the gold lacquer inkstone case were the reliquaries that prompted Teiko's memory of this most happy time in her life and continued to serve as symbols of her most important personal goals some sixty years later. "I still have them with me," she added.

"I enjoyed everything in school, but, as I said, I was very much preoccupied with getting good grades. When I look back, I feel that it was really a mistake, but there was nothing else that I wanted. I never wanted to have nice dresses or anything like that. I wasn't envious of anyone for anything. I just studied a lot. When I went back home during vacations, my brother used to tease me, saying, '*Neisan* [older sister], you are *tentori mushi* [a greasy grind].' It's so pleasant to recall those times," Teiko mused, as she reached back after years of deprivation and tragedy.

"I remember our principal," she continued. Like most older male figures in her life, he frightened her. She declared of him, "He was very frightening. We students were so afraid of him that we couldn't even speak to him. When we passed his office, we just bowed respectfully and walked by quickly.

"Our classroom teacher was a Miss Uyeda. I liked her very much. She came to our school immediately after graduating from Tokyo Women's Advanced Normal School. Even though she was a woman, she taught math. She must have been very bright.

"There was another teacher I liked. His name was Mr. Kobayashi and he taught Japanese literature. His lectures and explanations were excellent. I liked the subject very much and wanted to major in literature when I went to the women's advanced normal school.

"After graduating from Sakurai Koto Jogakko, I needed to go to a normal school to become a teacher at a girls' high school. At that time there were only two normal schools for women, one in Tokyo and one in Nara. When I graduated from junior high, my

teacher had told me that if I graduated from high school with honors, I might be chosen to go to the Nara Normal School without
taking an examination. Two such students were allowed every
year. This was another reason why I wanted to be an honor student; however, events did not proceed according to my plans.

"My mother had given birth to nine children and was very sickly from the time I was in elementary school. She suffered all kinds
of illnesses, including many abdominal diseases. I was often sent
to the village doctor for medicine. While I waited, I observed that
all the members of his household were healthy, and there was
much laughter. I wished that my family could be like that.

"Well, though I worried about my mother, I worried about
examinations even more," Teiko admitted. It is also evident that
Teiko's academic achievement was important to her father. "Once
when I went to take an examination," Teiko recalled, "my father
went with me. Even though we thought he was a fearsome man,
he was very soft inside and he worried about me. While I was taking the exam, he stood outside the classroom and read the questions which were written on the blackboard. He wrote them
down, and when we got home he said, 'All right, I'll give you the
examination again.' I gave him the answers that I had written in
school. Then he said, 'Well, I think you did very well.'"

Because every family member's achievements were considered
familial as well as individual, it was important for the sake of her
family's pride that Teiko attain her goals. The extent of her anxiety was like that of most Japanese students. "I didn't know how I
could face people if I did not pass the entrance examination for the
women's high school," she declared.

"During my first two years of high school, my mother was still
strong enough to sit up, but during my sophomore year, she
became worse." But Teiko continued her studies with subdued
concern because, as she explained, "My older sister quit high
school to take care of our mother."

Although the Matsuis were not a poor family and might have
hired a servant, attending to a sick parent was an obligation performed by a dutiful child whenever possible. "Grandmother
couldn't help much because she was very old," Teiko continued,
"about sixty-five. I'm eighty-two years old now, and I can do a lot
more than she used to do. In effect, my sister became our mother
and cooked and took care of the household chores. You see, ours
was the largest household in the village because of our grandparents and all the children; yet she managed all the family affairs.

When I went back home during the summer vacation, she used to laugh at me and say, 'You seem to worry a lot about studying, but you don't know a thing about household matters.'

"Sometimes I would help her, like when she asked me to get pickles from a barrel. We had so many people in our household that we had a special room for pickling. But there were so many barrels that I didn't know which one held what. There were cucumbers, nappa cabbage, *daikon* [a Japanese radish] and more. My sister laughed at me. She was right, you know.

"My mother's condition became worse when I was a senior. Then there was a marriage proposal for my sister. Even though she was needed at home, she got married when she was nineteen."

After graduating from the prestigious Sakurai Koto Jogakko with highest honors and being accepted into Nara Normal School, Teiko, a dedicated and conscientious student, continued to prepare for her next academic achievement. "I wanted to increase my knowledge before I entered the normal school and was taking a refresher course after graduating from high school," she explained. "Then my mother got worse and my sister got married.

"One day I received a letter from my father, who wrote, 'I am very sorry, but I want you to give up your plans to enter the normal school and come home. We need your help here. If you want to become a teacher, you can teach in a local elementary school. You don't need to be a teacher at a women's high school. Please discontinue your studies and come home, where you can still study if you want to.'

After years of hard work and concentration, Teiko was asked to abandon her personal goals. Deeply disappointed, she admitted, "I cried a lot. I thought about it over and over and couldn't sleep. Finally, I decided that I had to help my family. I was really disappointed and I cried," she repeated. "I gave up all my hopes of entering the advanced women's normal school." But as a Meiji woman, Teiko had no choice. The thought process was not for decision making. It was a means to reconcile the need to fulfill filial obligations with the disappointment of abandoning personal goals.

"A few days later I went to my teacher and told him I had to leave school. At first he simply didn't believe me. He thought that I had changed my mind and that I didn't want to study anymore. I told my teacher that I needed a few days to go home and assess the situation myself.

"While I was home, my teacher sent a letter to my father. He wrote, 'Your daughter, Teiko, has been studying very hard for the past four years. I have been helping her toward her goal, but now she has changed her mind. Please talk to her so that she will continue her studies.'

"The letter really surprised my father," Teiko recalled. But rather than use the letter to ask her father to reconsider his request, she chose to support her father, and by her actions, indicated her complete reconciliation to filial duty. "After he showed me the letter, I asked him to answer with a letter that I dictated. It said, 'I wanted to allow Teiko to accomplish her goal; however, my wife is very ill. Teiko is very disappointed because I have asked her to come home. We cannot let Teiko continue to study. Please understand our situation and accept our decision.' Before I returned to school, the teacher had received that letter. He didn't say anything more to me."

Teiko's father did not expect that such an accomplished daughter would abandon all of her academic inclinations. "From my home," Teiko continued, "I commuted to Tennoji Joshi Shihan Gakko [Tennoji Women's Normal School] in Osaka, passed the written examination and the practical teaching test, and received a credential to teach elementary school. "At home," Teiko added, "I helped with household chores, and grandmother helped some, too." It was obvious that the household tasks were not the reason she was asked to live at home, since, as she related, "I taught in elementary schools for six years." Mr. Matsui simply expected that as the eldest unmarried daughter, Teiko would assume the family position vacated by her older sister. Although Teiko had been indulged and allowed to study, she had also been taught compliance to parents and authority figures at home and in school.

Difficult as it might have been to abandon her personal ambitions, Teiko understood the importance of assuming family obligations, which she affirmed by simply stating her position in the family. "I am the second child," she said. "Besides my older sister, there is my brother, who succeeded my father. Then," she added, "came another sister, a brother, and another sister. Another brother and sister have died."

"At first I taught at a school about one and a half *ri* away from my house, and I walked to school," Teiko recollected. "Then I worked in the town of Kashiwada. I had to take a train to get there. Even though I was a teacher, I was still a young, inexperienced person, and my father felt that he still had to take care of me."

Teiko's father continued to intervene in her life, even when she was a young adult. Like all Japanese women of her time, Teiko lived in a world dominated by men. "One day," she continued, "I noticed that father was talking to the principal as I went into the teachers' office, and I wondered why he was there. I found out later that father had told the principal that the school was too far for a young woman to commute, and as a parent it was very difficult for him to let me travel that distance.

"My father was a member of the village council, so he knew about the education system and knew the inside information about schools. He had found me a position at the village elementary school and wanted the principal's permission to transfer. Without even discussing this with me, he negotiated my position with the principal. The principal acceded to my father's wishes. At that time, parents decided everything for you. It's very different from the present situation, isn't it?" she commented with no apparent memory of resentment or anger.

"This new position was close by. I enjoyed working at the village school very much and taught there about four years. I must have been around twenty-three or twenty-four years old by then."

Teiko's father and mother must also have been concerned about their daughter's marriage prospects. She was overeducated, oriented toward achievement, and her work away from home was considered somewhat improper. Whatever their reasons for restricting Teiko's living sphere, her filial duties required accession. Caught in the dilemma of a modernizing Meiji Japan, which offered educational opportunities to women, and balancing that education with the restrictions of traditional Japanese customs and mores, the young Meiji woman was challenged to reconcile the dichotomy that was created.

ONATSU AKIMAYA

The life story of issei Onatsu Akiyama, born in Hiroshima, unfolded as she unconsciously merged a Western and Eastern calendar. "I was born on September 10, in the thirty-third year of Meiji," she said. At the age of seventy-seven, with several decades and thousands of miles separating Onatsu Akiyama from her family in Japan, she continued to reflect the traditional virtues that had been ingrained in her as child.

Beginning her commentary by establishing her family's accomplishments, Onatsu underscored what Meiji women considered the source of their strength and the recipient of their most concerted lifelong efforts. "My family," she said, "had a store where we sold a variety of things such as fabrics, *sake*, and other goods.

This store has since become a large corporation which also owns at least twenty-two restaurants now. The main store had the highest gross sales on cigarettes and *sake* in the city. At one time this business was failing, but since the war these stores were brought up to prewar standards." After establishing the strength of her family background, Onatsu continued. "My maiden name," she stated with quiet pride, "is Okada. The family back in Japan is proud that the business has been built back up. I wonder if it was because my ancestors worked diligently," she speculated rhetorically, believing it to be true, and then declared, "It is very important to have respect for one's ancestors.

"Success and failure do come in waves," Onatsu reflected. "The other day I received a letter from my younger brother's wife, who wrote, 'Please rejoice with us because we were able to rebuild this store.' They must really be prospering," Onatsu added with cheerful pride. "But," she explained, "there were some rough times when my older brother managed it. Right after I came to America, the business began to decline. My older brother wrote to me and said that he had lost money in real estate but that the store was doing very well. He had gone into the *shoyu* [soy sauce] business. In order to get cheap lumber to make the *taru* [wooden containers] to store the *shoyu*, he bought a wooded area. That business venture did not go well and ended in failure; however, because the family worked diligently, they eventually were successful." Respect for the past efforts of one's ancestors and diligence and hard work to build on those efforts were among the traditional Meiji virtues that Onatsu learned as a child and maintained throughout her life.

"My father's name was Toyosuke," Onatsu recalled. Then, to indicate how well-liked her father had been, she repeated the affectionate nickname assigned to him. "People called him 'Toyo-san, Toyo-san.' He was such a popular man!" she said.

Continuing with affection and pride, she declared, "He was also a very honest man. He delivered rice by wagon to the *sakaya* [*sake* maker] or wherever, and had the responsibility to carry the cash for it. It was complicated to write checks in those days," she recollected.

In a country where literacy was still the exception rather than the rule, Onatsu said, "Father was able to write, and he was like a banker in a sense. He was the tax collector in the village and had the right to vote. In those days only persons in a specified status had the right to vote," Onatsu explained. It was not until 1925 that Japan adopted universal male suffrage.

"My father used to drink a little *sake* every night. He would invite me to drink with him, just one *sakazuki* [wine cup] though, now and then; and I learned to enjoy drinking *sake*." Obviously Onatsu enjoyed this special relationship with her father, and unlike most Japanese children she could declare, "I never was scolded by my father."

It was the unusual attributes of a mother that made a marked difference in Onatsu's life, as it did in Kiyo Miyake's. Modesty and homemaking skills were some of the characteristic traits in a good wife, but Onatsu enthusiastically described attributes usually considered negatives in a Japanese woman. "My mother was a very able woman. She could do anything that a man could do," Onatsu declared. "For example, she was able to climb up on a roof and nail down shingles. The only thing she couldn't do was write. But she did everything else. My husband used to tell me, 'Mama, you aren't worth the little finger of your mother.'

"There was a time when one of mama's nephews went to Korea to teach *kendo* [Japanese fencing]. My mother went along with him and stayed for three years. She went because her nephew didn't have a wife yet." In those times it was common practice for a woman relative to accompany a single man and run his household. Recollecting her mother's resourcefulness and aggressiveness, Onatsu related, "While she was in Korea, she went around the nearby villages and taught farmers how to make *mino* [a straw raincoat] and *mushiro* [a thick straw mat used to dry grains], *goza* [a thin straw mat], and *waraji* [straw sandals]. People used to dry red beans on the bridges, and pebbles got into the beans. When I bought *azuki* [red beans], sand used to be mixed in it. My mother taught the people how to make *mushiro* so they could dry beans on it. After that, there was no more sand or pebbles mixed in with the beans.

"I know my mother was a very able, resourceful person," Onatsu pronounced. "She was also diligent and kind. Whenever a `beggar came around for a handout, she would feed him. That really impressed me."

Onatsu also stated that, like a typical Japanese mother, "My mother was also a strict person. I took sewing lessons for six years and often had to go shopping for fabric, thread, buttons, et cetera. It was only five *cho* [blocks] to the store, and mother knew exactly how long it would take me to walk it. When I was delayed, she would come looking for me and be angry. She was very short-tempered.

"The most memorable aspect of my childhood, I suppose, would be that everybody took care of me so well. When I was small, my mother used to take me to visit shrines, but I had a bad leg and would get so tired that I couldn't move. Then I would sit down and ask my mother to hire a ricksha." As the only daughter in a family with three children, Onatsu recalled being pampered. "I was somewhat sickly, and my older brother used to carry me home from school on his back when it snowed or rained. When I got home, they had hot water ready in a washtub and soaked my feet."

Though very young Japanese children were indulged as much as possible, it was usually the male child who continued to be pampered. Rarely was a female child treated so favorably, and Onatsu basked in the attention. "My older brother was a very kind, gentle man," she continued. "I used to go to see shows, and he would take me and later pick me up. After he got married, my sister-in-law would go out early in the morning to gather up grass for the horses. My brother used to tell me to get up because his wife would be coming home soon from early morning work. Then he'd pull the *futon* [Japanese comforter] off of me," she said, recalling the wonderful, warm memories of a loving brother. "I was such a spoiled girl! Later on, when I came to America, I really regretted the fact that I was so spoiled," Onatsu admitted, "because I had a difficult time adjusting.

"I liked school very much and was well liked by my teachers. I used to go over to the house of one of my teachers to eat dinner and sleep there. These are the things," she reflected, "which I remember best."

Of her days as a student, Onatsu remembered, "I wasn't good in history because I didn't have a good memory, but I was very good at *soroban* [abacus]. It was my best subject. I used to stand in front of the class and call out numbers for addition problems as I worked them on my *soroban*. I can still do it. When I go to the store, I can calculate a lot faster than they do on machines.

"I got A-pluses in drawing and calligraphy. My older brother was also very good at it. He was asked to write words on gravestones. He was that good! My younger brother was also very good at calligraphy. He still writes to me with very neat handwriting.

"I graduated from the eighth grade. (I think my husband did the same.) In order to go to middle school," Onatsu explained, "we had to take an entrance examination. I felt that it would bring shame to my family if I didn't pass; so, instead, I asked my parents to send me to sewing school." A male student was encouraged to expend greater scholastic effort to sustain family honor; usually for women, the opposite was the case.

A resourceful Onatsu recognized that she had other valuable skills and capitalized on them. "I attended that school for over a year. Then I worked as a dressmaker and made a lot of money.

"I sewed garments like those for a man who pulls a ricksha. The pants looked like jodhpurs, and I made various kinds of shirts, similar to what we have now. I must have made at least six pairs like that each day. It was a long time ago," Onatsu mused, "sixty years ago, that I did all those things."

"I charged fifteen *sen* [about half a cent] for each pair," she continued, "and twenty-five *sen* for those which required more time and more difficult stitches. I kept a tally, and at the end of the month, I added the figures up, gave half to my mother, and saved the other half for myself in the bank. In six years I accumulated a little over 800 *yen*. Big money in those days! That's what I saved after buying thread and everything I needed for my business."

Though sickly and pampered as a child, Onatsu matured into a healthy young woman who developed important business skills. She enjoyed the monetary results of her work and took pride in using her money to help the family. "There's an interesting story concerning these savings: I had this sewing money that nobody knew about. I made bank deposits when no one was around, so none of my family knew about it. There was a very honest man in our village by the name of Mr. Kakuichi Harada. When I left the village for America, I asked him to keep that money for me, and told him that I would be back in three years. But it was nine years before I was able to return.

"When I finally returned for a visit, my father cried and said, 'I'm very sorry. I've done something wrong.' I said, 'I don't know what you are talking about, unless you explain.' Then he said, 'When Toichi [the oldest brother] failed in business, Mr. Harada told me that he had been holding 800 *yen* for you. He could not keep it a secret any longer because we were having such a difficult time.' I said to my father, 'Please don't feel badly. It was money I earned before I married into the Akiyama family, and I'm glad that it helped you.' Then he said, 'Thank you for understanding.'"

The ability to make enough money to contribute to the family expenses and to save for herself prompted Onatsu toward independent and almost shocking behavior for a young Japanese woman. "I felt that there was no future in our family business," Onatsu declared with confidence, "because there were twenty-two stores like ours in the village. That's why," she explained, "I went to Kobe for nine months and learned how to make men's garments. I lived with an aunt while I was there. I was eighteen when I went there the first time," she continued; then, almost casually, Onatsu revealed, "and I didn't have my parents' permission." Her aunt and her family must have been in a state of shock at her behavior. "When my aunt asked me why I didn't obtain permission first, I said, 'If I hadn't left home, my older brother would leave to go into the army. Then I'd surely have to stay home.'" Accustomed to having her own way, Onatsu accurately calculated that leaving so abruptly would ultimately produce the desired result complete with parental permission. "Well, they [my parents] promised me that when my older brother came home from the army, I could go to sewing school in Kobe. My aunt was my witness to this. When my brother returned two years later," she declared with satisfaction, "I went back to Kobe."

What her family thought of such willful behavior, Onatsu never revealed, but her personal ambition, determination, and devotion to her own family would serve her well in the long and trying years ahead.

SHIZU HAYAKAWA

"My name is Hayakawa, Shizu," the issei woman began, formally stating her name in the Japanese custom with last name first. "Hayakawa, Shunkei was my husband's name," she continued. I was born in the thirty-second year of Meiji, one year before 1900 in Fukuoka Ken, Kyushu.

"I graduated from higher elementary school. That means six years of elementary school plus two years more." For some Japanese girls, education provided a means temporarily to transcend the strict limitations of their society through the introduction of new ideas, but this was not the case for Shizu. Her memories of school were not happy ones. "I remember that my teacher was a very difficult, strict man. If we did not remember [our lessons], he would use his ruler to hit things, like the desk, and also kick with his feet.

"There were not too many subjects–*tokuhon* [reading], history, and science. Those were very difficult. And girls were taught how to sew," Shizu added. "We had a few track meets, but I did not like them very much.

"I came from a poor family and couldn't play too much with my school friends. When I got home from school, I would deliver milk and baby-sit.

"Though my parents were milk producers, my mother didn't let me drink milk," Shizu confessed, "because she was afraid that I'd turn into a cow!" With other Japanese sharing similar superstitions, it is understandable that, as Shizu said, "In those days there were not too many people who drank milk. Half of our milk was *shintei* [free samples]. This was to encourage customers. In nearby Yahata there was a steel mill. To get mill workers to drink milk, we delivered samples all around the surrounding neighborhood to Tobata, which had a large residential section.

"My father said that we must make the Japanese people drink milk or the country would never stand on its own. This was his own, unique idea." Equating milk consumption with modernization was faulty logic, but Shizu's father did impart the importance of being committed to modernization.

Unfortunately for Shizu, like other Japanese women whose fathers or husbands were possessed by some ideal or misguided vision, her lot was to work toward another's goal.

"Our house and dairy was at the bottom of the mountain," she recalled. "From the time I was eight years old, I delivered milk every morning on mountain roads before I went to school. It took more than thirty minutes to walk to school over the narrow roads. Then, when I came back from school around noon, I made more deliveries. We sterilized the milk. And in those days we sold hot, not cold milk, like here, so we'd have to run to get the hot milk to our customers. If the milk had cooled too much, the customers would really get mad at us.

"When I returned home from school, again I'd deliver the milk through those mountain roads. By the time I got home, it would be dark." Shizu volunteered no words of complaint, though the work must have been difficult. She simply added, "Because my life was such as it was, my childhood days were not very happy."

The business was understandably not very successful, and Shizu said, "When my mother passed away, we let the business go."

Despite her less than pleasant memories of school and the hard work involved in the milk business, Shizu never seemed bitter, for she, like Setsu Yoshihashi and other Japanese girls, learned that *kuro* or hardship was an inevitable, and even valuable, part of life that helped to build character.

Shizu accepted her burdens as a child without complaint and simply endured. The value of *gaman* or endurance learned as a Meiji child became a hallmark of the issei woman. Shizu never blamed her parents for her lot in life and spoke of her father with respect and gratitude. She saw his life as a model of the Japanese cultural adherence to duty and obligation and recognized that he, too, suffered *kuro* with endurance. After her mother's death, Shizu said, "My father made a lot of sacrifices. He did all kinds of work, because he had to look after and feed my brothers and me. There were nine children in all.

"My father," Shizu continued, "found out that he had intestinal cancer. In those days it was said that only three out of a hundred people who had intestinal cancer would live, but his physician, Dr. Noguchi, took a chance and operated on him. The doctor said that my father would be doing well if he lived three days because he had to look after so many children, but father lived until after I married and came to the United States. He wanted to come to America, too, but alas," Shizu added sadly, "he could not. He died three months after I left Japan."

MIDORI KIMURA

Adaptability, that quality so essential to survival in Japanese society, was a reliable constant in Midori Kimura's life since early childhood. "I was born in 1897, the thirtieth year of Meiji," Midori began. "I'm seventy-seven, and though I might look vigorous, I do have some aches and pains now and then," she admitted as she laid the groundwork for her life story.

"I was born in Nagano *Shi* [city], Nagano Ken [prefecture], Japan. It's a very cold place, very close to Niigata Ken, where I grew up and where the famous Zenkoji Temple is located. It is a temple of the Jyodo Shinshu sect, and they say that all the Jyodo Shinshu believers must make a pilgrimage to that temple once in their lifetime.

"There was a dark room in the basement of the temple where the pilgrims went to pray. The room was like a maze, and people used to go through the paths as they said prayers and groped their way to the exits. They believed that if you made your way through this dark path, you would be happy. I am embarrassed to admit that when we went through the maze, we used a flashlight."

Midori also explained that the strength of Buddhist practices in her hometown was reinforced by ties to the emperor. "A person by the name of Amamiya lived in the town. He was related to the emperor's family. About 5:00 A.M. he walked through the town to offer prayers at the temple. People were so grateful for his presence that they would go out to the street and view him with reverence. This was his work, you see, to go to the temple on Sunday mornings to offer Buddhist prayers. Some people went to see him and worshipped him. We just went to see him."

Because of Amamiya's presence in the town and the proximity of the Zenkoji Temple, Midori explained, "Buddhism was very strong in Nagano Shi. However," she revealed, "both of my parents were Christians. This was very unusual, especially at that time." In a society that valued the integration of its people above individual commitments, the practice of Christianity, a relatively new as well as a Western concept, was not tolerated, and Midori recalled the taunting she suffered as a child.

"In Nagano Shi we used to go to church on Sunday morning. When I went to Sunday School, kids in the neighborhood used to tease us by chanting, 'Amen *somen* [thin noodles].' They used to say, '*Yaso miso shoppaina* [Christian; soybean paste; salty].' They chanted these taunts and were mean to us at times," Midori recollected with distress. "However," she stated, "we continued to attend Sunday School."

The Kimura family exhibited the strength of conviction to weather the abuse and prejudice of their neighbors, but like all other Japanese, they were constantly striving to integrate themselves into the fabric of Japanese society, which did not value differences. The curious observance of some Buddhist practices, like visiting the Zenkoji Temple and celebrating festivals that had their origin in Buddhism, were the Kimuras' attempts to secure themselves to their society despite an unusual and strong commitment to Christianity.

As Midori continued with a description of her father and how his familial relationships differed from the norm, she also commented on how the family religion may have played a part. "My father, though a very strict person when he needed to be, was gentle most of the time. When he scolded me, I was made to stand in the corner, but he did not hit us. I do remember that. My parents got along very well, too. You see, back in those days some men used to treat their wives harshly; but my father was not like that, probably," Midori speculated, "because he went to church.

"My father was born into a Buddhist family. He wanted to go to college, but his parents would not allow it. I suppose they felt that he did not need to study since they wanted him to become a farmer. He left home and studied independently. I don't remember the exact story [about that part of his life]. At some point he came out to Nagano Ken, where he met my mother. It was," Midori revealed, "a Western-style love marriage."

As Midori continued with comments about her father, she once again revealed her family's tenacity in continuing to integrate non-Christian customs into their lives. "During the Russo-Japanese War, my father was dispatched to Korea as a member of the railroad corps for the Imperial Army. He was there for two years. We would prepare *ozen* or *kagezen* [meal for an absent person] every night.

"Instead of coming back to Nagano Shi after the war, father stayed with the company in Keijo [Seoul], Korea. That's when my mother took three children and a grandmother and moved to Seoul. Eventually there were four sisters. That's five children altogether in my family. All girls! And I am the oldest. I was eleven years old then.

Japanese women and girls rarely had a chance to travel. Midori accepted her unusual opportunity with relish, and it left her with wonderful memories. "Our move to Korea was the first time we had taken a long trip, and I was very happy because I could see my father," she said, recalling in detail the sights that impressed her. "We went by train to Tokyo, stayed there for a while, and then went to Shimonoseki, where we took a ferryboat to Fusan and then to Keijo.

"We stayed at an inn in Shimonoseki, where we had a delicious lobster dinner. Shimonoseki was very famous for lobster. My father came to pick us up at Fusan. From there we got first-class seats on the train. Korean trains were larger than Japanese trains so it was a very pleasant journey. We arrived at Ryozan and settled into special housing [for railroad employees].

"The first thing I noticed in Korea was that the households dried hot red peppers on their roofs. It was very beautiful. I still remember that sight. There were also many mounds in the fields. They must have been graves. I remember strong-looking, rolling hills, and I remember that Koreans always wore white clothing. These were very different sights from those in Japan.

"There were many Japanese who lived in Ryozan and also in Keijo. There was lots of special housing for railroad personnel and boarding-houses for single people.

"When we first arrived in Korea, it was summer and it rained a lot. When it rained, frogs croaked. The frogs there were really big, too. Once the Quan River flooded and water deluged the city. We lived close to the river, so our house was surrounded by water. Because we could not get out of the house, all the food was supplied by boats. I remember eating sandwiches that were supplied from Seoul. It was the first time that I had ever eaten a sandwich!

"Because of my father's occupation, we were able to attend an elementary school that was attached to the public high school while we lived in Japan. The school had a very good reputation, and I studied there until we moved to Korea, where I completed elementary school. Then I commuted by train to the girls' middle school, which was located in Seoul. Because I went to a Japanese elementary and also a Japanese middle school instead of Korean schools, I really did not get to know Koreans and didn't learn to speak the language. I wish I had studied it then.

"I attended middle school for four years and then a women's middle school. Finally I went on to a women's college, now Kobe University."

Though her comments about her mother are sparse, the maternal influences were strongest in Midori's life and extended beyond the grave. It was her mother who brought Christianity into the family and encouraged her daughters to be educated.

"My mother was a graduate of *jogakko* [girls' high school]," Midori explained. "She must have taught my father English, because he could read and write a little.

"Mother died of cancer one year before I graduated from middle school. She had wanted me to go to a Christian school, so after graduating, I entered Kobe Jogakuin, which was established by the Congregational church. I was there for five years and lived in a dormitory. While I was at Kobe Jogakuin, I took trips to Nagano Shi, where I was born, and went back to Korea to see my family." Then indicating her fondness and reverence for her dead mother, Midori added, "I also went to Tottori Ken, where my mother was born.

"My mother died about eight months after the youngest sister was born," Midori continued. "At that time my mother's cousin was living in our household to help the family. She was a very nice person. About a year later, my father married her." Second marriages were often difficult situations for Japanese children, who were never a part of the decision-making process and were rarely even informed of a new marriage until the ceremony was imminent. But once again, Midori, grateful for her father's exceptional manner, disclosed, "My father did not make this decision by himself. He consulted us. I thought that he was very sensitive to our feelings."

Midori had already left home to attend school and said of her stepmother, "I never lived with her, so I never experienced any problems with her."

Continuing her commentary with an explanation of her education, Midori said, "The middle school program was five years and the university was four years, but with my extra schooling in Seoul, I only had to finish two years to complete the middle school division. When I graduated from Kobe Jogakuin, I must have been seventeen years old. Then I went to Kobe Women's College, an old institution that was built by the American Congregational Church Board. I entered as a second-year college student. I had to catch up with those who had completed five years of middle school, but it was not that difficult. It was the best period of my life.

"I studied hard during my college years. Because I had gone through a different high school system, I was behind in English and I had to catch up. It was a lot of work. I also attended prayer meetings, and on Sundays we went to local churches. We had a free period in the afternoon but were not allowed to leave the school."

Describing further the limits of her social life in those days, Midori continued, "I did not have a boyfriend. There were some who had boyfriends secretly. But once you entered the dormitory, it was just like a nunnery. Once a glee club from Kansai University, a men's college, performed for us. These college students from Kansai attended church, too. They sang in the choir, and we really enjoyed their singing. It was the only time that we could see boys.

"We were allowed to attend the literary society productions of the Kobe Business School [also a men's institution]. When we put on a musical event, we invited students from these colleges to come in turn. There wasn't any chance to talk with the other [male] college students though. Not at all," Midori added adamantly, once again emphasizing the strict, protective life she and other Japanese young women experienced.

"We were never allowed to go out of the school by ourselves. When we went out with others, we had to get permission from our dormitory master, and we had to come straight back. I was twenty-two years old when I graduated from college, but I was always required to seek permission.

"There were some who got married and quit school before graduation. We attended some of those weddings. I don't recall anyone who got in trouble because of their boyfriends. There must have been some, but it was never a matter of public discussion."

An occasional Japanese family might have one of their daughters attend or complete college, but, Midori related, an advanced
education was a goal for all her sisters. "While I was still a student
at Kobe, my younger sister, the one next to me in age, entered as
a student. During a flu epidemic, she got sick and died. The next
sister went through middle school and also graduated from Kobe
Women's College. She lives in Kyoto now."

Overly educated, well beyond the optimum marrying age, traveled, and a Christian, Midori, though schooled in Meiji attributes,
was no longer tracked into fulfilling the destiny of a Meiji woman.

○ ○ ○ ○ ○ ○ ○ ○ ○ ○ ○ ○ ○ ○

Juxtaposing a feudal code of values with modernization, the
Japanese became masters at reconciling disparate elements of
their lives into an acceptable whole. Because of the effects of massive modernization in Japan, however, some Meiji women were
groomed for greater change than Japanese society could accommodate.

The common threads in the rearing of these issei women are
starkly evident. The feminine, courteous, modest, Meiji woman
was the outer shell of an inner self, disciplined by what the
Japanese characterize as rigorous moral training. They were strict-
ly disciplined, for the most part compliant, tidy, frugal, devoted to
their families, and schooled in the moral values of the ancient
samurai code. Issei women repeatedly emphasized an exacting
discipline to learn and complete every task or lesson with thor-
oughness and skill. Girls learned to accomplish chores quickly
and responsibly. They were not encouraged to ask questions but
to learn through observation and repetition. Oddly enough, the
goal, at least in the domestic realm, was to teach a girl to become
self-reliant. From a Western point of view, discipline, filial duty,
compliance, self-reliance, and endurance are character traits, but
for the Meiji woman, they were moral prerogatives.

These lessons learned in childhood were no different from those
learned by other Japanese girls of the time. But each of these issei
women possessed a quality or experience that propelled her
toward a very different future. For many, a higher education
became a critical factor. Better educated than the average Japanese
woman, issei women indicated that Western ideas had seeped into
their lives. Several mentioned mothers who were strong, influential role models. For others, ambition, aggressive personalities,
suffocating living conditions, or being Christian in a Buddhist

country were contributing factors. They had reached a critical time in their lives when the pressure to marry was increasing, but their differences made them less acceptable in a modernizing but still very traditional Japanese society. These women were good matches for issei men who had emigrated to the United States several years before and who were now seeking wives willing to take a risk.

CHAPTER TWO

From Meiji Woman To Isssei Pioneer

ONATSU AKIYAMA

What better candidate for an adventure than Onatsu Akiyama, who had already breached the boundaries of acceptable conduct by running away to Kobe without parental consent. She returned home only after securing a family promise to allow her to go back to Kobe in a year. When this unusually assertive, energetic, and willful young woman arrived in the city of Kobe a second time, she had what she had lacked before, parental consent. "About nine months after I arrived," Onatsu said, continuing her commentary, "a palmist read my hand and said, 'How strange! You should have left Japan for a foreign country a long time ago.' He said that I had already rejected many offers of marriage, and it seemed as if this man knew everything about my past. 'There is one more proposal left. If you reject this one,' he warned, 'there will be no other opportunities.'

"This happened in September. I returned home in November, and on the first of December my husband-to-be came back from America. A matchmaker came over and said that Mr. Akiyama had come back to Japan unexpectedly and asked if we [the family] were interested in an *omiyai* [meeting of prospective spouses].

"I didn't want to get married," Onatsu pronounced, "because I had heard that it was a very difficult life." What Onatsu knew was that marriage, though it promised children and ultimately fulfillment for a Meiji woman, was trying at best and often sorely tested the emotional resources of a young bride. Marriages were family alliances, and a newly married couple lived with the groom's family. It was the groom's mother who ran the household, and the Japanese mother-in-law was most often tyrannical in meting out duties and criticism to a new daughter-in-law.

Hisayo Hanato and Kiyo Miyake remembered their mothers counseling troubled brides who had nervous breakdowns. With no romantic bond between a couple, there was little communication between man and wife. The groom had little reason to be emotionally supportive of his new wife's position. Indeed, filial obligation required him to support his own parents first.

It would be difficult to imagine Onatsu obeying the every whim of a demanding mother-in-law! "I had told my parents," she said, "that I didn't want to get married. In my hometown girls used to marry when they were sixteen and seventeen years old. Because I was still single and almost twenty-one, people used to say, 'Yokosa Mise's girl is a tomboy!' Our store was called 'Yokosa Mise.' And they would laugh at me," she recalled with good nature.

"My family led a fairly comfortable life, and marriage proposals were coming to us from very well-to-do families. As you know, family life in the upper classes was very rigid and stifling, and I was pampered as a child. In addition, the in-law relationship used to be very difficult. It was more difficult then than now." But Onatsu recognized new possibilities in this arrangement with the Akiyama family. "Going to America was very attractive to me, because I felt that I could be free of traditional family rigidity," she declared. "I also remember thinking," she added, "that in our town they used to raise silkworms and make silk. It looked to me like such a tedious job. I dreaded the thought of it and felt that if I could go to America, I could escape from all those tiresome things.

"They said that this man [Akiyama] was big. My younger brother said, 'Will you marry him even if he is a six foot giant?' I was very shy talking about him with my brother. When he [Akiyama] came over, he was indeed a huge man. He had to lower his head to come through the door. Then we went upstairs to the *omiyai.* I was very fat, and when I got to the top of the stairs, I was out of breath," she recalled.

Recapturing the anticipation of that first meeting, Onatsu fluttered from one thought to another as though reliving that experience again. "I was twenty-one and he was already twenty-seven. I wanted to come to America very badly," Onatsu admitted, "so I let him know that I was interested." Because the prospective bride and groom often had no opportunity to speak to one another during the *omiyai,* Onatsu confessed a total breach of etiquette. "As I was pouring tea for him, I touched his knee, hoping that he would get my message. Well, you know," she declared in excusing her behavior, "we didn't have a chance to tell each other how we felt about one another.

"I didn't know how he felt about me then, but the next day they said that he was coming back to town because of some business." Unwilling to leave her future in the hands of others, Onatsu once again took the initiative. "I really wanted to tell him that I was interested in going to America with him. There were two roads to my village. One was the regular street, the other a shortcut. I waited for him on the regular street all day, but he must have come the other way, and I missed the opportunity to speak with him.

"Then trouble started at home. Because I was the only daughter, my father and mother did not want me to leave Japan. And, of course, they wanted to check out Akiyama. My mother went to see Mr. Nobuso, who lived in Ono-machi, about three and a half *ri* from our house. He had come back to Japan with my husband-to-be." Indicating the serious concern of her parents, Onatsu reported, "Mother went to visit him three times, but he was never at home. When she finally met the Nobusos, they said that my husband's father had property worth 3,000 dollars. If Akiyama took a wife, he could start a business or do just about anything.

"The Nobusos have passed away," Onatsu explained in an aside, "but their children still live here [in Sacramento, California]. I feel I still owe them something," she said, expressing the Japanese imperative that all *on* [favors or acts of kindness] must be repaid, usually by reciprocating a favor when possible. Some favors, like helping to negotiate a marriage, continue to exact a reciprocation until both husband and wife have died. In this case Mrs. Akiyama acknowledged her continued obligation to the Nobusos and said she would make a recompense, whenever appropriate, to the Nobuso children, who have inherited the good deeds of their parents. "When we lived in Florin,"[1] she continued, "I used to visit the Nobusos and report to them on how we were getting along. Mr. Nobuso was a good friend of my father-in-law, Motoji-jisan [grandfather].

"I was very nervous and worried because I knew that Akiyama could stay only a short time in Japan," Onatsu recalled, as she continued to relate the circumstances of her marriage. "Finally, the go-between came to tell us of the marriage proposal. Well, it was quite an ordeal. My father kept saying that I didn't have to go to America to get married. He also said that he could find a good match for me around the village. It was so hard for me to listen to him." Satisfied that Akiyama could provide financial security for

[1] Florin was a small farming community south of Sacramento, California, where many Japanese emigrants had settled.

their beloved daughter, the family, Onatsu reported, "signed the marriage contract on the eleventh day.

"My father didn't want me to go, so he began drinking three or four *choshi* [sake bottle] per day. I really had to make myself numb and tear away from my family to come to America. After the wedding ceremony, I left home with my husband to go to Kobe nine days before the ship was to depart, because I felt that my father might change his mind. It was a lot easier on my mother. She must have accepted the fact that I had to get married, but I must say that I had to be brave to do what I did."

Away from her family, there were indications that Akiyama's financial status was not all that had been reported, but Onatsu was not even remotely suspicious at that time. After the wedding, the newlyweds traveled to the port of Yokohama, where they would complete the necessary health exams, obtain visas, and depart by ship. "My husband and I stayed at an inn outside of Yokohama. I didn't know at the time that he had very little money. He said that he didn't want to go out on the town. Instead he slept all day and pretended that he was drunk and sleepy with whiskey. Actually," she said, she discovered later that "he didn't have enough money to take me out. It must have been very difficult for him," Onatsu added understandingly. "He also pretended that he had a cold and stayed in bed for several more days. If he had gone out, then he would have had to buy something for me. The only things he bought me were stockings and some facial cream. I kept them until World War II as mementos. I had been such a spoiled girl that I suffered a lot later on.

"But my husband was such a good person that when my older brother went bankrupt, my husband sent him a lot of money. My father used to say that if he could, he would have walked until his feet were destroyed to reach America and thank my husband."

Before the marriage, Onatsu had reason to believe that Akiyama was a man of impeccable character, a belief she maintained throughout their lives together. "Before we got married," she related, "Papa [Akiyama][2] would work till midnight on his father's

---

[2]Another indication of how much more importance the Japanese place on the family unit than on the individual is that when a man and woman first marry, they live in an identity limbo. They rarely refer to one another and do not call one another by name. It is only after the birth of a child that a couple speaks more directly to one another. They still do not call one another by name, but use the terms "Mama" and "Papa." To avoid confusion, the older parents in the household, who also do not call one another by name, refer to one another as "Grandma" and "Grandpa."

forty-acre grape ranch. Then Papa would go and pick up Ojisan [grandfather] in the town of Florin. He would be at a *rioriya* [Japanese restaurant] being entertained. He'd be drunk, and his hat, clothing, shoes, and other belongings would be all over the place. By the time Papa brought Grandpa home, it would be about 2:00 A.M. Then Grandpa would play the *taiko* [Japanese drum] and drink even more, though Papa had to get up early in the morning to take care of the ranch. I suppose that's why a Japanese newspaper wrote an article about an *oyakoko seinen* [young man who loved his father].

"I knew about the article because Mr. Nishi, who was chairman of the Japanese Association in Florin, had the article printed in my village paper. While visiting Japan, Mr. Nishi happened to drop into my father's store, and I heard him talk about this famous young man whose story was in the paper. Mr. Nishi said, 'I read about this model young man, Akiyama, and I'm really impressed. I hear he is back to visit, so I'm going to bring my niece from Kyoto so that she can meet him.'

"Well, this Mr. Nishi had also lived in America, so he must have known the Akiyama family well. I really felt I had lost the chance to meet Akiyama. But you never know your fate. It's so unpredictable," Onatsu declared with relish. Still it remained to be seen whether this pampered, favored child, who believed her husband was financially secure, could maintain her sense of determination and initiative when her new life circumstances became known.

TEIKO TOMITA

Unlike most young Japanese women, Teiko Tomita did not consider marriage an important addition to her life. She had happily taught school for six years. "I wouldn't have regretted it," she staunchly declared, "if I had taught school the rest of my life and never got married."

Teiko had earlier revealed an ability to work with determination toward a singular goal when, as a student, she earned high academic honors. That determination also gave her a spirit more independent than that of most Japanese women, who felt that adult life without marriage was an aberration. Although Teiko acceded to her parents' wishes and married, the seeds of independence and inordinate determination that were part of Teiko's youthful character flowered later in life in response to harsh necessity; however, at age twenty-four Teiko was enough of a

Meiji woman to defer once again to parental wishes and custom. "My parents thought that a woman must get married. Even though I was already twenty-four, a bit old for marriage, I did think my parents were right, too, and accepted their decision.

"At that point in time," she related, "my marriage proposal surfaced. In those days young people had no choice about getting married [or about whom they would marry]. Marriage arrangements were made by parents, and there was no socializing between a man and his fiancee. [Although I knew many men teachers, dating was out of the question.] A *nakado* [go-between, matchmaker] would try to match young people. He would make inquiries about prospective brides and grooms.

"One of our relatives became our *nakado* and brought us together," Teiko explained. The matchmaker, usually a trusted family friend or distant relative, made overtures and arrangements for a possible marriage. Using a third party in these negotiations ensured minimal embarrassment to both families should the arrangements be unsuitable or the prospective bride or groom be rejected. "The *nakado* was the same person who had arranged a match for my older sister and her husband," Teiko related. "He was a friend of both our families. He had approached my father and said, 'Mr. Tomita is in America, but he is such and such a person. Would you be interested in matching Teiko with him?' The Tomita family is distantly related to us. You can see that when you study our family tree.

"The *nakado* also told my father that Mr. Tomita had gone to America with the support of his older brother, who was living and farming in Wapato [Washington], near Yakima. He had several hundred acres of hay and other crops. Then the *nakado* told me about my husband's situation. He said that Mr. Tomita was already thirty years old and was looking for a bride. Later he showed me a picture of my husband.

"It took about ten months to conclude the arrangements. Then I was directed to exchange letters with him, because the only thing I had from Mr. Tomita was his picture. Ours might be considered a picture marriage, even though my husband came home for our wedding."

It is evident from Teiko's comments about picture brides that she had less reason to be apprehensive than the average picture bride, who would not meet her husband until she crossed the Pacific Ocean. But in a society where arranged marriages were the rule, a picture marriage was simply a practical extension of an existing social practice. "There were quite a few picture brides at that time," Teiko commented; in fact, most Japanese emigrant women were picture brides. "Brides were coming to America by boat, and prospective husbands waited for them at the dock. They had to find each other, and the only help they had was one another's pictures. There was a lot of trouble because some looked different from their pictures." Some of these immigrant men sent photos of themselves taken when they were much younger. Hoping to create the best possible impression from across an ocean, some were so desperate to obtain wives that they sent photos of other, better-looking men. Fortunately for Teiko, Mr. Tomita said that he would come to Japan for the wedding ceremony if all the arrangements had been completed.

"My parents and grandparents were very happy. The *nakado* had said, 'He [Mr. Tomita] is a big farmer in America. We know he has become very successful because the older brother was able to return to Japan, as his help [on the farm] was no longer needed; and Masakazu [Mr. Tomita] says that he will return to Japan again in three years.' Whenever I recall what the *nakado* said, I also think of my mother and grandmother's words before I left, 'Even if it takes five years, it will be wonderful for you [Teiko] when you return.'" With grim sarcasm, Teiko added, "I laugh about it." She was never to return.

Circumstances for most of the issei men were similar to Mr. Tomita's. After spending as many as ten years or more in the United States, they were anxious to marry, but increasing prejudice, antimiscegenation laws, and Japanese custom directed the issei man back to Japan in his search for a wife. Because they required wives who were willing to leave Japan, the most "desirable" women according to Japanese standards were not available to these issei men. Beyond the usual marrying age themselves, their choices were also women who, like Teiko, were older. Educated women, also less desirable as wives in Japan, were also more available.

Most of the issei men did not have the financial resources to make a return trip to Japan. As a result, the practice of picture marriages became common. Westerners are sometimes appalled at the idea of marrying someone sight unseen; however, this practice resulted in only slight modifications of the very formalized, well-established Japanese marriage customs, which did not include romantic love as a condition for a good match.

Japanese marriages were not viewed as the union of two individuals but as the perpetuation of a line of descendants who brought honor (or disgrace) to a family. Consequently marriages were arranged by two families in a formal negotiating process that did not directly involve the prospective bride and groom. They trusted their fate to their families.

Of course, a marriage involving as drastic a move as emigration to a foreign country usually involved consent of the prospective bride, but the fact that she would not meet her husband until she crossed an ocean was not nearly as traumatic as a Westerner would expect, since in a normal situation with the bride and groom in Japan, there would be little or no opportunity to become acquainted.

"I married Mr. Tomita without meeting him, but I knew him through our exchange of letters, so I was neither surprised nor disappointed," Teiko stated. "He came to Japan, we got married in October, and we came to America in February. During that time I got to know him better. He was a dependable, single farmer, very similar to my father in character. He was a quiet man of very few words who spoke only when necessary. His speech was awkward, but because we did exchange letters, I knew his thoughts. I began to understand him better later on, and I was very much impressed.

"After we got married, we stayed in Japan for four months. We went shopping, amused ourselves, did some sightseeing, and also visited his relatives, since he was back for the first time in ten years. When I left for America, my mother traveled with me to Yokohama, where she said her farewells. She cried and cried. It was the last time I saw her," Teiko said sadly. "She died a year after I left.

"We boarded an old, dirty ship called the Manira Maru in Yokohama," Teiko recalled. Because the Tomitas traveled third-class, like the vast majority of emigrants, "The men and women were segregated," Teiko said, "and we had to sleep in bunk beds." Raised to be fastidious, the emigrants were plagued by infestations of lice, almost inedible food, and seasickness. "It was February, the sea was very rough, and my husband got seasick.

"There were many picture brides in my cabin. We talked a lot about our schools or things that happened when we left Japan. Most of the women on the ship had never seen their husbands-to-be. One said, 'I'm from such and such a place, and I'm going to Canada. When I arrive at the port, my husband should be there to pick me up.'" Despite their understandable anxiety, Teiko and the other issei picture brides were filled with youthful optimism for the most part.

Upon their arrival, these young pioneer women faced a bewildering and sometimes misrepresented reality. Teiko remembered with distress the confusion and fear that surrounded her first days in America. "Most of the men had been in America before," she recollected, "but the women were here for the first time, and we were detained at the immigration office. I remember crying there.

"They gave us thorough physical examinations, also checked our urine. I can't quite remember exactly what they did. Some people got out in three days. Others had to stay there for two or three weeks. The only people left there were women, and we all cried. We didn't understand the language, and though they gave us three meals a day, their food did not agree with us. There was a store, but we could not buy anything because none of us had money. I might have had a Japanese coin or two, but those were useless. We all cried and cried because we didn't know when we'd be free, and because we couldn't understand anything they said to us."

SHIZU HAYAKAWA

With her marriage and voyage to America, a new phase in Shizu Hayakawa's life began. Although she was sometimes anxious, Shizu seemed to regard this time as full of interesting experiences with opportunities to socialize.

"I came to America in March of 1919. Our marriage was a *shashin kekkon* [picture marriage]. I knew of my prospective husband already because my husband's elder sister[3] had married my father. My husband's elder sister had two children also.

"I had been writing to him [Hayakawa] from the time there were definite plans for marriage, since I was seventeen.

"I was nineteen when I got married in Japan, and I was twenty by the time I came to San Francisco," Shizu recalled. A proxy stood for the groom during the wedding ceremony. "I had registered as his wife and in his family name a year and a half before I came to the States." This registration or *koseki* is an official record of family births, deaths, adoptions, and marriages. "The regulations in Japan required a wife to be legally married for six months or more before permission was granted to emigrate to this country," Shizu explained.

In traveling alone to the United States to live with a man she had never met, Shizu experienced the common lot of the Japanese

[3]Japanese emphasis on placement in the family rather than on relationships is reflected by the phrase "husband's elder sister," which, if translated into common English usage, would be "sister-in-law."

picture bride. "When I left Japan I knew that I was going far away. Everyone told me I was brave! I sailed on the *Korea Maru*, and it took over a month to get from Nagasaki to here." Before leaving Japan, Shizu spent time in Yokohama obtaining a visa and the necessary health clearances. "I was very lonely, because I stayed by myself at hotels and inns in Yokohama," she confided. "I was traveling to places I had never been, and I did not know anyone. I was very much afraid.

"Our ship stopped in Hawaii overnight. There were a lot of picture brides on board. We did not know if we would ever see Hawaii again, so we went ashore." Happily she recalled, "We all dressed in Japanese kimono and went *shan shan* [walking with pride] to a restaurant where we ate delicious *sukiyaki* [a Japanese dish]. The women were very attractive, and everybody was young, about twenty or so. None of us knew what kind of husbands were awaiting us, but we had a great time talking about our future husbands," Shizu recalled and then added reflectively, "We were so young.

"Most of the ship's passengers were picture brides, but there were also *saitoko* [persons who had emigrated to the United States, had gone back to Japan to visit, and were returning to the States]. Some were parents who had left their children with relatives in Japan because they could not support them at the time.

"There were quite a few young men on our ship who were coming to the States because they were summoned by their parents. They would say to the girls, 'Why don't you come with us rather than marry a man who is fifteen or sixteen years older than you?' That created all kinds of problems on the ship," Shizu observed. But the vast majority of the picture brides, like Shizu, honored the commitments negotiated by their families.

"My husband," she said, "was sixteen years older than I. I did not think about whether he would be a suitable husband or not. In Japan it was the custom for parents to arrange marriages. This being so, there was no alternative," she affirmed. When Shizu Hayakawa stepped onto the ship to leave Japan, she had already accepted alternatives to her Japanese way of life. And life in the United States would present more alternatives that she later would not ignore.

Recalling her anxiety and confusion, Shizu described the difficulties of her first week in the United States. "When I first arrived at Angel Island, the immigration station in San Francisco [Bay], it was somewhat frightening." Angel Island was the Ellis Island of the West Coast, where Asian immigrants were processed. "We all had to go into the clinic for a physical examination," Shizu recalled. "Before we left Japan, we were, of course, checked to see if we had any diseases, especially hookworms or trachoma. Well, the immigration authorities were on a holiday. What with one thing and another, it took a whole week before I was cleared."

Stranded on Angel Island during that first week, Shizu found everything different, even something as simple as bathing. "We took a bath," she recalled, "and bathed as we did in Japan. We washed ourselves outside the tub and then soaked. We got into trouble because there was water all over the place!" The bathing facilities were located on the second floor, and water had leaked through the floorboards into the administration offices below.

Surrounded by water and barbed wire fences, the immigration station on Angel Island must have seemed like a prison to these scared, young issei women. The multitude of detailed life differences often left these picture brides in a state of shock, but Shizu also recalled the small kindnesses that eased the confusion on Angel Island. "Reverend Terazawa's wife was working at the immigration office on Angel Island, and she looked after us [picture brides] until she passed away," Shizu noted. "My husband," she continued, "had come to meet me. He brought *sushi* [cold rice specialty] which Mrs. Mizuno had made. Mrs. Mizuno is still here [in San Jose] and has a *tofu* [soybean curd] shop. She is famous for her *sushi.* Rice had been scarce, and it had been a long journey, over ten days, since we left Yokohama, so everyone was happy to be able to eat this delicious food.

"My husband did not recognize me immediately. But there were some men, *saitoko,* on the ship, and they helped me find him. When I first met my husband, I did not say much.

"After the ordeal on Angel Island we were ready to be on our way. But since it was considered almost a crime to wear and be seen in a Japanese kimono," Shizu said, indicating the extent of prejudice and the immigrants' need to conform, "we were whisked away in a well-covered car to the Nichi Bei Bussan [Nichi Bei Shop]. There we were stripped of our Japanese kimono and footwear and were given dresses and shoes to wear. The shoes had high heels, and we were used to our flat Japanese footwear, so we could hardly walk! Americans can wear the Japanese *zori* [thonged sandal now, but when we came, a person couldn't wear such things."

Issei women recalled what were then embarrassing, but later became amusing stories of young brides who were so taken by the lovely lingerie that they wore it over their dresses or tried to walk in high heels slipped on backward.

As if all of these differences weren't overwhelming, Shizu had to modify religious practices. "In Japan we were Buddhists," she explained. "We had heard about Christianity in those days, but we didn't go to church. We were told not to associate with false religious groups. My husband had become a Christian and was baptized in the San Francisco Presbyterian church in 1914. As soon as I came to the States, we had our wedding at this church, for we felt it was the right thing to do. Usually with picture marriages, the bride was taken immediately after her arrival to a farm [to live and work] and she didn't know whether or not she had had a proper ceremony. But under the leadership of Mr. Takayama and Mr. Abiko,[4] picture brides in San Francisco were cared for properly. I was able to stay with a young women's group for about ten days until the wedding. During the ten days, Mrs. Noza taught me how to use an American toilet and many other practical things."

Shizu must have had some initial apprehensions about her rapid introduction to Christianity, but, raised a Meiji woman, she had been taught to obey her husband and support him in every way. The kindness of her husband's Christian friends also eased her anxiety. "The people at the church were so good to me," she related. "There was one lady who helped me get ready for my wedding. This lady really treated me like her younger sister and was so thoughtful that I thought Christian people were wonderful."

Although Shizu's life had already changed dramatically, her Meiji rearing was sometimes in dramatic opposition to her new life and at other times adaptable to the circumstances of that new life across thousands of miles of ocean.

KATSUNO FUJIMOTO

Combining the traditional custom of an arranged marriage with the belief in new ideas, opportunities, and travel, Katsuno Fujimoto's parents negotiated a marriage for her with a Japanese who had emigrated to the United States. "I didn't get married in Japan. I was a picture bride," Katsuno explained. "We had a go-between who arranged everything and we exchanged pictures." All wedding arrangements were conducted according to established custom. Katsuno, still considered a child, was rarely con-

[4]Japanese community leaders.

sulted, because it was assumed that her parents knew best. Negotiations between the prospective bride and groom's family were sometimes lengthy, but once engagement gifts were exchanged, the bargain was considered sealed and the marriage ceremony only a formality. "It wasn't until after we had exchanged betrothal gifts that we found out the man I was marrying was twenty-three years older than I was."

Katsuno was shocked and reacted in panic. "My uncle thought that it was too much of an age difference," she recalled, grateful for the support, "but my mother said I could not change my mind because it would affect my younger sisters' marriages and would disgrace the family." Katsuno had earlier described her father as a "progressive" and "way ahead of his time." He was supportive of education for women, but in the social realm he remained steeped in tradition and offered no support to Katsuno in her dilemma. In desperation Katsuno searched for a way out. "I considered going to Osaka to become a nurse; I even thought of committing suicide, but I was watched at all times. Then, suddenly, without letting us know, my husband-to-be returned to Japan. The go-between came after me and took me to him." Stunned by the suddenness of her husband's appearance and without support from her mother, Katsuno said, "I cried for two days, but finally came with him to America." It was no consolation to Katsuno that this age difference between issei husband and wife was a common one and that in many cases such as hers, the age deception was calculated.

HISAYO HANATO

Though Hisayo had expressed no passionate desire to emigrate, she had listened to others talk about the wonders of America, seen photographs, and was favorably impressed. Fulfilling obligations of filial duty after expressing early admiration and devotion to her mother provided Hisayo with a practical and acceptable reason to consider emigration. "My older brother in America fell ill, and my mother worried about him day in and day out, so much so that I thought if I could go to America and take care of him, my mother might regain some peace of mind. It was toward the end of the picture bride era when my husband-to-be returned to Japan for a wife. We were," she verified, "paired by a *nakado* [matchmaker]."

Marriage, a much-valued social institution, coupled with emigration, provided Hisayo with an acceptable means of travel and change, as it did for so many young issei women. But as Hisayo recounted, it was far from ideal. "The attitude toward marriage then and now is different. I would like to have dated some of the men who had proposed, but dates were not allowed in those days. When I saw my husband for the first time, I was not impressed. He was fifteen years older than I." But the match was concluded because of practical rather than romantic considerations. The two families had agreed to the arrangement, and the marriage was finalized.

SETSU YOSHIHASHI

Recounting the beginning of a new chapter in her life, Setsu recalled the circumstances of her marriage. "My brother-in-law had been earnestly looking for a Japanese wife for his brother in America lest he marry a white woman. His brother was already thirty-one years old. There were many eligible girls, but he didn't want to marry just anyone. A farm girl wouldn't do. He was looking for a girl from a more prominent family. His brother had approached some good families for brides but they had all refused and said, 'No, we don't want our daughter going to a far-off country.'" But for Setsu, who had been shunted from household to household and who was living a life of physical comfort but one that was devoid of any emotional support, the opportunity to leave an exacting and emotionally volatile aunt must have seemed like the light at the end of a tunnel.

Setsu recalled, "The Matsuis did not want to give me up either, but other relatives believed that life in America was fantastic and pressured the Matsuis until they couldn't refuse. My uncle told me that I didn't have to go to America. He said, 'Think very carefully before you make your decision.' But I didn't concern myself with such thoughts. I was a Japanese child, and if my aunt wanted me to do something, I obeyed. I had never had to do any deep or serious thinking in my life before this, so I was unable to make such an important decision on my own. I didn't have the presence of mind to think so deeply."

Though Setsu stated that the choice was not hers, she repeated a second time that her uncle gave her several chances to change her mind. "As I look back, I guess my uncle really didn't want me to go. He said, 'If you don't want to go, just say the word. Think about it carefully.' He said that to a person like me who had never had to do any serious thinking. But, you know, I now believe a person's path is set. It led me to America, and I'm very grateful. My parents had nothing to do with the decision, since I was in the complete care of the Matsuis. In the end my aunt decided to give me away as a bride." And surely Setsu must have breathed a sigh of relief when she left her aunt's household.

"My husband's elder brother's wife [sister-in-law] was also my mother's younger sister, so my husband's brother was my uncle by marriage. His wife was my blood-related aunt. They were not on the Matsui side but were Yoshihashis. Later, my husband's eldest brother was conscripted into the army and died in the war [World War II]. He and his wife were kind to me and took good care of me. They took me into their family and gave me to this younger brother as a wife.

"I became a Yoshihashi before I graduated from high school, and I attended school while I lived in the Yoshihashi home," Setsu explained. She, too, had been married by proxy, without the bridegroom present, and was therefore a responsibility of the Yoshihashi family.

After years of emotional deprivation, everything pointed toward positive changes in Setsu's life. "Life with the Yoshihashis was just marvelous," she said. "They were the best kind of people. He was a fine soldier, a military man, too; but he didn't drink. I'm very proud to belong to such an honest, upright family. I'm very proud to be a Yoshihashi. My husband was a very strict man and life with him was very hard, but the Yoshihashis never drank alcohol–for thirteen generations. In Japan this is very rare. My children don't even drink beer to this day. The Yoshihashi family is a serious, honest family, and I'm very grateful to have been taken in by them.

"I was with them a year and a half. Both this aunt and uncle were very kind to me. Basically I felt that whatever they decided was in my best interests, and I didn't worry about my future life in America."

Setsu's marriage was typical of Japanese marriages. This marriage was unusual only because the bridegroom was not in Japan at the time. "We [my family] had told my husband that if he did not come for me in person, I would not marry him. He replied that he owned a laundry business in Hollywood [California] and that he could not leave his business at all. My family responded that if he sent a first-class ticket, I would be allowed to go to America. So, I came to America first-class on the *Nihon Maru*. I came to America in style."

After spending a year and a half with the Yoshihashis, who had treated her so well, Setsu looked forward to her trip and to her new life in America. She couldn't have helped but think that her fortunes had definitely changed for the better, especially after her time with the Yoshihashis, and now she was one of the very few emigrants who would travel first-class!

"I had to go to Yokohama several times for a physical exam. The head of our district was very strict about the regulations. Also, an official from the Ministry of Foreign Affairs came to question us. The inspector asked my uncle many questions. I remember that clearly.

"I really never gave any thought to what I was doing. Oh, yes, I was sent to have English lessons before I left. I had studied English as a third-year high school student but I hadn't learned enough. And my aunt Yoshihashi had tried to teach me to cook before I left Japan. I cooked rice one day, and it came out raw. She said, 'Setsu, how can you possibly go to America when you can't even cook?' They gave up and let me go out and play. My aunt wondered what would become of me in the end."

Throughout her commentary, Setsu refrained from any bitter criticism of her Matsui aunt, but added in quick contrast to her treatment at the Yoshihashis, "When I stayed in the Matsui household, I got yelled at, but I stayed with them for several years and worked hard." Still bearing the emotional scars of that time, she added, "I couldn't have been all that bad."

"Many people saw me off at the port when I was about to sail," she continued. "I wish we had taken pictures then," she said and recalled the partylike atmosphere. "My cousin, an officer, oh, just so many people came to send me off. I traveled alone, but my uncle Matsui's friend who was in the military service was on the ship with me. He was going to England via America to serve in the Japanese legation in England. He was from Akita, too. My Uncle Matsui asked him to look after me.

"All we saw was the ocean, day in and day out, but my life on the ship was so much fun. Because we traveled first-class, we were treated very well. There were about seven first-class passengers-- a head librarian from Yamaguchi Prefecture, members of the Japanese legation, and people like that. I made friends with the rest of the passengers in first-class but had no contact with second- and third-class passengers. I had never been treated so royally and had the best time of my life. We landed in Hawaii for a day and ate at a beautiful restaurant by the shore. Oh, what a life! I was awed by such luxury."

The trip made such an impression on Setsu that she recalled in detail the events of the voyage. "We sat at the captain's table for each meal. I wore my kimono for dinner and sat right next to the captain, and Miss Ono, my cabin mate, sat on his other side. He had to have a lady at each side. The other first-class passengers sat around on the remaining seats. We had ice cream for dessert every day. In fact we got sick and tired of ice cream. Life on the ship was so extravagant! I really enjoyed that trip.

"Yoneko Ono shared a cabin with me. She was a Eurasian who had been a student at an English college for women and was going to attend Columbia University. We parted company in San Francisco.

"I saw America for the first time and was totally enthralled. I was sent to an immigration station–Angel Island." Because Setsu traveled first-class, she was given preferential treatment and did not have to endure an extended stay. "We were released that evening," she continued, "for the processing was not complicated. A woman, the wife of a Japanese minister who worked at the immigration office, told us about sanitation and other necessary things."

Setsu's life had changed dramatically since she had married and become a Yoshihashi. She described her year and a half with her new family as "wonderful." Her voyage to America was "the best time" of her life, and now Setsu had only to meet the husband who seemed to promise a continuation of her newfound good fortune.

KIYO MIYAKE

"One summer vacation when I returned home from college, there was a middle-aged woman staying with my mother," Kiyo said as she began her account of how she had married. "She was the wife of a dry goods wholesaler. She had such a mean mother-in-law that she was exhausted." This particular mother-in-law was apparently ruthless in dispensing duties and criticism to her son's wife. "It was decided that this woman would stay with my mother for a while. At that time about forty peddlers came to her store to check out materials from her. In those days peddlers carried merchandise on their backs and walked the streets to sell their wares. Well, the woman was really exhausted from the work and stress and needed a rest. I didn't understand much about her circumstances. I was such a naive person. But soon this woman became well and strong, regained her health, and went home.

"Sometime after she returned home, I saw this woman again and she said to me, 'If my son was a little bit older, I would like you to marry him. Unfortunately he is just too young for you. But there is a fine young man I know. I have been looking for a nice girl for him. In some ways he is a very difficult person, but he is a very good person, too. If you are willing, I would like to make an *omiyai* for you two. I think you would make a very good couple.'" When Kiyo learned that the young man in question had emigrated to the United States, she exhibited an enthusiantic interest.

Already a confident, assertive young woman, Kiyo responded, "I would like to associate with him for six months and then I'll make up my mind." The woman must have been surprised at Kiyo's straightforward ability to declare her own wishes. "It was the modern style," Kiyo declared. "My children say it was a romance. Well, it was not quite like that, but at least it was an American-style courtship," she added, and then displayed the sense of humor that was an integral part of her energetic personality. "Sometimes I joke about it and say, 'I failed! I made a mistake! I should have done better than this.'

"Well," she continued with a renewed freshness that memories of her courtship evoked, "this young man came back from the United States and we dated for six months, just like young people today. The difference between the American-style courtship and ours was that Americans fall in love with one another in a natural way, but we had marriage in mind from the beginning. Even so, it was also quite different from the Japanese traditional marriage."

Mr. Miyake was as frank as Kiyo in his response to her suggestion of a six-month association. "He [my husband] said to my parents, 'They say that if a person graduates from a women's high school, there is less chance for her to get married. Then, if we went out every night unchaperoned and I decided not to marry your daughter, her reputation might be hurt.' It was such a period in time. Therefore we didn't go to see shows or anything like that. We went for walks in quiet places and talked."

Formal negotiations for marriages were the rule in Japan. Courtships were rare. But during this courtship, Kiyo learned much about Miyake and was obviously impressed. "We talked about religion, literature, and other things. He could talk about art, too. He was a very learned man and he had a deep understanding of many subjects."

Despite the modern flavor of the Miyakes' courtship, Kiyo remained steeped in the traditions of Japan. Establishing social position had primary importance. Once married, a Japanese woman validated her own position in society through her husband's family lineage. The longer the lineage, the more respected the family. Kiyo recounted with specific detail the Miyake family's lengthy history.

"He [Miyake], whose family line goes back for 300 years, was the son of a *kendo* [sword fighting] master in Awaji," Kiyo related, and therefore was a member of the samurai class.[5] "When the feudal system ended with the Meiji Restoration, his father lost his position," Kiyo explained. Despite the dismantling of the samurai class, great prestige continued to be attached to being its descendants.

"His mother was the daughter of the principal retainer [general to a feudal lord] of the Awaji clan, so his mother never went out of the house without being carried in a palanquin. She was the youngest of six children. Their house was huge with a large, beautiful garden. In the garden, sparkling water from the mountain formed a waterfall and fell on a boulder." Then, once again subtly emphasizing respect for the family's lengthy lineage, Kiyo added, "The water had fallen on the rock for the past 300 years and had created a large hole.

"My husband's father was also a fine *haiku* [a seventeen-syllable verse form] and *waka* [a thirty-one syllable Japanese verse form] composer as well as a painter. After the Restoration, he received his severance pay in a lump sum. He then built a beautiful house and frequently invited friends over for dinner and held poetry meetings. Unfortunately he had no sense of business, and his money ran out rapidly. Soon he had to borrow. The moneylenders were very mean if they were not repaid. One day his father's house was seized, and everything was confiscated except a rice chest. My husband remembered his mother crying over the rice chest."

As Kiyo concluded her comments, which established her husband's, and therefore her own, family lineage, she began to outline her husband's character. "As a young child my husband was treated with respect because he was the son of such a prominent man. But then later on, no one paid any attention to him, and a spirit of rebellion grew in him. When he was in grammar school in Kobe, he had many small followers. When a boy was asked by his mother to go and buy *tofu* [soybean curd] in the evening, my husband and his sidekicks would not let this boy pass. He [my husband] was really a bad boy. As a teenager, he was such a rascal, though he eventually became a good Christian."

Because Kiyo's ideal marriage involved her Christian beliefs, she felt it was important to recount the circumstances of her husband's conversion. "One day my husband decided to go to church

[5]Dismantling of the samurai class was accomplished by first allotting them a pension, and then, as Kiyo indicated, by simply paying them off with a lump sum to start a new life.

and interfere with the service. He took his friends to heckle the minister. He went every Sunday, but the minister never got mad. Meanwhile he began to think, 'There is something to respect in this Christian minister!' He began to listen to the sermons. Then he began to criticize them. As he listened, he was influenced more and more. Finally he was baptized. Later on he took care of this minister.

"He was sixteen at the time of his conversion, and the congregation of Hyogo Kyokai had begun a project to build a new church. Although the minister organized many fundraisers, there was not enough money. During the coldest part of the winter, a sexton noticed that each night around midnight, dogs started barking. One night this sexton went out with a lantern to see what was going on and looked around. He saw the figure of a person praying and found out that it was my husband, who had been going to the church every night to pray for the new building. The minister told this [story] to the congregation, and the people were so moved that they decided to work together and build a new church.

"My husband was very poor, but he had saved about a hundred dollars to come to the United States. He donated all that money to the church anonymously. We were married in their new building."

Kiyo had taken great pains to weave herself into the fine web of Japanese society despite her Christian beliefs, her advanced education, and her admiration for Western culture. But as she spoke of her wedding arrangements, she revealed an independent streak not common to most Japanese of the time but found in varying degrees in issei women.

Kiyo explained, "My husband's brother was a Buddhist priest, and my husband's best friend was a Buddhist priest, too. But I wanted to have my wedding ceremony in a [Christian] church with the 'Wedding March' and all." Eliminating any explanation of the conflicts of which there must have been many–involved with a wedding that combined a variety of traditions, Kiyo added emphatically, "I insisted on that!

"It was kind of strange," she continued, "with two Buddhist priests wearing *kesa* [formal priest's attire] sitting right in the front pew.

"We also had a reading of a poem by Madam Aiko Jaku. She was a very famous poet but was confined to a wheelchair."

Taking delight in revealing how unusual her marriage arrangements had been, Kiyo asked rhetorically, "Where do you think we went for our honeymoon?" and answered, "A temple in Awaji!

That temple is still there. It belonged to my husband's brother. We stayed there for about two weeks. I liked it. I like things like that."

Then Kiyo struck a more serious note, "But I was a very inadequate wife. My dream was to live like the picture of *The Angelus*, to work in the fields and be able to pray together and return home at the end of each day. I thought that this was the most beautiful life that I could hope for. However, you can't hope to match your dreams with reality. I had no sense of farming. While hoeing, I sang hymns. When I came home from the fields and my husband asked me the condition of the plants, I couldn't remember. I had been too busy singing. A farmer cannot afford to have a wife like me. I didn't make an ideal wife."

Kiyo's assessment of her husband was much more generous. "By the time we were married, my husband had already graduated from a commercial school, worked for an import-export company, and had emigrated to the United States, where he had a dairy farm in the Imperial Valley. He was a very energetic person, who had to educate himself because his family had declined."

Kiyo was, however, realistic and recognized that Mr. Miyake's greatest strengths were also what made him difficult. "When someone asked me my first impression of him, the first thought that came to me was, 'He is the most difficult person in the whole world! I cannot keep up with him.' On the surface he was a very gentle, quiet person. And even though he looked very tough, like a person who wouldn't even care about culture, he liked poetry and art. By difficult I don't mean that he complained a lot or was financially tight or anything like that at all. It means that he was a person with a vision, and he lived for it. I mean that the present was not in his calculations.

"His dream was to make lots of money and build an orphanage. He suffered a lot when he was young, so he wanted to help unfortunate children.

"He used to send all his earnings to a friend who lost his job because he was mistaken as a Communist. He did all these things without telling others.

"He was very straightforward, could not flatter anyone in order to make money or get ahead, and would express his opinion even though he might be the only one who felt that way. When he thought he was right, he would not listen to other people but would sacrifice for a cause if he agreed with it. He went overboard sometimes. He was such an idealist, and sometimes it was too much for others to go along with him. I used to tell him, 'Don't decide everything yourself. You must be able to listen to others.' I could talk to him like that. Even though he might scold me, I could fight with him and insist on my viewpoint."

In sharp contrast to any other issei couple, the Miyakes were a rare match sharing a zest for life, spiritual goals, and intellectual compatibility.

IYO TSUTSUI

As a student Iyo Tsutsui had been impressed by a geography teacher who had urged students to emigrate. "When I was fifteen," Iyo said, "I had already made up my own mind to come to America before my parents made their decision." Still, as a Meiji woman, Iyo could not and would not emigrate alone. Marriage presented the only opportunity to fulfill social expectations and her personal dreams.

"I did not know my husband before I came to America," Iyo continued. "My mother's cousin lived close to Tsutsui's house, so my mother asked her about the Tsutsui family. She found out that even though they did not have much property, Taro [my husband] had always been a very earnest person, even from childhood. I felt," Iyo declared, "he would be good enough for me.

"A go-between and Mother Tsutsui came to see me, and Tsutsui's mother inquired whether or not I might be interested in coming to the United States. I thought it was a good chance for me to get out of the country. In fact, when the go-between began to discuss my going to America as a bride, I said, 'Oh, yes. I was thinking about going to Manchuria, but it would be better to go to America!'

"They had brought a picture [of Tsutsui] and I said, 'He looks like he is a man of steady and earnest character.' Everyone agreed that he looked like a very fine person. It was at that time that I decided to become his bride, and sent him my picture. I was twenty years old according to the Japanese custom of determining age, but I was really nineteen." And although Iyo added a typical Meiji woman's response to the events, "I did not question anything," she strongly asserted that the decision to marry Tsutsui and emigrate was her own.

Iyo was married in Japan with a proxy for the groom. Her name was then entered into the groom's family register, and the formalities were considered complete. "After I married into the Tsutsui family," Iyo explained, "I lived with them in Yamaguchi for a year and one month." Her new life with the Tsutsui family was not fraught with a difficult in-law situation, for, Iyo added, "Mother Tsutsui was a very nice person.

"Although my family were farmers, my father never worked hard at farming and neither did we children. All the work wa done by laborers. However, at the Tsutsuis' I had to help out, especially during the busy times, spring rice planting and during the fall harvest. That's how I learned to farm." This practical experience would be of inestimable value to Iyo in the United States.

"In 1915 I left the Tsutsuis in Yamaguchi and went to Yokohama, where I stayed at the Fukuokaya Inn." Like other emigrants, Iyo needed a health check before a visa could be granted, so she remained at the port of Yokohama until she was cleared.

"The ship I sailed on was called the *Korea Maru*. It was a picture brides' ship. Most of us on the ship were going to be brides to unknown men in an unknown country, not knowing the language or the customs. We knew nothing about how Japanese people lived in America and were all like blind snakes trying to find a path." But like the other picture brides on board, Iyo enjoyed the camaraderie and looked on her trip as a great adventure.

"During the trip we talked about things back in Japan. One bride said, 'I wasn't supposed to come to America; then, after I married into the family, I discovered that I also had a stepchild. After the wedding I saw a small boy. I asked who he was, and my husband said that the boy was his son. He hadn't said anything to me about the child before the wedding!'

"Well, we also talked about the joys and troubles of the events after our marriages. We talked about our future and wondered, 'What will we do when we get there? What kind of food are we going to eat? They say Americans eat meat all the time, but I don't like meat! When I get there, we may have to change from *kimono* to Western clothes. I don't think I can wear them because I'm fat.'

"I didn't talk with the other brides much. I talked with Mrs. Iwashita, who came from Yamanashi. Her husband operated a laundry business in San Francisco. We had just met, but we became good friends for some reason; maybe it was because of our similar backgrounds. She talked about her experiences at school and about her home. I asked her all kinds of questions about Yamanashi Ken because I knew nothing about the area." Iyo enjoyed this relaxed camaraderie and remembered little jokes and bits of conversation with her friend.

"As we walked on deck and talked, we met an Englishman who had been teaching at a university. He said that his wife was Japanese and that they had a daughter. He was going to America and knew a lot about the country. Though he was traveling first class, we often met on deck and he told us many things about England and America. He knew a lot about both countries and kindly answered all the questions that we had."

Although no longer at the mercy of rumors and half-truths about their new home, Iyo and Mrs. Iwashita could not have known that the life of an educated Caucasian professional would be far different from their own.

"As soon as we landed," Iyo continued, "we were taken to the immigration office on Angel Island in San Francisco [Bay], where we were examined for hookworms." In her urgency to get to the United States, Iyo admitted to a small deception. Prior to obtaining a visa for the United States, emigrants had to be free of hookworms. "When in Yokohama, I knew that I had hookworms," Iyo said. The manager of the inn where I was staying said, 'Mrs. Tsutsui, if you want to leave for America as soon as possible, take Ochiyosan's stool sample. She doesn't have hookworms.' I did and that's how I got to come to the United States.

"But when I arrived at the immigration office in San Francisco, I knew that I might be detained. Tests showed that I had hookworm eggs, and I had to stay there [Angel Island] for two weeks, though most other immigrants were there for only about a week. It wasn't too bad. I didn't have to work or anything. A guard stood at the door during mealtimes," Iyo remembered, "and we ate only Chinese rice and boiled potatoes. When I was cleared, I was allowed to land.

"I met Mr. Tsutsui for the first time–well, in the very beginning they called my husband's name and made him sit down in the waiting room. Then the the immigration officers came to get me and questioned me. They also asked if I had *mise gane* [money to show that the immigrant is not indigent]. Then they called my husband and asked him questions. They had to make sure that he was the right man.

"My husband was eleven years older than I was, and he was just average looking. He had already been in this country for ten years and was accustomed to the American attitude of 'ladies first.' He carried my things," Iyo said, and recalled her most pleasant reaction to the gesture. "I thought, 'Oh, he is very kind! If this is my real husband, everything will be fine.' I felt that if this was my husband, I could endure anything." Issei men were raised to expect service and deference from women, and Iyo was pleasantly surprised to find her Japanese-reared husband catering to her needs. Though the vast majority of issei men continued to be served by their wives, some, like Mr. Tsutsui, opted for changes in their marital relationships.

MIDORI KIMURA

As Midori briefly outlined family events during her college years, she also began to explain the circumstances of her marriage. "One of my uncles, my mother's brother, was living in the United States already. Although he had a middle school education, he worked for a blacksmith. He had to take a job like that!" Midori exclaimed, revealing her great regard for learning and education.

"My uncle and Mr. Kimura were good friends. Mr. Kimura was a bachelor, and it was an appropriate time for him to get married. They thought that I would be a good match," Midori continued matter-of-factly, "so we were engaged before I graduated from college."

Midori continued with a description of her rather typical arranged marriage. "I went to the Kimura family for the engagement ceremony. From that time on, Mr. Kimura and I exchanged letters and within a year I got to know him very well.

Mr. Kimura lived in San Jose. He was a New York Life Insurance Company agent and also was a newspaper reporter for the *Nichibei Shinbun,* an English/Japanese language newspaper published in the United States.

"At that time newspaper reporting was a voluntary job. Because most of his insurance clients were farmers, my husband had to work at night. As a result he was free during the day for newspaper work.

"There was a fourteen-year age difference between me and my husband," Midori revealed. This common age discrepancy in marriages of Japanese immigrants caused major marital difficulties for some couples, but for Midori there were other more important compensations.

"My husband was not a college graduate because he left Japan when he was very young. He did take some correspondence courses from Waseda University and was able to read English. Many [issei] women who came here to marry were high school graduates, but most of the husbands were farmers and did not have very much education. Their levels of education were so different that it caused problems.

"When I left Seoul [Korea] for my schooling," Midori recalled, "I was very emotional because I was leaving my family. But afterwards I did not think about it too much because the future was more pressing." In contrast, Midori stated, "I don't remember any sadness in leaving Japan [for the United States]. I suppose I was rather naive.

"I didn't know too much about what America might be like," Midori reflected, but her college, supported by an American Christian organization, was also staffed with some Americans. "My English teacher was an American, and so was the principal of the school. They were very fine people, and from their example I did form an opinion of America, but I didn't give too much thought to it. I was actually surprised to find so many Japanese living here.

"Just before I left Japan, I needed to go to the American consulate in Tokyo. I stayed there with an aunt for a few days and then left Japan from Yokohama. I sailed on the ship, *Shunyo Maru*. It was in 1919."

Mr. Kimura, like Setsu Yoshihashi's husband, sent Midori first-class passage, a rare luxury for an issei picture bride, most of whom traveled third-class. "The voyage, which took seventeen days, was very pleasant. Even though I had first-class passage, I asked to be with four other girls in one cabin. There was a woman by the name of Yamashina. She was a graduate of the Toyo Eiwa [an English/Japanese college]. We used to go up on deck and talk a lot. When the sea was rough and I got seasick, I just stayed in the cabin and had my meals brought in.

"I was introduced to one of the ship's officers by a distant relative, so I received special treatment. I was able to visit the captain's cabin and other interesting places on board.

"When the ship arrived in Hawaii, we got off and went sightseeing. Then we came to America."

Although Midori was technically a picture bride, she did not consider herself one, because of her different situation. "There were picture brides on the ship," she recalled, "but I did not have a chance to meet them because they were in third-class. I saw them when we arrived in the [San Francisco] harbor.

"We landed at Angel Island. Mr. Kimura came up on the ship and we met for the first time. We recognized each other quickly because we had exchanged pictures. I don't remember what we said. I suppose, because we were Japanese, we just bowed formally to each other. We were rather serious at that time. I wasn't afraid of him, because we had corresponded for seven or eight months, and I felt that I knew him very well. Sometimes he wrote to me in English.

"After meeting my husband, I went through the immigration procedure. I felt as if we were detained in some place for suspicious persons," Midori commented, because of the barbed wire, poor food, and barrack-type housing. "However," she added, "I was a very optimistic person, so I didn't worry too much. There were many Japanese women there. Some had to stay there for a long time. Luckily, I only had to stay overnight. They [immigration authorities] were also checking some of my husband's documents. Because his papers were burned in the San Francisco earthquake, it took a while to track down his records.

"When I finally landed," Midori recalled, "an uncle and cousin came to see me. I was taken to my husband's house by car. It is the house that I still live in now. I was lucky that I didn't have to live in a labor camp [like other brides].

o o o o o o o o o o o o o o

As these issei women have described, revival of the ancient samurai code of conduct in a modernizing Japan, which also allowed for the education of girls, produced some women who found life in Japanese society increasingly confining. Cautious, but encouraged to be outspoken on certain issues, Iyo Tsutsui was also prompted to emigrate by the remarks of a geography teacher. Katsuno Fujimoto's father encouraged a progressive attitude in his daughter despite her traditional rearing, and Setsu Yoshihashi's compliant manner covered a growing determination and a will of steel. Kiyo Miyake came from a well-educated, Christian family, which marked her with significant differences from childhood. Her idealistic and decidedly Western concepts of marriage would mean a difficult future for her in Japan. Teiko Tomita, far too ambitious for a young woman, doggedly pursued a teaching career despite familial obligations and societal restrictions against women with careers. Yet these young women needed to mold their lives in ways that were acceptable to their families and their society as well as themselves.

The expectation–indeed obligation–for every Japanese girl was marriage and children. Success and fulfillment were possible only within the confines of marriage and child-rearing. Complying with such expectations, these women also revealed the means to accommodate their training with the modern ideas that crept into their lives. As emigrants to the United States they bridged the gap from Meiji women to issei pioneers.

CHAPTER THREE

Life In The United States

A suppressed desire for adventure, fed by a few stories and photographs, and colored with imagination, gave these Meiji women the courage to take that first step from ship to land. These young issei women came from a society homogeneous in language, race, and customs. In most instances they left close family units to live with new husbands whom they had never seen or scarcely knew. That first step became a giant leap when these pioneer women began to cope with the reality of their new lives.

KATSUNO FUJIMOTO

Katsuno Fujimoto's first months in her new country were filled with misery. "I was unhappy because my husband and I were so different in our ideas," Katsuno said, as she recalled the desperation she felt when faced with the thought of living the rest of her life with a man twenty-three years older than she. "I thought of committing suicide sometimes," she admitted, "but after our first child was born, I decided that I had to bear everything for my child's sake."

Katsuno's decision to devote her life to her children's welfare was a choice common to many brides who lived in Japan, as well as many an unfortunate issei bride. But the choice was one that left few regrets. Raised to accept hardships as part of life, to hold family welfare before individual need, Katsuno demonstrated the basic characteristics of a Meiji woman and channeled her efforts into her children. "Now," she added, "I think I was fortunate that I came to America." The outline of Katsuno's initial disappointments were repeated by many issei women, and most, like

Katsuno, molded their individual experiences into lives that were focused on the support and welfare of their families and their communities.

Hisayo Hanato recalled her first disappointment. "After the ship docked in Seattle, I went sightseeing. I was a tall girl and thought America was for tall people. Well, I felt as if I had shrunk because, you see, everybody [here] was very tall."

Hisayo had commented earlier that she had come to the United States to ease her mother's anxiety about an ailing, immigrant brother. As she continued her story, it became understandable how her initial disappointment grew to despondence.

"At first I did not feel good about coming to this country. You see, right after I came, my brother died. He had been living in Nebraska and I never even got to see him."

Fortunately for Hisayo, she had another source of support. "My older sister [and her husband] had a rather large dairy farm between Seattle and Tacoma. They had worked very hard, overcome many difficulties, and had become very successful. When someone wanted to borrow money from a local bank, people said that if Yamada (that was their name) cosigned, then the bank always approved the loan. I felt that this was a measure of success. Well, my older sister went back to Japan for a visit and caught the flu," Hisayo said, recalling her sadness as she revealed, "During that visit she died.

"One of the reasons that I came to the States was because I had an older brother and sister here. But within the first two years, I lost both of them, so I changed my mind about living in America." In addition to her personal losses, Hisayo confronted a racial prejudice that was completely unanticipated. "Because there was such strong anti-Japanese feeling here," she confessed, "I was very much afraid of the people and wanted to go back to Japan as soon as I could."

But Mr. Hanato moved her to Southern California and settled on Terminal Island, where a highly competitive fishing industry was thriving. Competition between fishermen of varying national origins was keen, and the resultant racial tensions often ran high, as evidenced in the almost yearly introduction of bills in the California legislature to deny fishing licenses to aliens. "My husband, his friend who had a boat, and another man became partners in a fishing business. I didn't like it very much," Hisayo recalled. She seemed happier when her husband gave up fishing and moved the family to Long Beach, where the Hanatos lived until World War II. With the birth of two daughters and a busy life running a small restaurant, Hisayo's despondence abated, and a generosity of spirit reminiscent of her mother's is reflected in her commentary about the Depression.

"I remember the Depression. It was a time when there were breadlines in the park nearby. Since we had a restaurant, we did not have to worry about eating, but it was different for others. We were located on Ocean Boulevard, and people who didn't have jobs would hang around at the beach. They were all white people. We expected those who came into the restaurant to be customers. Instead they begged us to feed them for free. Most of the time we fixed them something, like a sandwich. Well, when we'd give one person something, he'd tell others that he got food at our place. So many people came to our restaurant that we finally had to tell them to go to the breadline in the park. Still, we gave them as much as we could.

"We, too, had a hard time. Sometimes there wasn't enough cash to pay our workers." For Hisayo and other issei women, this was a period when the Meiji lesson of endurance was sorely tested.

SATSUYO HIRONAKA

After her arrival in the United States, Satsuyo Hironaka worked so hard that it never occurred to her how terribly difficult her life really was. When asked about hardships, she seemed to cast around vaguely and mentioned child-rearing. Then she stated simply and emphatically, "I was just too busy living!" And indeed she was.

Satsuyo had married her childhood friend at seventeen and had borne her first child a year later. Her husband had emigrated to the United States and began farming. Satsuyo soon followed her husband but left their baby in Japan until the child was four years old. She found herself pregnant soon after her arrival and eventually gave birth to eight children, five boys and three girls, including a set of twins.

Besides caring for a large family, Satsuyo recalled, "I got up at four in the morning and never went to bed before midnight. We had twenty to thirty field hands who had to eat breakfast at six. We hired a cook, but I took care of making the rice and washing the dishes. After breakfast I gave instructions to the field hands and told them where to work in the orchard [100 acres]. Then I came back to the house to do whatever was necessary. That included washing by hand for all the employees and cleaning their rooms. We had a house as big as a barn, and all the hired hands slept upstairs, though eventually we built a bunkhouse. Every night I had to heat hot water on a wood fire for everyone's bath, twenty to thirty people every night," she said, referring to the large, Japanese-style tub that required steaming hot water. "After I had two or three children," she added, "the cook did the cleaning."

Even as her family grew, Satsuyo through economizing and frugality was able to save five hundred dollars to help finance a trip back to Japan and fulfill her father's wish to see Satsuyo again. Her treasured memories with childhood stories about filial piety add poignance to her commentary. More than seventy years after she left her home and family in Japan, she acknowledged that she had not completely fulfilled those most important filial obligations. Satsuyo, at age ninety, said, "I still recall this incident once in a while: When I left Japan [first traveling by rail to a seaport], I leaned out of the train window to wave good-bye and heard my father say, 'Don't stay too long in America. Come back and see me while I am still in good health.' I thought, 'When I have saved two thousand dollars, I will return to Japan.'"

With the five hundred dollars in savings, the Hironakas bought some land during the Depression and hoped to increase their investment, but as the Depression worsened, the goal to save two thousand dollars continued to elude Satsuyo. "How hard I worked," she exclaimed, "but the money could not be saved! Just enough to eat every day," she added sadly.

"My father had said, 'Don't stay in America more than five years.' I remembered his last words and tried to go back to Japan, but I just could not do it," Satsuyo said and added regretfully, "We are undutiful children."

The ensuing years brought Satsuyo a measure of prosperity and happiness. "Recently [ten years earlier] our land was sold for a housing development and I have a small fortune now," she revealed. Had this windfall occurred earlier, she could have made her visit to Japan. The missed visit was the only regret she expressed in the commentary of her long life. Then she added, as though fate had reprimanded her, "It was destiny that when my husband was about seventy years old, he went back to Japan for a visit and never came back. He got sick there and died."

Setsu Yoshihashi

Because of her cooperative and obedient nature, considered great assets in Japan, Setsu had never complained when she was shunted from one household to another. Her longest stay, "seven long years," was with an aunt who provided a harsh and trying emotional environment. But this experience was somewhat offset by a privileged social and financial situation.

Setsu emphasized that she, like other Japanese women of her time, was lulled into a belief that after marriage her new life in America would be with a secure businessman of a fine family. Her new husband, unable to escort her to the United States because of the demands of his business, provided Setsu with first-class passage, a rare extravagance for a picture bride. Setsu obviously enjoyed the luxury and comfort. Demure and refined, dressed in a beautiful new kimono, Setsu stepped forward to meet her future. When Mr. Yoshihashi came on board to claim his new bride, the contrast between the new bride and groom was startling. Always careful of her own appearance because her uncle, a military man, demanded meticulous grooming, Setsu noted immediately, "When I first met my husband, he had a stocking hat on his head and dirty shoes on his feet. He was not a handsome man, and he had extremely short legs," Setsu recalled, registering her disappointment and shock at his general appearance. And then she noticed that he was much older. "There was a fifteen-year difference in our ages," she was to learn later. "I'm sure we greeted each other, but I don't remember. I had come to a foreign land. I was now in the hands of a stranger and I was in a daze.

"Then Sho-san, the diplomat who was entrusted to take care of me during the voyage, met my husband. He looked so sad for me. I still remember that look on his face.

"The Matsui side of my family is very distinguished looking, but the Yoshihashis are not physically attractive people. They have such short legs. I was so embarrassed that I couldn't walk next to my husband. I was very vain and had high expectations. I never could fall in love with him. But he was very strong-willed, and I could not change his mind, so I gave in to him."

Caught in the confusion of adjusting to a new life and her shock at finding that her husband was not what he was said to be, Setsu did indeed succumb to her husband's dictates. But those characteristics that had enabled Setsu to stand up to her Aunt Matsui would emerge later when she desperately needed every ounce of strength.

"I remember everything in such a confused frenzy," she continued. "After I was released from Angel Island, my husband and I stayed at the Kumamoto Inn in San Francisco. We went to the World's Fair, where there were a lot of mechanical exhibitions," Setsu related. It was a rare opportunity for any young person, but in shock at her encounter with Mr. Yoshihashi, the excitement of the fair only contributed to her confusion. "I didn't understand what was going on, because I didn't know anything about machines. I was in a daze," she repeated.

"Because there was a fifteen-year age difference between us, I knew nothing of life, but he [my husband] had experienced the hardships of life. He probably thought I was just a child and wondered, 'Oh, my God, what have I gotten myself into.'

"My daughter, who has since passed away, used to say, 'Mother, how could you possibly come to a foreign country and marry a man you'd never met? I just don't understand.' But, you know, women in those days were not allowed to live by their own wits and strength. We could only do what someone told us to do. All we could do was to say 'yes' and be obedient. It was so different then. Modern women can do what they want and say 'no' if they don't like something. Modern women have the right to decide whom they want to marry. But in my day we could only obey our parents or relatives. If they said, 'Do this,' we had to do it. We were brought up and trained that way from childhood. It's difficult to understand if you think in terms of modern customs. Setsu added a brief reminder, "I was brought up in the olden times."

"We went by boat from San Francisco to Los Angeles. Then we went to live in Hollywood. After that the hardships began. That," the usually reticent Setsu pronounced, "was the beginning of a living hell.

"My husband had a laundry business in Hollywood and employed about twenty people. Everyone [back in Japan] had told me that Yoshihashi, being able to send me a first-class ticket, was a successful man. Considering the standards in those days, it was extremely expensive to send a first-class ticket from Japan to America.

"My husband wouldn't take me to his house for a long time. He was afraid I'd be upset, so we stayed in a hotel in Los Angeles for a while. Sometime later, he finally took me to his house. I was appalled!" The degree of Setsu's distress was such that she never once described the house that was her first home in America. "But," Setsu continued, "because he was so finicky, his room was absolutely clean and spotless. He was a picky, neat man," she stated, and bit by bit described a husband whose self-absorption did not allow any emotional sharing.

"My husband had high ideals–he hated to work for anyone. He would suffer anything as long as he could be his own boss. He used to say, 'There is no way I would ever work for the whites.' Because of his stubbornness, he never made any money. My daughter would ask him, 'Papa, with that kind of attitude, why did you ever come to America?'

Setsu's list of disappointments grew longer as she described her difficult marital situation with the following incident. "Not long after I started working in the laundry, my husband's elder brother, who was in the military, committed suicide over the cavalry issue. This brother was a senior member of the *kiheitei* [cavalry]. He was an inspector general. Another officer who had gone to France as a government envoy during the First World War reported that, from what he had seen, the cavalry would not be useful to Japan because the next war would be a war in the air–a war using planes. He said the period in which cavalrymen marched to Manchuria was over. There was a fierce discussion between our brother and this officer. One argued for the glory of the cavalry and the other on the side of the airplanes. The discussion became bitter, and struggles ensued. Our brother had never been in France, and all he cared about was his cavalry. He had many followers, but of course, the other officer was correct in his prediction. It was because of this bitter controversy that my husband's brother committed suicide. He was a very dedicated officer with a one-track mind.

"He committed suicide according to the traditional samurai code, by disemboweling himself. The event was even covered by the American newspapers. Now there is a statue in his honor in Toyohashi. Even to this day, young officers still pay homage at the place where he committed suicide and say that his military honor and tears are buried there. He was that famous a person. His son also became a general years later.

"Well, when my husband heard this news, he suddenly fell ill. He said that continuing the laundry business wouldn't give him the rest he needed, so he said we had to move to a rural farm area. He took me to live on a farm owned by a Mr. Nappa in Anaheim. We went by wagon.

"When we arrived at the farm, we stopped under a chestnut tree, and my husband put up a tent. He told me that this was now our home. I felt like we were tramps. Real tramps. Other Japanese people had put tents up nearby, too. There were some from Hiroshima who worked on the farm. My husband told these people that they wouldn't be able to get ahead and raise a family in America without knowing the English language. He said that he would teach them, and every night in our tent he held classes. He was really a strange man."

Despondent and dispirited, Setsu revealed, "I cried every night in front of our makeshift home, and between the sobs I taught ABC's to the Japanese. I really felt like a beggar."

Living according to the whims of this difficult man as well as the natural elements, Setsu said, "When it rained, the water would seep into the tent at the corners. I caught a cold and became quite ill. I couldn't even get out of bed. A friend, Mrs. Kagawa, nursed me. She told my husband, 'Really, Mr. Yoshihashi, I don't know about your circumstances, but must you live like this? It's your fault that your wife is ill.'

"At that time the man who had been looking after the laundry for my husband finally insisted we return. After two or three months in the country, we went back."

Rescued from her vagabond life, Setsu found she had only exchanged one life of suffering for another just as difficult. "Then I worked at the laundry for seven years," she said. "I worked until midnight every day, all those years. Life was very hard."

Setsu had lived in a household full of servants and had never learned to cook, but life in the United States brought dramatic changes. "I got up early and had to cook for twenty people," she said. "We had many single employees, so I had to feed them. I cooked twice a day, breakfast and lunch. Oh, what a chore that was! They all went out to have fun on Sundays and didn't return until Monday," she said, as she recalled the relief of not having to prepare those huge meals one day a week. "We had a lot of problems with the business, too. It wasn't an easy way to earn a living."

In Meiji Japan, a woman was rarely a wife and mother exclusively. When a woman married into a family, she was expected to help on the family farm or in the family business. But living in an extended family, she also had the help of other female members of the household and was seldom expected to do everything herself. Setsu had no help, but her husband obviously did not consider the possibility that she could be overworked.

"I had five children in all and three were born at the laundry. I took the children to the babysitter's in the afternoon, and I worked until midnight ironing clothes. I thought my husband was a horrid, cruel man." If Setsu had been in Japan and had been the only woman in the household, she would at least have managed the household finances. Unfortunately, Mr. Yoshihashi did not allow even this possibility until much later. "'You have me work like a man, get me pregnant, and won't give me any spending money,' I said to him. His business partner told him that even though I was a family member, he should at least give me some spending money. Then my husband gave me forty dollars, and I went right out to buy some clothes for my children.

"I worked from morning till night. My life was hell in those days, but it is because of those years working in the laundry that I was able to survive in America. The hardships I went through then paled in comparison to my life later, because later I had to support my family of seven when my husband became ill and couldn't work."

Setsu's earlier attitude of obedience and acquiescence gradually faded as she bore the shock of substandard housing, living in a tent for three months, and then working for years in a laundry from dawn until midnight. Whatever hopes she might have had of an easier life vanished as she learned to live by her "own wits and strengths."

Then Mr. Yoshihashi became ill. "During that time," she said, "I worked at the desk and put up advertisements in front of the store offering customers a ten percent discount. As a result," she stated proudly, "we increased business. Then I had to work until four in the morning to get the work done, washing and ironing the clothes. And because of what I did, all of us were able to eat and survive." But even the strongest of Meiji women couldn't rear children and work those hours indefinitely without a husband's help.

"My husband was physically too weak for that kind of work, so we sold our business and he started selling insurance in Pasadena. Our eldest son, the third child, was six months old when we moved. We were able to start the insurance business because we had some money from selling the laundry.

"The insurance business was extremely good in the beginning," Setsu said, as she recalled the brief hiatus from her grueling existence. "We had saved some money, which we used to lend to those who didn't have enough to insure themselves." But fate tested her once again. "Then, the Depression hit and we were caught up in it. No one could pay back the money we had lent. We were hit hard and landed on the bottom again.

"My husband became even sicker [with asthma] and he wasn't able to do anything. The doctor had to come and give my husband three shots a day to relieve him. I didn't know what to do," Setsu said, as she recalled the anxiety of nursing her husband, caring for young children, and needing to find some way to support the family. "All my children were too young to help out [financially]. The oldest child was twelve. I found work at a white family's home for half a day and took my children with me to work. I would then do laundry for customers after I got home. It was the only work I could do at home and still look after my children. This is how our family of seven was able to survive."

Setsu was now in charge of the business, and though her life was once again physically taxing, she obviously derived some satisfaction from controlling some of the family's economic resources. In Meiji Japan, the husband earned and the wife managed the household finances. If the couple lived with in-laws, the mother-in-law managed the household finances. With most issei couples, the delimitation between earnings and management was maintained. Given freer circumstances in the United States, however, the management of money extended beyond meeting immediate domestic needs, and eventually the money manager became a controlling power in the family.

"I made a sign," Setsu explained, "put it in front of the house, and customers began to come. I didn't have a washing machine and couldn't do all of the clothes by hand with so many customers. What happened then was strange. I picked up the telephone book and leafed through the washing machine advertisements and called one of the places listed. I said in my broken English that I wanted to buy a washing machine and asked if I could try one for a couple of weeks. They said fine and brought a washer to my house. I was able to do the laundry, but the machine was too small for all the business I was doing. I called the shop back and told them I wanted to buy a bigger washer. He said the price was two hundred dollars and told me how much the down payment and monthly charges were. I was able to make the down payment from the money I made from using the smaller machine and then bought the larger washer. I'm still shocked at the courage I had then. Imagine! I called a shop and asked for a deal over the phone in my broken English. I am proud of myself! I was able to pay for the machine completely and feed all the members of my family.

"Oh, how lucky I was that my husband's employees had taught me how to do laundry. If I didn't have that skill, we would all have been in deep trouble. I washed, ironed, and folded, sometimes until 4:00 A.M.; otherwise the laundry wouldn't be ready on time.

"My husband didn't work a bit. He never got well. He had asthma each spring and fall, and I knew I couldn't depend on him to hold a steady job. I then realized he couldn't even support himself, that I could not rely on him, and that he could not assume responsibility for his own family." With a determination dredged from still-untapped strength, Setsu recalled, "I made up my mind that I had to work as though he was dead. So that's what I did." Transplanted to another cultural realm, the compliant, well-bred Meiji woman shed much of her shell to rely on those traits necessary to become a strong, self-assured issei woman. Setsu managed the family's affairs and began to make major decisions.

In Meiji Japan, a woman had no social freedom. Instead, when her life became difficult, she accepted the *kuro* or hardship as life's necessity. Setsu, like other issei women, turned to resignation that freed her emotionally and gave her the psychological energy to continue. "I just accepted," she said with Meiji resolve, "that he wasn't alive, so I wasn't too sad for myself. I didn't mind working myself to the bone or going down to the depths of the ocean if it was for my children, but I felt like I carried a load of stones on my back."

Accepting the burden of *kuro*, Setsu continued with dogged determination. "I learned that people do not go crazy easily. I was able to make it through these hardships because I had children, and I loved them so. My will to survive was solely for them. I never knew my parents' love for me, and it was painful for me. I was determined never to be separated from my own children; so I was able to survive anything. I felt just like I was dead, but kept on going. That's all. I had no time to think about my condition. I just had to survive, and I did it all through sheer will."

Though long hours of grueling labor were common in the lives of issei women, and often their lives were made extremely difficult by the circumstances of their marriages, Setsu Yoshihashi's life was particularly harsh.

"I did laundry work for some time. How many years. I don't remember. Just about the time my life got a little better, the city of Pasadena passed a law prohibiting commercial laundries at home, but by then I was better off and didn't have to do laundry work." The contact with customers and successfully supporting her family had built Setsu's confidence, and she began to trust her acquired economic savvy.

"I had started working for a greengrocer and sold vegetables at the Farmers' Market in Pasadena. The market was very popular then and stretched out for four or five blocks. Competition was very stiff. I worked for three different bosses during that period of time. I sold vegetables in my broken English, but my customers all liked me. They all asked for the 'Oriental' and all wanted me to serve them. My boss couldn't fire me or his sales would have declined sharply.

"Everything seemed to be going pretty well for us until one day a policeman came to where I was working, arrested me, and dragged me to the station." Frightened, confused, and unable to understand the legal problem, Setsu said, "I had no idea what was going on and called my daughter. The policeman explained that I had not paid some sales taxes. He was referring to a time before I started to work at the Farmers' Market and after I had quit the laundry business. A friend had come to us with a business proposition to start a grocery store. I had withdrawn some money from my children's savings. With this money, my friend and I went into business. We bought a truck and started a grocery store on Green Street. The store failed and we went bankrupt. By law, we were supposed to have charged a sales tax, but my partners never did. Come to find out, they had bought the business in my name because the partners and my husband had debts and couldn't get credit in their names. Well, the police arrested me because the business was in my name.

"The [revenue] officer said, 'I don't know anything about your circumstances, but the store is in your name. We must, therefore, ask you for the government's share of the taxes. However,' he continued, 'I see that you can't pay your taxes, so you may pay the government in monthly installments. As long as the debt is in your name, I can't release you from this obligation.'

"Well, because the sales taxes hadn't been paid for so long, there was a lot of interest, too. My daughter was working for the Department of Education by then, and I was working at the Farmers' Market. Both of us paid three dollars or five dollars a week on what we owed." The legality of the ownership was surely questionable, but Setsu was a Meiji woman whose primary concern was moral responsibility. If her husband used her name, it was as if she had signed. "When the war started," Setsu continued, we went to the revenue office and found that we still owed one hundred and thirty dollars. I wanted to pay it off completely, because I knew the interest on the debt would just grow. My daughter and I settled the debt before we entered camp. I ended up paying all the taxes because they had put the business in my name. I was so angry then!" Setsu stated with a vexation that would make it difficult to conjure up that compliant child who had spent years being agreeable in various households back in Japan. As a measure of what it cost her in pride and economic difficulty, she declared in strong but measured words, "I still keep the receipt.

"Life was very hard, but the government was very understanding," she continued. "When I think of all the things that have happened to me, I'm surprised I kept on going. And," she added reflectively, "even though we went through such hard times, I couldn't reproach my husband."

Attempting to come to terms with her ambivalent feelings about Mr. Yoshihashi, Setsu explained, "My husband came to America in the thirty-eighth year of Meiji–during the time of the Russo-Japanese War. He had gone to Tokyo to study to became a military officer. But his legs were too short, so he couldn't become a soldier. He was a stubborn man with the unrealized ambition to be a soldier, a man who hated to lower his head to anyone. On the other hand," Setsu generously added, "he was a serious, hardworking man who would never do anything crooked. He had asthma and he was in no condition to be criticized.

"I just worked and cried. When I started to work in the grocery store, I worked from six in the morning, and on Saturdays until eleven at night. I would be exhausted on Sundays, but when I tried to sleep in, my husband would say, 'Mama, what are you doing sleeping so late? You are a bad example for the children.' Then my elder daughter Fumiko would say, 'Papa, please,' and she would try to calm him. He never drank or gambled so I just couldn't reproach him for his behavior." The epitome of endurance, Setsu Yoshihashi drew from the spiritual resources taught to her in Meiji Japan to help her weather a life and marriage that made immense physical and emotional demands on her.

"Just before the war," Setsu said, continuing her commentary, "I went to work for a white family. They were very nice to me. Dr. Cramer, a millionaire and the head of the house, trusted me completely and treated me very kindly. He would send me to work upstairs where there were diamonds all over the place, but the family never allowed other maids to work upstairs. I worked for three or four families, all Dr. Cramer's relatives."

Though Setsu's material resources continued to be limited, her strength of will and ingenuity were boundless. "I was very worried about leaving my two older sons home while I was out working. So, I asked [my friend] Mrs. Fuyumi if she would let my eldest son work at her grocery store after school. But she told me that it was very difficult to work for Mr. Fuyumi and that Ichiro, my son, might not last very long. I told her it was much better for him to work for a strict man than to play outside every day after school. I told her that I would buy all my groceries from their store if she did this one favor for me. I told her to pay him very little if she liked. My son, therefore, worked at the grocery store for three dollars a week. He saved his earnings and was able to buy a bicycle for himself. He was so happy and proud.

"When I started to work at the Farmers' Market, someone there was looking for a boy to help out during the summer. I said that my son had experience working at a small grocery store and asked that person to hire my son. My son started to work there making eighteen dollars a week. I had my younger son work at the Fuyumis' store where his brother had worked."

Reducing her eighteen-hour days with a new job and finding work for her sons brought some measure of relief and security to Setsu, but misfortune continued to haunt her. "Then," Setsu stated, "the war started."

KIYO MIYAKE

Kiyo Miyake had led a sheltered life in Japan. Nurtured in a warm and supportive household, she married a man who matched her in energy and intelligence. She recalled a comfortable sea voyage to the United States, where she saw the wonders of San Francisco before confronting a life so different that she could never have imagined what it held.

"When he [my husband] came to meet me in Japan," Kiyo recalled, "he must have had someone manage his dairy farm in the Imperial Valley [California]. After our marriage, he returned to the United States alone. I came later and was in the care of the president of Doshisha University. When I lived in Japan, my circle of associations was very limited. But on board ship I met all kinds of people. I was sometimes surprised and sometimes shocked.

"My husband met me in San Francisco, where we stayed for a while. We went shopping for clothes because I came in kimono. I also went to Koshado, the bookstore. The owner of the store had been on the same ship. He helped me send a telegram home.

I was not really surprised at what I saw in San Francisco. I had lived in Kobe and Osaka, so I was used to city life. However, I was somewhat disappointed when I was taken to the Japanese section of San Francisco. It was very dirty. I was surprised to find it so, because houses in Kobe were really beautiful. Kobe was a very graceful town. Osaka was a very high-class area, too. Even schools were very nice places.

"In Japan we had electricity and gas in our house, of course, and we used to cook our meals on a gas stove. When I came here, there were no such things. Well," she added as an afterthought, "it was understandable in the countryside."

Living on a farm was a huge adjustment for Kiyo, whose life had been centered around intellectual pursuits rather than physical labor. "When I first arrived [in this country], I was very quiet and looked frail. I was very fair, even pale, and must have looked unfit to do farm work," Kiyo said. This delicate, educated, refined young woman recalled, "People told me, 'You'll die if you go the the Imperial Valley and farm!'

"After I came to the Imperial Valley, my husband switched from dairy farming to raising cantaloupes. My husband asked me if I'd help with the field work. Since I was his wife, I had to follow him. When I was told to hoe for the first time, tears rolled down my cheeks because I had never even seen a hoe before in my life, and I didn't know how to use one. I couldn't say, 'I cannot do it.' If I said that, then he [my husband] would say, 'You are no good, because you were educated in such a way that no matter what the task, as long as you pray for it, it will be done for you.'"

Naive and sheltered, Kiyo also admitted, "I was also really scared. We had many Japanese field hands and those men looked very rough and dark. And I didn't know American ways very well yet," she added. At this point in her life Kiyo was unable to distinguish what was "American" and what was simply the difference between her rather comfortable life in Japan and a life of strenuous physical labor.

"We had to get up very early to work and had to finish by 10:00 A.M. because the temperature would reach over 110 degrees in the afternoon, and no one could work then. People used to die from the heat!

"There was very little water in the valley," Kiyo recalled and what little they had for [domestic] use needed to be processed. "We had a huge storage container that the menfolk used to fill. After the sediment settled, I would climb up a ladder and scoop out the upper part. Then, I would carry the water back to the house and pour it into a water purifier. The water dripped through layers of material and then into a pail. I had to cook for ten people with this water.

"I never had to cook meals when I lived in Japan, because I lived in a dormitory. My cooking was often criticized," Kiyo said. Japanese men were used to being served and expected to be served well. "When I was scolded, I became terribly vexed and upset," she admitted, but she held her temper and tried harder. "I wrote, '*Kanchi meshi taite otto o okorsuna* [Don't make your husband mad by making bad-tasting rice],' and posted it on the kitchen wall. Then I tried even harder to cook good rice.

"The workers used to say, 'Hey, old woman, the *miso* [soybean paste] soup is too salty!' Or, 'The pickles are too sour!' Then I'd say, 'I'm sorry! I'm very sorry!' One day an old man who used to work for us said, 'You are a very admirable young woman.' I replied, 'No, I don't know anything about cooking. Please teach me.' Then he said, 'Don't worry about cooking. They don't know what they are talking about. Besides, they shouldn't call you an old woman. Don't get angry. It's the way they talk in the Hiroshima district.'"

Buoyed by this old man's kind attention, Kiyo was reminded to maintain her self-esteem. "I replied, 'Yes. No matter what they call me, my worthiness as a person will not change.' 'That's right, that's right,' he replied. Yet when my cooking was criticized, I was really hurt and upset, and he tried to console me. Well, I just decided to become a good cook.

"That old man used to say to me, 'Why did you come to America? You came here to suffer. You made a big mistake.' I said to him, 'Not at all. I don't mind working, cleaning bathrooms, whatever. I accept it. I'll do anything.' We talked a lot together."

Kiyo might have hoped for some encouragement from her husband, but knew better than to expect it. Mr. Miyake was a product of Meiji Japan and his expectations were high. But Mr. Miyake never pretended to be other than what he was or to offer Kiyo a life of ease. During their marriage negotiations, Kiyo recalled, "Once my husband wrote me a letter [from America] and said, 'There are many educated women who are disappointed with life in America, because there were no decent houses, no pianos, no this and no that. I don't have any property except my own self. If you expect more than that, I can't help you at all.' I still have that letter somewhere. When I read the letter, I was very impressed. I thought if he could write that well, he must be a person to be respected. I didn't think the average college graduate would be able to measure up to him.

"Yes, I was lonesome sometimes," Kiyo admitted, "because I was far away from Japan. It was so. If you called your family as loud as you could, they could not hear you." Despite the occasional melancholy times, Kiyo always rebounded with optimism and determination. Recalling Millet's painting, *The Angelus*, she said, "But I came here with a dream, so I didn't discourage easily. I never thought of giving up everything and going back home.

"Even if I had to sleep in a tent," she declared, "I could see the stars, and I thought it was very beautiful. Yes," she declared, "we lived in a tent house, you see." And probably as a result of her efforts Kiyo could say, "It was clean, not that bad. When you think about it," she bubbled with irrepressible spirit, "it was even romantic. We lived in it for two years.

"During the summer we had to get out of the valley. Otherwise you would become sick or die from the heat. We'd take a rest and stay with friends. Then around 1927, we moved to this place [Livingston, California] because my husband knew that I was not in good health. My husband heard about the Yamato Colony from a friend in the Imperial Valley."

The Yamato Colony was a Japanese Christian farming community established in Livingston. Two additional Japanese farming communities were also started near Cortez, and Merced, California. At that time the California Alien Land Act of 1913 prohibited the purchase of land by any immigrant ineligible for citizenship, and prevailing immigration laws did not allow Japanese or any other Asian immigrants naturalized citizenship. But the Yamato Colony lands were purchased as a corporation and in turn sold shares to Japanese aliens.

"We bought twenty acres, and at first," Kiyo said, "we lived in a small shack. People wonder how we could live like that. Now we have just a garden left from that farm and there remains only the frame of our house. That's all. We lived there for a long time."

Despite the hardships, the life of a farmer's wife in a Japanese Christian community was reminiscent of, if not strikingly similar to, Kiyo's earlier recollection of *The Angelus*. "We grew grapes in Livingston and were given many children, our treasure," Kiyo affirmed. "I do like this kind of quiet life, but for three years we did not have much income. We used money from the sale of our ranch in the Imperial Valley, even though it was not much.[1] My husband found other work, too, and we leased out a part of our land. Our living conditions began to improve little by little," Kiyo

[1]Mr. Miyake had probably purchased this property in someone else's name.

said, but she also confirmed that the lessons of frugality were deeply ingrained. "Once I remember thinking to myself, 'For the last ten years I have not bought anything for myself.' It wasn't just me. It was the same for all the people in the Yamato Colony. If you didn't have that much determination, you couldn't live here or accomplish anything.

"During those years my seven children were born. I was very busy and it was very difficult. There were some housewives who didn't have to work outside [their homes] but I had to. I used to make thirty-two tons of raisins every year. My son used to make over fifteen tons. But I never worried about finances and depended on my husband, although there were some [issei] women who were very knowledgeable about the family finances." As in Japan, where wives controlled the household budget, many issei women assumed that responsiblity, and some like Setsu Yoshihashi eventually assumed total financial control. Kiyo, who felt she had enough responsibility with her child-rearing, household duties, and farm work, recalled in detail her busy workday.

"Because my husband went out to work about 6:00 A.M. in the morning, I got up earlier to cook for him. Then I would clean up and get ready for lunch. I would nurse the baby and then go out to hoe between feedings." Decades later, as Kiyo Miyake sat in her house in Livingston, California, and unfolded her life story, she stated matter-of-factly, "I did all the hoeing by myself," and gestured as she spoke, "twenty acres here and forty acres over there."

Explaining that in some ways Mr. Miyake held true to the character of a typical Japanese husband, Kiyo stated, "My husband never praised me. When he got sick and could not get out of bed, I did all the work with one Mexican laborer. I inspected the raisins and set up all the things the worker had to do ahead of time, so that we could work with the greatest efficiency. I did it all by myself and produced thirty-two tons of raisins. For the first time my husband said, 'Oh!' That's all. It was the first time he said anything that was close to praise."

Neither Kiyo nor her husband could throw off all the old Japanese attitudes that governed relationships between husband and wife, but the mutual respect, honesty, and sharing with which they began their lives flourished in their new setting. As Kiyo continued to describe how harsh and difficult her life was as an immigrant, she also described the sharing and building of a marriage filled with mutual respect and energetic caring. "My husband could discuss anything in depth," Kiyo declared. "He studied hard, so he knew a great many things. I often said to my children, 'Papa made a big mistake. He should have studied to become a doctor.' I still think so. He was really sharp and diligent. He was never surprised by anything, even if it had rained rocks and fire. Had he gone to a university and met professors, he could have sharpened his mind. If he had been a man of average intelligence and effort, this life would have been all right; however, he should have been disciplined by educated people in order to realize his potential. He also needed to be more humble and to be able to listen to people. I used to argue with him about this and say to him, 'This is what's lacking in you most. You could have been a great man,' but it was too late.

"I still have many of his writings. When he thought he was right, he expressed his opinions eloquently on paper and sent them out. I told him, 'You must wrestle with theologians who have studied far and wide in order to sharpen your own thinking. You have no such opportunity, so you have created for yourself a small world of your own.' This was the most difficult thing to deal with for me. He needed some challenge. If a man runs ahead of everybody, then he becomes irrelevant. He finally amounts to nothing. I really felt sorry for him.

"'You know,' I said to him once, 'you are a very difficult person to be with. It's a shame. You have such talent, yet you have not had a chance to develop it. Just as you have said, I'm not a very gifted person. Your wife should have been the wisest or the most foolish woman in the whole world. I am neither of those extremes. That's why you have so much trouble with me.'" Then Kiyo added with relish, "We were a very interesting couple."

It was rare in those days that a Japanese wife spoke up to her husband, and had the Miyakes remained in Japan, their relationship would surely not have developed in the same way. Though Kiyo never felt herself the intellectual equal of Mr. Miyake, she had enormous regard for her own self worth and powers of assessment. Kiyo would caution Mr. Miyake about his idealism and debate with him regularly.

"Once the Okuyes [neighbors] had a worker, a graduate of Doshisha University, who used come to our home to talk," Kiyo recalled with amusement. "One day my husband said to him, 'I haven't made too many mistakes in my lifetime, but I did make a big mistake in my marriage.' The worker said, 'Oh?' My husband explained, 'They say when you are looking for a spouse, you should believe only half of what she tells you. I believed only a quarter of what my wife said, and that was too much.'

Taking her husband's bait, Kiyo recalled, "Then I spoke up, 'You had better not judge a person too quickly. You see my children are still small. When they grow up and become like St. Augustine, then my real value will be recognized. Right now they're only babies. Their lives have just begun. The race is on from now. You'll see how effective I can be in raising my children.' Then this Doshisha graduate said, 'Wow! You've got a really fine wife!' Everyone came to my aid, and my husband was terribly vexed." Then Kiyo exclaimed with mischievous glee, "It was really fun!

"Once," she continued, "Mr. Seo asked me, 'How long have you been married?' I replied, 'Well, we have been married a long time.' He said, 'It's really wonderful that you can still talk to each other.' I answered, 'Oh, yes. We talk every night.' Then our neighbor said, 'You have your lights on every night until early in the morning. What do you do?' My husband replied, 'Oh, I talk to my wife every night.' Then the neighbor asked, 'What do you find to talk about every night?' Imagine asking a question like that," Kiyo reflected with pleasure.

"We talked about government, politics, and other things. Once I just could not come to an agreement with my husband, but I had to leave for a Bible study meeting. When I came back, I found his note: 'It seems as if you had the better argument in our discussion tonight. Good night.' And he was sound asleep.

"The other area where I had trouble with my husband was in the education of my children. He was raised in the pure Japanese style and wanted to raise his children that way. However, children nowadays cannot be taught in the Japanese style, even if they are *nisei* [American-born children of the issei]. This was a problem for me. Everybody here [in Livingston] knows how hard nosed he was.

"I used to teach our children Japanese every night for about thirty minutes. We had only one room in that small house, and my husband declared, 'This is the place where the kids study, where we hold speech contests, and also the place where we fight!' It was really funny," Kiyo recalled with amusement and then added reflectively, "We were a very different couple, weren't we?"

As Kiyo completed this segment of her life story, she concluded, "Even though he was an *issei* and even though he was a very difficult person at times, our life together was excellent because we could talk to each other. He was a rare man in this respect." Kiyo's dream of life as portrayed in *The Angelus* came close to reality and she declared, "I never had any problems with him. I just thanked God for the gift."

TEIKO TOMITA

Mr. Tomita, Teiko recalled, had made some attempt to prepare her for life in America. "My husband had told me earlier, 'When you get to America you'll experience *kuro* [hardships].' I knew what the word meant, but I'd never experienced it, and I asked him to explain. Even if my family was not rich, I was given money to go to school and thought it was a matter of course. The idea of becoming independent and putting myself through school never entered my mind. I never knew any financial hardships. I had never experienced hunger, never cooked. The only thing I had to do was to study hard and get good grades.

"At that time it was said that America was experiencing a recession. This news was in all the newspapers we read. I asked my husband, 'Please tell me, what is a recession?' He replied, 'I can't explain it simply. You wouldn't understand. In any case when you get to America, you'll learn all kinds of *kuro*.'

"I asked him again, 'What do you mean by *kuro*?' I knew how to write the character for it, but I didn't understand it concretely. He answered, 'You must experience it on your own. When you face up to it, you will know exactly what *kuro* is all about.'"

Recalling her confusion, fear, and distress on Angel Island, Teiko said, "When I cried at the immigration office, I thought, 'Oh, this must be *kuro*.' After I was released from the immigration office," Teiko continued, "I went to stay in a hotel with my husband for a week. I suppose we were very unlucky from the very start. My husband said, 'Let's go out shopping to buy necessities. We need to get everything ready and go back to Wapato [Washington].'" Recalling the exact date, Teiko said, "Right before my husband went to sleep, he said, 'Today is February 28, the last day of the month. Let's count the money we have. Bring your money here, too.'

"He kept money in various places—in his pockets, in his suitcase, in mine, and in my handbag. He took out his bank passbook, too. We gathered everything together before we went to bed. 'We have enough money for one week,' my husband decided. 'Let's get our shopping done and go back to Wapato by train.' We put most of that money and the passbook on a shelf and the rest in his pants pocket.

"The Pacific Hotel, where we stayed, was a second-rate place," Teiko continued, "We had to go down the hall to get to the bathroom. When we finished, we came back, locked the door, and went to sleep. My husband returned first and asked when I got back, 'Did you lock the door?' I answered, 'Well, it closed with a big bang, so it must have locked.'

"We fell asleep and slept late. When morning came, both of us opened our eyes and lifted our heads. We noticed that the door was slightly ajar. The pants that my husband had placed on a chair was on the floor close to the door. We were startled and jumped up. Well, someone had stolen all the money we had including the bankbook! We had been robbed!

"'Don't worry,' my husband said. 'The savings will be all right, but we can't do anything about the cash. You'd better stay in bed, because you will be very hungry.' We didn't even have coins to buy breakfast. Then he went out to seek Mr. Shimanaka's help. He was a man from Nara Ken who had brought me some Western clothes to wear. I thought what a terrible place America was and cried. Fortunately my husband was able to borrow some money because he was a dependable person.

"We went out to get breakfast and did a little shopping. That night we took a train and left for Yakima. This was one of the first difficulties I confronted."

Though these initial experiences left her stunned, Teiko was comforted somewhat by her husband's consideration. "I came here knowing no real hardships, and my husband tried to keep me from worrying too much about it. He said to me, 'Oh, this is nothing. If we work hard for a couple of years, we'll get it all back.' He really tried hard not to worry me." His comments are spare by modern, Western standards, but to a young Japanese bride whose feelings were seldom if ever considered, the words were appreciated.

"I was shocked by many things, and I could not write about them to Japan," Teiko continued. But a letter from her father, a rare paternal acknowledgment to a daughter, alternately cheered her and left her with feelings of regret. "I had received a letter from my father, and was very happy. It was so kind and considerate of him. Whenever I thought about it, tears rolled down my face.

"Well, as soon as I arrived [in Wapato], I was told to get out in the field to work. As I weeded, I thought about my father's letter. I used to think of him as a fearsome person, but I realized he was a kind father, so I cried and cried all day.

"I guess my husband must have been watching me because he came over to me later and said, 'Poor thing! You must be thinking you shouldn't have come to America.' 'No,' I said. I'm not thinking about that at all.' He said, 'You've been crying all day long.' 'Ah,' I said, 'that's because I got a letter from my father and he said such kind things. He never said such things to me in Japan. I always thought that he was such a fearsome person and never had a chance to *amaeru* [exhibit affectionate behavior] in front of him. Whenever I had to talk to him, I had to think about what I was going to say beforehand. Otherwise I felt as if I might be scolded. I am truly moved by the discovery that he is such a kind person. I was crying because I was happy.' My husband replied, 'Is that right?' But he looked as if he was not convinced." The work of a schoolteacher in Japan could hardly be compared with the physical labor needed in farm fields. Mr. Tomita might have been grateful for his young wife's assurances, but he also knew she must have had at least a few regrets.

"Well, the hardships that followed could hardly be described," Teiko commented with a resignation akin to that which must have accompanied her early ordeals. "You just have to imagine them," she added. No longer the honor student teased about her lack of household skills, Teiko began to define the realities of her new life. "It was enormously difficult, but I learned how to cook," she declared. "Normally I prepared meals for three or four hired hands, but during the hay harvest, we hired about twenty young, strong men. It really was difficult for me, but I learned."

Adding to Teiko's difficulties were fears that were simply the result of new experiences. "When I first came to America and white people were around, I hid from them because I couldn't speak English. Even though my husband was not very good at it, he was used to talking to them, so I depended on him completely. Many of the people we had to hire were white."

As Teiko recalled how frightening the harvesting machine was, she described the sight. "It was big and could tie up hay in bundles. There was so much that the bales were piled high as a mountain. It was stacked up high all around Wapato and Yakima.

"Everyone worked. We had leased over a hundred acres and also grew watermelon, cantaloupe, corn, and other vegetables that we shipped to Seattle.

"I had babies one after another, so I didn't have to go out to the fields every day then, because cooking and taking care of babies was more than a full-time job. But during the harvest, I had to go to pick potatoes. When we weren't harvesting our own crop, I had to work for other farmers. Of course I got paid, but it was exhausting work. Fortunately we were still young, and we didn't think of it as *kuro*."

When Teiko left Japan for the United States, she left an entire way of life. An honor student and teacher who had known only books and little about the details of housekeeping, physical labor, and child-rearing, she learned each task painstakingly, sometimes only through trial and error.

"Making *sake* [rice wine] was another difficult thing for me to learn. When we moved to Wapato, we were with a lot of people who loved to drink. And even though my husband didn't like to drink," Teiko explained, Japanese etiquette dictated "I had to offer something to the workers. We had three to five field hands all year around and had to offer them *sake* every night. There was no problem when I could buy it, but during Prohibition I was in trouble.

"I learned to make *sake* from the other [Japanese] housewives who knew how. There are ways to make it from fruit, but the real Japanese sake had to be made from rice. I had to steam lots of rice first and then spread it on a table. When it cooled, I mixed it with yeast. There was a set ratio between rice and yeast. Then we put it in jugs.

"I wanted our workers to enjoy *banshaku* [a light evening drink] at supper time. When I made good *sake,* I was very happy. When the workers drank it and enjoyed it, it made me very happy." Teiko tackled each new domestic problem with the same dedication and pride she previously lavished on scholarship. "Once I made a batch that was sour and had to throw it out. Unfortunately this failure was repeated two or three times. I asked my friends what was wrong, and they said that once the *sake* turned sour, the jug was no longer usable. I had to buy a new jug and start all over again. They also advised me not to throw away the sour batch, which could be distilled into spirits. I borrowed the equipment, including the rubber tubing, to make rice spirits, and I boiled the sour *sake,* letting it drip into a bottle. It was harder than working in the field, and I didn't get any help from my husband. He knew nothing about the process. The only ones who could help me were my friends. After this experience, I very carefully measured the ingredients and," Teiko pronounced, "I became a very good *sake* maker."

"In 1929, about the time when America was entering the Depression," Teiko continued, "my husband was hired as head foreman of a nursery." Because she was no longer needed in the fields, Teiko's life was easier for a short time. "At the time the only thing I had to do was cook and care for babies. Then we moved to Sunnydale to start our own nursery. It was the worst possible time to begin a business."

Each difficulty seemed to precipitate a greater hardship as Teiko repeated, "Before I came to America, I didn't know what *kuro* meant. My husband had said that if I came to America, I would learn. Well, I did experience *kuro* and the Depression.

"We didn't know that the Depression was coming, so we threw away a good job and began this nursery business. We piled into a big car and drove out along the Columbia River. When we came out to this farm, I was holding a baby and my two little kids' hands. We had to live in a house that used to be a saloon and was about a hundred years old. It was near a very quiet, sparsely populated village. None of the other Japanese people lived in nice houses, so it didn't seem too bad in comparison. It was a two-story building that rattled when the wind blew hard and scared us.

"We were prepared to take a loss the first few years, figuring it would take some three years before we could realize a profit. The land had been farmed about ten years before, but had since turned into a wilderness. It was very hilly with lots of brush, not even flat land. Right behind our house there was a small hill with a lot of big trees. It took a whole year to plant it properly. Each day we cut down trees and cleared away the branches. Then we used dynamite to destroy the huge roots of the trees. We cultivated the land with horses and then seeded and planted small trees the size of chopsticks.

"That period was even more difficult because we didn't have any income. There were lots of Japanese people who lost jobs because of the Depression. We asked those people to work for us. They worked for less, but we still had to pay them, though we had no income. When our savings were gone, I understood what the Depression meant.

"There was a bank, the *Taiheiyo Shogyo Ginko* [Pacific Commerce Bank], which was owned by Mr. Masajiro Furuya, the owner of *Furuya Shoten* [Furuya Store]. This bank closed [during the Depression]. At that time many Japanese people banked with them. Fortunately–well–I don't know whether or not we were fortunate, but we didn't have enough money left to save in the bank. We had already taken out all our money and were using it for our daily expenses.

"In a way it was a blessing in disguise that we went through that much poverty. My children understand the hardships we endured. When they were in high school, we gave them a small amount of spending money, but they had to find work. They worked in the school office a few hours, or they did housework for white people. At that time I worked hard in the fields and also at home.

Beginning her day at five in the morning to cook breakfast for the hired workers, Teiko then sent the children off to school and finished the daily wash before working in the fields. "I washed everybody's clothes, including those of the workers," Teiko recalled. I washed 365 days a year," she said, and added in exclamation, "even on New Year's Day," which is the most significant Japanese holiday. "After I washed, I hung the clothes outside and then went out to weed. Lunch was at noon and dinner was at six. I cooked those meals for the workers, too. I tried to get to sleep as soon as I could, but my bedtime was usually around eleven. I had to clean up in the kitchen, get ready for the next day, and put the kids to sleep. I had to bathe them, too, and that wasn't easy. We had built a *furo* [a large Japanese tub] in one of the rooms and I pumped water into the big tub in the afternoon. When I think about it, I don't know how I was able to do everything, but everyone else worked just as hard.

"I was taught *naijo no ko*, that a wife is supposed to assist her husband. It really means that a wife is to help her husband even in areas where it is not obvious. Young people would not know what that means. We were educated in that way. As long as what I did helped my husband, then it was good. Sometimes I feel as if the whole thing was a dream.

"While we were still in the old, dilapidated house," Teiko continued her commentary, "my husband got sick. I'll never forget that time. It was on a Saturday night. About twenty-five Japanese families lived in Sunnydale, and we had a Japanese school in one corner of our field." Many Japanese communities organized schools to teach the Japanese language and culture to their children. Classes were held after regular school hours. "Our women's organization was meeting in the school that night," Teiko explained.

"When I left for the meeting, my husband was asleep. He had caught a cold and had stayed in bed. During the meeting one of my daughters ran over to get me. She said, 'Papa is in pain. I want you to come back!'"

"By the time I got home, Papa was in bed, doubled over with pain. It was so bad he couldn't even speak. We asked a Japanese doctor to come and examine him. 'Acute appendicitis,' the doctor diagnosed. 'He must be taken to a hospital immediately!' The doctor called an ambulance and my husband was taken to the hospital and operated on that night.

"During the operation some friends had gathered in the waiting room. After an hour and a half, the doctor and a nurse came out. (I was pregnant then with a child we lost later on.) The doctor made me stay in the waiting room while he called some good friends of ours outside and talked to them. I couldn't hear what was said, but I felt very insecure. They all came back afterwards and looked very disheartened. I didn't have the courage to ask them what the doctor had said. After that we went home.

"They gave my husband a special nurse around the clock for two or three days. On the day he came home I was told by a friend, 'The doctor said that he had a ruptured appendix. The infection had spread throughout his abdomen. If there was fever, then he might not have lived more than a week. The doctor told me not to tell you because you were pregnant.'

"Fortunately my husband survived, and his fever subsided four days later. He regained consciousness and began to talk to me."

"Well," Teiko hesitated as she relived the burden of those years and then painstakingly resumed her commentary, "hardships seemed to continue during that period. I have four children now, two boys and two girls, but I had five altogether. I lost a young child when she was two years and nine months old." In halting, short sentences, Teiko recounted the circumstances of the loss. "It was so tragic. I'll never forget. It was December 23. I had sent the older kids to school. The others just hung on to me as I worked in the field. It was under those conditions that I lost my child.

"I knew that Christmas was near, and I felt that I had to finish weeding that patch before the holiday, so I worked very hard. About eleven o'clock I started back to the house to fix lunch. My five-year-old girl and the youngest one were playing and singing in the field. I said, 'Mama is going to go back to the house soon. You start ahead.'

"Even though it was the middle of winter, it was a very nice day. That's why I really wanted to finish weeding in that patch. If it snowed, the weeds would be covered up. The children started walking toward the house. I thought I would work a little bit more, then a little bit more, but finally I quit and walked back home.

"When I got to the house, the older child was reading a book in the kitchen. 'Where is Yaechan?' I asked. She said, 'Yaechan was playing in the garage.' We looked around the garage and the house, but we couldn't find her. We asked the neighbors; we looked in every corner of every field; and even though it was just before

Christmas, all the village people came out and searched. There was no trace of her. It was so strange, and we were all puzzled.

"We searched for her in the hills and looked for her in every bush–anywhere she might have gone. Still she was not found. Then the police came out. In Japan the police department would not abandon a search until some kind of evidence was found or a conclusion was reached. They would have searched everywhere for many days and nights.

"When the villagers first began to look for my daughter, the bread man came by. He used to deliver bread every morning. The searchers asked whether he had seen a little girl who had been missing for a few hours. He said, 'No, I haven't seen her.' After being questioned that day, he just turned around and went straight home. He didn't finish his normal route. Others thought that he acted strangely and said, 'He is a suspect!' By then I was beside myself, and I thought nothing of it; but later," Teiko admitted, "the thing nagged my thoughts. But there was no evidence, so what could we tell the police? In this country, you must have evidence before you can accuse anyone.

"The villagers continued to look everywhere. There was a deep channel of water by our house and people used to say, 'What a nice river you have nearby.' They were envious," Teiko said recalling that the Japanese place great value on certain natural or recreations of natural phenomena such as running water. The villagers could not find my child anywhere, so they decided to drain the ditch. It was in vain. Finally there was nowhere else to search.

"The police department gave up the case. There was no evidence of a kidnapping. There was no ransom note and the parents were not rich or famous. We lived in the oldest, most dilapidated place. We were poor dirt farmers.

"The day before Christmas arrived, and we told the villagers to stop searching to observe Christmas. From that time on, I was so sad that I lost the will to live," Teiko confessed. "Yet," she added, "I had three other children, so I couldn't die and leave them.

"I became disillusioned with America and wanted to go back to Japan. I was so insistent that my husband became angry with me. He said, 'You are thinking only of yourself. All the townspeople, even strangers, came to search during their busiest time. They all worked as if she was their own daughter, and here you are thinking of abandoning all those people and going back to Japan. Are you in fact going to do that? You must overcome your sadness,' he said, 'and return *on* to them.'[2] Reminding Teiko of her moral obligations may have seemed harsh, but she responded to Mr. Tomita's appeal. He added with cconcern for his wife, 'You could go back to Japan for a while, but you shouldn't think of going back for good.' Well, I realized that he was right and decided to stay.

"It happened such a long time ago," Teiko added. And as she tried slowly to shake off the stray thoughts of this tragic event, she repeated, "As long as it wasn't raining or snowing, I went out to work. I got up at five in the morning and made breakfast for my husband and the workers. Then I would take care of my children. I wanted to feed them, clean up, and wash clothes as soon as I could, so that I could hurry outside one minute sooner to pull one weed more. I held this thought in mind all the time.

Later on, I said to myself, 'That must have been the thing called *kuro*.' Yet while I was going through it, I didn't recognize it. I had to do what needed to be done."

The memories of a life with books and teaching had faded completely, replaced by grueling hours of work and the nearly obsessive thought of "pulling one more weed." The near-death of her husband and tragic disappearance of her daughter made *kuro* Teiko's dreaded companion in life; but, raised a Meiji woman, she knew that a life of ease, a life without *kuro*, would never be her lot.

In those years between 1929 and 1942, Teiko worked eighteen hours a day, seven days a week, but the years of labor began to show some promise. Combining the diligence of a Meiji woman with a pioneer, issei spirit, she said, "When the Depression was over, we were able to sell young plants from the nursery. The income was not enough for us to eat on yet, so my husband farmed about an acre. The harvest came and we sold our produce to a wholesale market. This helped to feed our family. My husband would say, 'My burden is getting lighter. My oldest child drives the truck to the field and he helps me out a great deal.' The next year our son could get a driver's license and go to the market for us. He could use horses and a plow," Teiko added proudly. "He was bigger and stronger than I.

"Well, it was still difficult for us to pay the taxes," she continued, "but we finally started selling trees from our farm, and we began to look forward to the day when we could take life a little easier." Yet prosperity continued to elude the Tomitas.

[2]*On* are the obligations a Japanese incurs over a lifetime as a result of favors or acts of kindness. These obligations must be repaid but not necessarily in kind. *On* and *giri*, the repayment of moral debts, pervade every aspect of Japanese life and are the mortar of Japanese society.

"I was in the field working as usual," Teiko recalled, "and went back to the house to prepare lunch when a friend of ours from the village ran over. She said, 'Oh, Mrs. Tomita, stop working! Stop working! All your hard work will be in vain!' 'Why?' I asked. She replied, 'Japan and America have begun to fight!' It was December 7, the day when Pearl Harbor was attacked."

ONATSU AKIYAMA

According to a Japanese newspaper article, Michiharu Akiyama was a young man whose respect and duty to his father knew no bounds. Back from the United States to find a wife, Akiyama appeared to be of impeccable character, financially sound, and for Onatsu Okada, a good match. Independent, and by her own admission a "spoiled, pampered child," Onatsu eagerly anticipated a new life in America free of the rigid rules that characterized Japanese society. There was no way the new bride could anticipate either the discrepancies in her perception of Akiyama's status or the accidents of fate that gradually revealed themselves as she traveled across the ocean.

"When we [my husband and I] arrived in Hawaii, the ship docked there overnight. We could have stayed in a hotel on the island, but I found out later that Papa [my husband] couldn't afford it." Onatsu continued to be unsuspecting of her new husband's dire financial status because, as she recalled, "When we arrived in San Francisco, Papa's relative, Tsutsuyo Hasegawa, bought a dress, shoes, and everything for me.

"Well, what happened was that while we were in Hawaii, the grape ranch burned down and Papa lost everything he had. Mr. Hasegawa knew about this. When we arrived in Florin, Dr. Tsuda gave Papa fifty dollars. I thought," Onatsu said, as she remembered her naiveté, "'They say there are money trees in America, and it must be true.' I didn't realize that my husband was borrowing money. His debts were increasing rapidly."

Although Onatsu rarely complained and never blamed her husband for these shocking circumstances, she graphically described the life they led. "As soon as we arrived in Florin, I started working hard. We worked and worked and were in the depths of poverty," this favored daughter of a comfortable family disclosed. "Carrying our blanket rolls and moving from one camp to another, we worked as farm laborers for three years. We'd stay one or two months here, and a few months there. It might sound crude to say, but we were so poor that I patched up my underwear so

many times that I could not see the original cloth anymore. It was
very difficult for us," she stated simply, and then affirmed, "but I
didn't regret the fact that I came to this country. I really wanted
to come here.

"My husband had borrowed three thousand dollars from a
shoten [store] owner in Florin and we worked the grape ranches to
pay off the loan. There was no bank in Florin, so we asked Mr
Mori,[3] a store owner, to hold our money for us. He knew then how
much we had and would ask us to pay off our debts. All my husband's paychecks were signed and given up to Mr. Mori. It must
have been very difficult for my husband," Onatsu added with
understanding. "This is the reason we didn't even have a nickel in
our pockets at that time.

"Papa used to say, 'I borrowed money and was helped; however,
there is no distinction between persons who would pay and would
not pay.' What he meant was that he had to turn all his checks
over to Mr. Mori. It was regrettable that he seemed not to distinguish between people who would pay off a debt and those who
would not.

"When I went back to Japan for a visit later on, Mr. Mori
brought a box of oranges and a fifty dollar check." This custom of
giving money to friends as a farewell gift to express best wishes for
their journey is a common one called *sembetsu*. But Onatsu
explained, "I could not accept that money because we still had
[part of] that three-thousand- dollar loan to pay off. I did accept the
oranges though."

Struggling with physical and economic difficulties, Onatsu
learned of some rather shocking news about her husband. "Well,
during this difficult time, I also learned that my husband had been
married once before to another woman. She was well liked by his
father, *Motoji-jisan* [grandfather]," and as a result Onatsu worked
hard to be a "good" daughter-in-law despite her spirited nature.

"My husband must have been around twenty or so at the time,
and she was only fifteen years and seven months. She got up late
in the morning and must have been spoiled. When my husband
tried to help her wipe the table in the morning, she would throw
things around because she didn't want him to help her. They were
married for three years and worked a forty-acre grape ranch.

"My husband was a very diligent, serious person," Onatsu
explained. "He must have thought that they did not have a future
together, because he signed a three-year contract to work on a pear

[3]A pseudonym.

ranch as a sharecropper in Lincoln and did not take her with him. He did this all deliberately so that his wife could reject him and leave him. It was a difficult situation because he had to make her leave him, even though she cared for him."

After she learned about her husband's first marriage, Onatsu gradually pieced together some of the puzzling aspects of her husband's earlier behavior. "I recalled that back in Japan my husband had told us [my family] that he was going to see a friend in Okayama, and I remember thinking that he was a very considerate person to make that visit. He went to Okayama by taxi, though it was quite a distance and therefore cost a great deal. Well, we were very impressed. Later on I asked him about that trip. It turned out that the real reason for the trip was to check the *koseki* [family register]. His former wife was from Okayama and her name was returned to her original family register. Then he felt he was free to marry me. If her name was not returned to her family, that meant that she was still married to him." Registration of family names, a custom once reserved for the nobility but required among all classes during the Meiji Restoration, assumed particular importance. The status-conscious Japanese wished to emulate the samurai, and if one were to comply with the spirit of the samurai code, it was basic to record scrupulously all family births, marriages, and deaths.

"She [the first wife] was a sickly, tiny person. I used to look around the house to see if any of her things were left. I suppose I was jealous," Onatsu begrudgingly admitted. "I found a stocking that had been cut off at the top. It was too long for her, so she must have been a tiny lady," she surmised.

"Mr. Yamasaki, a family friend, felt sorry for my husband because he was such a fine young man, and loaned money to my father-in-law, who in turn gave it to my husband to go to Japan [and find a new wife].

"My husband's friend used to say, 'Akiyama is a lucky man! He is able to change horses [meaning wives] in midstream.' Well, people don't understand what goes on inside of you," Onatsu lamented in a rare display of personal pain. "They used to say a lot of things about us and about the other woman, and I didn't like it. However," she added generously, "when I consider Papa's feelings, then I'm glad for what happened."

For many issei women, laboring in the fields as an equal partner with husbands eventually promoted a sense of self-worth in them rather than hampering their spirits. On the basis of six years of backbreaking labor and her successful sewing venture in Japan,

Onatsu expressed her opinions in economic matters with confidence. A Meiji bride in Japan might, after years of living with in-laws, finally manage the household accounts, but she would hesitate to give direct advice about business ventures.

"It was six years after I came to America," Onatsu recalled, "that we bought the store. Papa came back to Florin to make *mochi* [rice dumplings] for *Ojiisan* [grandfather, Onatsu's father-in-law] for the New Year, and that's when he heard about the store. I thought it was a very good omen," Onatsu said. Eating *mochi* and other specific foods for the New Year has special significance for the Japanese, and immigrants continued these customs.

"I knew something about business," she continued, "and said, 'I don't mind working in the fields, but we should go into business. I'd like that better.' The price was only one thousand [dollars] or so. We talked to *Ojiisan*, my husband's father about it and asked him to loan us five hundred dollars. *Ojiisan* had quite a bit of money. You see," Onatsu explained, "before we were married, Papa would save as much as possible and give the money to him. Papa worked as a gardener for four months, and we made nine hundred dollars more. That's how we started our fish and grocery market," she said, as though gathering the money had been relatively simple. What Onatsu did not mention was how frugal she was and how hard both she and her husband worked to accumulate the money.

"We began with a partnership that included two other people. I had to be very sensitive to the other families, so my nerves were wearing thin. By then I was pregnant with the second child, too.

"There was a big labor camp near Elk Grove[4] where 230 workers lived. There must have been 400 acres of grapes to be worked. I had to deliver food to the workers by 9:00 A.M. I had to make *tofu* [soybean curd] and other food things. When I got there, I unloaded all the food and cut up the meat and vegetables.

"If the *tofu* didn't have enough brine, it got too soft and fell apart, a real mess. I used to make a four-gallon can of *tofu* and it was really difficult. A very unpleasant lady used to be the cook there. If I was a few minutes late, she would complain in an endless harangue.

"For three years I delivered sea bass or meat, and vegetables, and I drove the truck without a driver's license. Once I was delivering a can of *tofu* and had to put the container on the driver's seat. I held the can with one hand and steered with the other and drove

[4]Elk Grove was a small farming community south of Sacramento.

the truck into a ditch. I couldn't get out for a long time since there was very little traffic. Then a gasoline truck passed and the driver helped me get out. When I think about it, it is a miracle that I was able to manage without a major accident.

"In those days Papa worked so hard that he had very little time to sleep, sometimes only two hours a night. We worked with all our strength, so we have no regrets. Even though he died rather young, I don't think in terms of, 'We should have done this or that differently.' We opened the store at about six in the morning and closed it at nine in the evening. Sometimes we couldn't close till eleven. On New Year's Eve, by the time we cleaned up, it was already 2:00 A.M." Because the Japanese celebrate the new year by entertaining and visiting on the first day of the New Year, Onatsu said, "Then I had to make New Year's *gochiso* [party food] like *sushi* [cold rice specialty] and roast turkey to sell on New Year's Day." Once the store's business increased, I quit making food deliveries. It was a very hard life. Now I don't do anything. It's like paradise.

"Human life is amazing," Onatsu stated, as she continued to reflect on the past. "I feel that the suffering and pain that I experienced back in those days taught me a great deal." And with irrepressible optimism and zeal she added, "I'm truly thankful. My husband was a very strict, serious person. He used to lecture me for hours about all kinds of things. Sometimes I look back and say to myself, 'That's right. He was quite right about this or that,' though I didn't like being scolded at the time. Now I feel a sense of gratitude. I'm very happy because I feel thankful about those things that happened in the past. I don't think of past events as just hardships," she stated and affirmed that the quality of endurance instilled in her as a lesson for the young Meiji woman had served her well.

"During the Depression there were many Japanese people who could not buy food. Some families only got paid once or twice a year as the strawberry crop was harvested. Papa used to sell them lots of food. There were families with eight or ten children, and they could not pay. I said to Papa, 'Are you sure that they can pay for this?' He'd answer, 'Don't talk like that. They are having such a hard time.' And he'd let them buy on credit.

"In those days Papa used to sell rice by the ton, but he only made fifteen cents a ton. I said, 'Papa, you can't even pay the gas bill with that!' But he'd reply, 'Don't worry. There will be a time when this will help us.'"

Continuing her recollections of the Depression, Onatsu related, "Once I visited a family, and they were drinking something like tomato soup with nothing else in it. We felt so sorry for them that we let them buy food on credit, even though we had no idea whether or not they could pay us back.

"There were some who never paid us what they owed. I remember one person who used to turn away from me when he saw me on the street or in a store. When he discovered that I wouldn't ask for his money anymore, he got real brave. He saw me a while ago and said, 'Oh, you're still alive?'" He passed away recently. There were such people.

"There were also people like Mr. Kamada[5] who had eleven children. In those days people didn't know too much about contraceptives. This man once said, 'I use a condom, but it doesn't work. I keep having children.' I answered, 'Well, probably you aren't using it.' I used to tell Papa to buy a lot of condoms for people who didn't want more children. I gave them to those who were having a hard time as they came to buy vegetables.

"In any case, Kamada had eleven children. They came back [to California from a relocation camp] after the war. Mr. Kamada died about ten years afterward. After Mrs. Kamada died, her sons and daughters sold their property and had a family meeting to decide what to do with the money. A few days later the oldest son and daughter came to ask me how much they owed before the war. I didn't remember the amount since my books were confiscated by the FBI.

"Well, later they sent me a letter and I still have it. It was so beautiful that I want to keep it for my children's sake. The letter had all their signatures on it. It said, 'On behalf of our parents, we would like to express our gratitude for your kindness shown to us in the past. We will never forget what you have done for us.' There was a six hundred dollar check included. They must have remembered what their parents used to tell them. They were wonderful people.

"When I saw them [the Kamada children] later, I said that because they were such fine people, their children would also grow up to be good people like them. A few months ago, one of the daughters who lives in Fresno wrote to me and said, 'Please be happy for me. My sons have grown up to be such nice young men. They are good judoists.' She enclosed two pictures of them. These

[5]A pseudonym.

people who don't forget *on* will someday become very successful. I really learned so much from them. It was the debt from times when things were very difficult."

When Onatsu first began her commentary, she expressed a belief that the continuity of family history–its responsibilities, obligations, and successes–continues through successive generations. This particular relationship with the Kamadas is especially dear to her because it confirmed her husband's faith in others and reinforced her ties to him, though he had been dead for many years.

"I keep that letter in the drawer of the *hotokesama* [a household Buddhist altar]. I'm sure it will be a very good lesson for my children, and it was such precious money that I offered it to Papa at the *butsudan* [another reference to the household altar]," she said, though the usual offerings to the spirits of the dead are food and flowers. "I had it put in a saving certificate. I just can't bring myself to spend that precious money," she said and added, "so there were those people, too."

Ever realistic, Onatsu recounted the difficult times as well as those when she claimed the rewards of her diligence. Because of her strong desire for a life free of the tedium and restrictions of Japanese society, Onatsu opted for a life in the United States, and she did not complain when that new life introduced her to poverty. She worked hard as a field hand and then helped her husband with their small market. She also worked hard at being a good wife, which, for a Japanese woman, meant being a good daughter-in-law. Unfortunately for Onatsu, her father-in-law was not only colorful but extremely difficult as well; yet her lengthy commentary on this man is cheerful, conveying his zest for life, with which she might have identified.

"Papa's father was a soldier for a while. He fought in the Sino-Japanese War and also the Russo-Japanese War. Ojiisan used to tell us that when he was marching during the Russo-Japanese War, he had made up his mind to die there. During the war he was wounded in hand-to-hand combat. He lay there pretending that he was dead and had his gun ready to shoot himself in case an enemy soldier tried to stab him. Later he was decorated for his bravery. This was his favorite story. He kept a diary and it is with his bones in the family grave.

"Ojiisan had a good [singing] voice, was able to write well and was very popular. He remembered everything, and people used to call him a walking history book.

"He was also a very good carpenter and had once worked repairing a castle. [When the repairs were nearly completed,] he climbed on top of the highest roof by the symbol of that castle, which happened to be a fish, and showed off to the people down below asking who was higher, he or the fish." Although the crowd might have enjoyed this prankish joke, Moto-jiisan's act was a grave insult to the lord of the castle.

"That night," Onatsu continued, "at a celebration for the completion of the project, a maid told him to run away because the chief of the construction crew was furious with him for standing at the highest point. That's how his life was spared.

"He was also quite a lover. In Japan he had married five times. He must have been a tremendously able person. He used to say, 'I have had seven and a half wives.' 'It doesn't make sense,' I said. 'What does that half mean?' Then he answered, 'Well, the last one went back home before she reached my house.' He used to laugh about that."

Onatsu then added a comment about how her father-in-law's family judged this colorful, roguish rebel. "Ojiisan was made *bunke* [loss of the right to inherit family property] by his parents," she disclosed, "so he didn't have any possessions at all; but before he died, my husband built him a beautiful house in Japan.

"Ojiisan was a very difficult person to live with, even for a Japanese," Onatsu stated and then emphatically declared, "he was just terrible. When we had a grocery store, he used to cut a good piece of meat for himself, bring it to me and say, 'Hey! Barbecue this for me! I like it rare.' So I'd charcoal broil it for him. If I said, 'Ojiisan, we'd better broil it a little longer,' he would say, 'What! You don't want me to eat a good piece of meat. You think it's too good for me!' Then he would throw it down on the ground, dish and all. He was that kind of a man.

"After Papa settled down with his first wife, Ojiisan was very lonely. He took up with a widow in her home, but he had to have a place of his own, so [after we were married] we leased a house for him." Onatsu advised her husband to encourage Ojiisan to marry, but the dutiful son refused to interfere. "Ojiisan did get married," Onatsu related. "He bought a piece of land. He and his new wife were together for a while and then he suffered a slight stroke. He was in his late sixties then. I told Papa that it was our duty to send Ojiisan back to Japan." When elderly Japanese immigrants felt that illness might result in death, they often chose to return to Japan, where their remains would be disposed of proper-

ly. "But Papa said, 'What are you talking about! We don't even
have enough money for ourselves.' You see, it was during the
Depression and it was such a hard time."

Ever resourceful, Onatsu also managed to be a good daughter-in-
law, as well as to rid herself of a difficult relationship with her
father-in-law. "But I insisted that we send him, and brought out
seven hundred dollars! When I presented the money, Papa asked
suspiciously, 'Where did you get this?' He thought that I might
have come by it dishonestly. I told him that I had saved up the
money from the sale of empty boxes, you know, those lettuce
crates and fruit boxes that people used to buy back for five cents
apiece. Well, Papa was really happy." The lessons of frugality
learned in Meiji Japan had paid off.

"My husband had already had a house built for Ojiisan in Japan,
and a cousin's name was entered into the *koseki* [family register]
so that he could take care of Ojiisan." The cousin was adopted as
a son, and therefore assumed the filial duty of taking care of an
aging parent, since Onatsu's husband could not care for his father
long distance. Having the cousin's name entered in the family register formalized the adoption. "When Ojiisan went back, he
received Papa's cousin as his son. The only relative [of Ojiisan's
family] left in Japan is this cousin. He inherited most of Ojiisan's
estate. There is some property left in Japan. We tried to sell it, but
it's such trouble.

"By that time Grandpa's wife was elderly, too. He wanted to
take her back to Japan with him, but she put conditions on her
accompanying him." Onatsu reported that he was true to his independent nature. "Well, the terms didn't suit him, so he went home
by himself. He told his wife that if she wanted to follow him, she
could sell the land she had and come with that money. When his
wife wanted to go back to Japan later on, she asked her daughter-
in-law to get some money for her because the land couldn't be easily sold. The daughter-in-law brought the old lady to us."

Even after her father-in-law returned to Japan, Onatsu, ever cog-
nizant of her filial duties, continued to provide what she could and
to settle the old man's affairs. "This old lady was a very unfortunate person," Onatsu commented sympathetically. "At that time
we had the grocery store in Florin. Because we had all kinds of
merchandise, we gave her lots of food. She lived very close to us,
close enough to see our water tank. They said that every time she
saw our water tank, she would express her gratitude saying,
'*Arigato gozaimasu* [thank you very much]!

"The old woman worked for a while at a hotel in Stockton and finally went back to Japan. I don't think she went back to Ojiisan though, because I heard that she died in Hiroshima."

Onatsu's relationship with Ojiisan was the focal point of the conflicts she faced when inevitably her independence and sense of Japanese duty clashed. The conflict reached its climax in the days just preceding Ojiisan's departure.

"Well, I had four children," she explained, "and I had to cook for fifteen people [because we had workers to feed], so it was impossible for me to do everything right away. We were getting ready for Ojiisan's trip and were packing candy and other things for him to take." Japanese custom dictates that each relative be presented with a small gift, and it was Onatsu's responsibility to purchase and pack these gifts for Ojiisan.

"We had some money so that he could buy a kimono as soon as he arrived in Japan. 'Ojiisan,' I said, 'making a kimono for you is very difficult for me because I haven't done it for a long time. The only sewing I've done in the last few years is to mend socks. I'm sorry I won't be able to do it for you. Besides, I know your taste and I'm afraid what I make would be unsatisfactory for you.' Then he got very angry and said, 'What! You can't? My son's wife is a big fool.' It was 9:00 P.M. and Papa came over to us after closing the store. 'What's going on?' he asked. 'What are you fighting about? Let's hear from each of you.' We sat there for two hours and expressed our feelings. I gave him credit for being a patient listener. Then Papa said, "I understand now. But [whatever the issue], Mama should not have made Ojiisan angry. You had better apologize to him. Sit on the floor, bow, and apologize,' he instructed." Disgrace, as well as honor and achievement, is shared collectively by the Japanese family; therefore, apologies are carefully avoided because they signify family disgrace.

"I cried and cried and was very chagrined," Onatsu recollected, and then revealed how much of her Japanese past remained with her. "I felt that I had been well disciplined and taught correct behavior at home in Japan. My parents sent me to school to learn sewing, flower arrangement, and the tea ceremony," Onatsu stated to emphasize that these activities were used to instill order, discipline, respect, and proper conduct. "But now," she continued, "I was placed in a very embarrassing situation. I didn't know what explanation I could make to my own parents. They were being reprimanded along with me at that point. I just couldn't stop crying. Still, my husband insisted that I should apologize.

"In those days the floors were dirt and people used to spit on the floors as well. That's where I was to sit and bow my head. It was late, around 11:00 o'clock. There was nothing else I could do, so I apologized."

Still, Onatsu was troubled over the family breach and couldn't sleep. "About 4:00 A.M.," she continued, "I woke up my husband and said, 'I better go over and apologize again.'" This time the apology was sincere. "I wrapped up some *sashimi* [raw fish] and *tako* [octopus] to take to him," she said ever mindful of the Japanese custom of bringing a small gift when visiting.

"Ojiisan's house was about seven blocks or so from ours. It seemed that he couldn't sleep either, and we met midway between our houses. 'Ojiisan,' I said, "I'm truly sorry for what I said to you. I apologize. I was wrong.' He answered, 'I'm satisfied if you understand.' After that we didn't have any more trouble.

"He was such a character," Onatsu stated with exasperation and understanding. "Before he went home to Japan, he bought a new car and took it back with him. The entire village came out to welcome him."

The reward for Onatsu's patience was the praise she received years later. "When we went to visit Ojiisan's home village after the war," Onatsu recalled, "he said to his neighbors, 'My son's wife is a very wise, good wife. I've been a mean father-in-law to her, but she has never fought me and was always faithful.' He said this to everybody in the village," Onatsu added with enormous satisfaction.

Onatsu could never be totally free of the family rigidity from which she tried to escape, and many of the strictures of Japanese society were so ingrained in her that she never questioned them. Yet she believed in her own resourceful abilities and continued to act independently whenever the opportunity arose.

"Papa went back to Japan with Ojiisan because he couldn't go by himself," Onatsu continued. "When they left, Papa took all the money we had, so I had a very difficult time operating the store. Because Papa did not like to ask for payments," she explained, "I took one of the workers and went around collecting money from our customers. I explained the situation, but some of them said, 'What are you saying? You loaned money to us because you had money.' I replied, 'Because Ojiisan and Papa had to go back to Japan, you need to pay cash for any new merchandise. You may settle what you owe on your payday.'

"Many said that they could not trade with us any longer. It seemed to me that because they owed us a lot, it would be natural that they should continue to buy from us. Well, there were many who stomped loudly on the boardwalk as they passed in front of our store and then walked on to another store." Still smarting from the snubs and breaches in etiquette, Onatsu fortified herself with the comment, "The most important thing in life is sincerity and honesty."

Revising the store's credit policy was not the only change Onatsu made. "While my husband was gone," she stated matter-of-factly, "I improved the store: I let workers go, remodeled, took inventory, and organized it. You've got to do this when you have your own business. When my husband came back," Onatsu said with some satisfaction, "he was really surprised."

Then, needing to reconcile her independent action with her Meiji ideals, Onatsu added, "A woman has to serve the family from the shadows. In any case, we couldn't let Ojiisan go back home by himself. So I let Papa accompany him." It seemed that Onatsu may have created the opportunity to "serve from the shadows."

Onatsu obviously appreciated the freedom to make changes in the business, but being without her husband had its hazards. "When Papa went to Japan," she related, I was still very young, about thirty years old. One night–it must have been after midnight–I heard a knock on the door. It was a man I knew and he said, 'Please, sell me some ice cream because my child has a fever." I sympathized and let him in. But he wasn't interested in ice cream, he was interested in me. I headed for the door and ran away. He was such a crude man. After that [incident], this man hadn't the courage to look me in the eye and looked away when we passed on the street. It was such a shameful thing he did. He was a respected man in the community, too.

"A woman must be on guard all the time. It was terrible before I came, they say. Florin was a very nice place to live and there were many Japanese there. I must be a lucky person because only once did I have trouble like that.

"The store was very popular," Onatsu stated, and then gave the credit to her husband, though it was she who had made the improvements. "I think it was because Papa was such an honest man."

The Akiyamas did not grow wealthy from their business, but there was enough financial security to allow Onatsu a trip back to

Japan a few years after her father-in-law left. "We were very poor at that time," Onatsu maintained, "but my husband borrowed some money from a friend and sent me home [to Japan]."

Despite her years in the United States, which provided her with freedom from the restrictive and rigid rules of Japanese family life, and the opportunity to develop and exercise her own business acumen, Onatsu did feel a responsibility to maintain and enhance the reputation of the Akiyama family.

"I took a fifty-day vacation, but I didn't go out sightseeing or for entertainment. Instead, I made contributions to the village school and for the building of a strong wall to prevent mud from sliding behind the village shrine and improved the family grave sites. We had two of them. I also gave something for the village fire station. I contributed all over the place in Akiyama's name.

"I knew that my father-in-law wouldn't live much longer, so I also made a *rekidai bako* [a family crypt with a large room to house the remains of many generations] for the Akiyama family. I think it cost 20,000 yen at that time. Relatives said that there were other brothers there and the cost should be shared by all. I replied that they were taking care of my father-in-law and would also care for the grave. I wouldn't be able to do that because I was going back to America.

"My father-in-law said that I should do something for my own village, but I had already spent all the money I had for the Akiyama family memorial.

"When we went back to Japan after the war, we were very poor and couldn't do anything for the village." Onatsu then reflected, "We should contribute to the community when we can. I was very happy that I was able to do something for other people then."

Decades later, Onatsu continued to view the family welfare above any personal gain. She considered whatever she earned as a family possession rather than a personal one. "It didn't take too long to bounce back from the Depression," she continued, "but we were not able to collect money from many who owed, because of the war. There were those who returned money with thanks, but there were also those who were not willing to pay us back. Years later, after my son took over the business, some people paid their debts to me instead of to my daughter-in-law," Onatsu stated, as she continued to reach back to her Japanese ways and recognize that because her son was now head of the household, her daughter-in-law should control the finances as she had. "I gave the money to my son's wife because we are all one family.

"All my sons have forgotten about those difficult days, but I am very thankful that we can live without worry now," Onatsu added, as though concluding her commentary on the Depression might have brought some stability to their lives at that point. But her addendum indicated otherwise. "I never had any unpleasant experiences with white folks, even though we had many white customers, at least," she added, "not before the beginning of the war."

IYO TSUTSUI

Like Setsu Yoshihashi, Iyo Tsutsui had married in Japan with a proxy for her groom and then lived with her new in-laws for a time before she set sail for America as a picture bride. Iyo liked her mother-in-law and remembered her concern over Iyo's well-being once she left Japan. "Once," Iyo said, "a friend of ours visited my mother-in-law and told her about America. He told her that it was considered shameful to have your wife work in the fields in America. So Mother [Tsutsui] thought that I would not have anything to do once I got to America. She was told that my husband had twelve horses and that I would have to water the horses. That's what Mother Tsutsui thought my life would be like," Iyo remembered. But like most other picture brides, Iyo found reality much different.

Traveling first-class like Setsu Yoshihashi, Iyo left a life of leisure and luxury when she stepped off the ship. Much to her pleasant surprise, Mr. Tsutsui was not the typical, gruff, demanding Japanese husband. Because he exhibited courtesy and kindness toward his new bride, she followed him willingly. "My husband was farming near Stockton on the Holland Tract about a half an hour by automobile from Sacramento. He and a partner grew beans. He brought me by steamboat from San Francisco to Stockton. Then we went to Holland, Camp No. 7. The trip took a half a day, and we arrived there in the evening. When I landed and looked around, to my surprise there were not any houses that were suited for human beings. They all looked like stables. I asked my husband, 'Where are we going to sleep?' He answered, 'In that one!' I was surprised again. It was terrible! Even the poorest family in Japan didn't live in a house like that!

"When the wind blew," Iyo continued, "the inside of the house turned black with peat dust, because the walls were made of one-by twelve-inch boards with spaces between. I was terribly upset. In the evening people began to come back from the fields. Their faces were black with the peat dust. I felt that I could not do that kind of work, and for a time I did not go to the fields to work.

"In the camp there was a main building, and people who were farming as sharecroppers ate together in the dining room. The camp boss charged room and board according to the number of family members. The camp had a cook and helpers. There were individual houses for families and there was also a dormitory for single men. Mr. Nomura and Mr. Hironaka had some land that they subdivided and leased to other Japanese farmers in a share-crop arrangement. Sharecroppers took sixty percent and the boss took forty percent. From that the boss paid the rent."

A patient, caring husband, Mr. Tsutsui did not press his wife to work immediately. But, Iyo recalled, "One day my husband said, 'In America, women work in the fields. If you stay in the house like a rich man's wife, people will laugh at you.' I realized it was the opposite of what our friend had said about American women. Well," she said, chagrined, "I began to work outside. I was obedient at the time. I went out to hoe but I didn't know whether or not I could do the job. Well," she said with a sigh, "it was hot and it was very hard. I was the slowest because it was the first time I had ever used a hoe. Then a lady next to me said, "Mrs. Tsutsui, hoe-ing is the easiest job in this country.' I thought, 'If this is the easiest job, the rest must be very hard!"

Despite her shock at the change in living conditions and the hard labor, Iyo's picture marriage was basically a successful one because of her husband's considerate nature. But Iyo recalled the difficulties in other picture marriages. "In picture marriages, the main trouble was the the picture and the real person were sometimes very much different. When we worked on the Holland Tract, there was a man from Kyushu who worked with horses. He had burns on his head and had scars, like that of smallpox, on his face. When his bride, a tall, beautiful woman, came from Japan, they were brought together for the first time by an immigration officer, who asked the bride, 'Is this you husband-to-be?' She said, 'No, he isn't' because the picture she had in her hand looked a lot different from this man. But this man had borrowed someone else's picture and sent it to her. When she understood the situation, she said that she was going back to Japan. There was an influential person there at the time whose wife talked to this picture bride and convinced her to stay.

"The couple married and had children. Everybody felt sorry for her because she was a tall, beautiful woman. The man was small and had that scarred face. It must have been very difficult, but they adjusted well.

"There was a woman who came to Stockton when I did," Iyo continued, "and didn't like her new husband. She said that she would leave her husband; however, she, too, stayed," Iyo said, "because of the children."

These issei pioneer women had been raised to believe that mothering was almost synonymous with womanhood. Once she became a mother, the Meiji woman's life became child-centered to the point that events in her own life were recalled by stages in her children's development. Her highest priority was her family, not her husband. The father's role was to provide for the family financially. An abused or neglected Meiji wife would remain in a difficult marriage for her child's economic and social welfare. She might suffer nearly a lifetime of living with difficult in-laws or a philandering husband. Whatever the trial, she had a moral obligation, for the sake of the family, to endure. The issei woman did likewise. "Once couples have a baby," Iyo affirmed, "it is very difficult to separate."

There were also a few picture brides who could not manage the difficulties. "Those women who left their husbands," Iyo claimed, "became greatly disturbed. They would latch on to other men and run away. There was a woman who said to me, 'I wish I could walk down the street with a man like Mr. Tsutsui.' He was indeed a nice-looking man. This woman ran away with a man from Kochi Ken, leaving her husband and children. There were some women who did that.

"If my husband had been an irresponsible person, I might have left him, too," Iyo declared. "I could have gotten a job as a domestic worker. However, I cooperated with my husband."

Though her husband was supportive, Iyo's life was like nothing she had anticipated. As soon as she started working in the fields, she recalled, "I got thirsty and drank ditch water from the Sacramento River. I was sick the next day with a fever. Tsutsui had gone into town," she remembered, and the other workers missed her when she didn't appear for meals. "Mr. Nomura came to see how I was. I told him that I felt very bad and was resting. He said, 'Oh, you must have malaria.' Then he called my husband for me.

"When you get malaria," Iyo explained, "you get a chill first. Even though it was a hot day in June, I was cold. I piled up one *futon* [Japanese comforter] on top of the other and it wasn't enough. I still shivered. Thirty minutes later, I was hot and so feverish that I took off all my clothes. I was sick in bed for about ten days.

"The Caucasian boss asked my husband where I was. He said, 'She is in bed with malaria.' The boss said, 'Oh, then I'll go and buy medicine for her.' The medicine made my urine purple, but it cured me.

We stayed in Holland for a year. Before that, my husband had farmed in Stockton and had lost a lot of money. The year I came was a good year for beans, and we made enough money to pay off our debts.

"Then we farmed in Stockton, where we grew onions and made more money. After finishing the onion season at Barnhart Tract No. 7, we moved to Holland Camp No. 1 to grow beans. We stayed there for a year. After that, we went to another camp and then we returned to Stockton.

"We moved from place to place because we had to look for good land," Iyo said in explanation of her nomadic existence. "The toughest period of my life was when we were renters. At that time I got up at 4:30 A.M. every morning and cooked for the Russian workers. I cleaned up the kitchen and went out to the field one hour later. At 11:00 A.M. I had to come back and cook lunch for them. When they went out to work in the afternoon, I did, too. Then I had to come back a little early to cook dinner for them. In the evening after cleaning up, I had to make *ofuro* [Japanese bath]. I had to make a wood fire for it. I also burned wood for cooking, too. My work was hard labor and I had to use my muscles."

As her days passed in an endless, arduous grind, Iyo admitted, "Sometimes I thought if I had stayed in Japan, I wouldn't have had to work that hard.

"When I first came here, I didn't even know how to cook! I couldn't even make rice. In Japan I had a mother and older sisters, so I never had to learn. I didn't know how to do the wash either. In those days we used a washtub and a board. We boiled the water outside first, shaved soap into, and then boiled the clothes, white things first, of course. Then the clothes had to be rinsed. My husband taught me all these things," Iyo explained. How difficult those times must have been! Yet there is no trace of self-pity or complaint in Iyo's commentary.

As she paused to reflect and collect her strength for the telling of a most painful episode in her life, Iyo chose to find support in the memories of the many years she spent on the land that continued to be her home. "We bought this land in 1940, I think," Iyo said. Although the California Alien Land Laws of 1913 and 1920 prohibited the Tsutsuis from purchasing land, their children, referred to as "nisei," if citizens by birth, could purchase land when they became adults. "We bought this land in my third daughter's name," Iyo explained. "She was already an adult then."

"We had six children," Iyo continued and then recounted in short, measured sentences the tragic loss of one child. "Our youngest son, Saku, died in this river," she said sadly. "He drowned. You see, we didn't have a fence there. We used to wash everything in the river and pumped water from it for a bath. We also kept a raft on the river.

"One day I went out weeding in the celery field. My youngest daughter asked, 'Is Saku over there?' I answered, 'No, isn't he over there?' When we could not find him, I asked her, 'Did you scold him?' because he would hide in his room when he was scolded. But she said, 'No.'

"We searched again but still couldn't find him. Then, Minoru, my son who lives with me now, said, 'We put some pears on the raft.' I said, 'He might have fallen in the river.' We started searching down by the river." By then, Mr. Tsutsui had joined the search, and Iyo remembered vividly, "When he poked the bottom of the river with a long stick, the boy came up.

"We took him to the emergency [room] at the hospital. I asked my husband how Saku was, and he said that they were trying to resuscitate him. About ten minutes later, they brought him out in a basket. That's how Saku died."

Within a few short years, the exuberant, young picture bride from Japan had faced startling disappointments, the grinding demands of a farm laborer, and the tragic loss of her youngest child. In order to recover from the pain of recounting this loss, Iyo characteristically focused on the positive memories. It was her continuing respect for her husband and his values that helped sustain her.

"My husband was a very serious, earnest person," Iyo declared. [Before we were married] he worked for a railroad in Utah. He went as far as the Mississippi River from here. Then he worked for a sugar factory in Colorado. From there he went to Brigham, Utah, to work in a mine. The reason why he worked so hard was that he wanted to save money and come to California to start farming.

"At that time gambling was very popular in places like Brigham, because there was nothing else for the men to do. My husband worked there with a good friend, and they promised each other not to gamble. The gamblers would bring them *botamochi* [rice cake dumpling covered with sweetened bean paste] and did all kinds of nice things for them. But still they did not gamble. Later on, the gamblers said that they just couldn't take away Tsutsui's and Sano's money.

"He was such an earnest, serious person. That's why even during the Depression, we had some savings to help us out. We did not have to buy food on credit.

"I heard that life for some issei women was terrible. Men got so involved in gambling that they couldn't even afford to buy shoes for their kids. There was one case of an issei fellow who later was saved by the Salvation Army. One day his wife cut her hair like those women did who had lost their husbands. When her husband saw her, he was enraged, but even this did not keep him from gambling. At that time Rev. Masasuke Kobayashi traveled through this area. He was a major in the Salvation Army. One night he spoke on the 'Movement to Eradicate Gambling Places.' That gambler was saved that night and finally came to his senses.

"I felt fortunate that my husband was not a gambler; so I helped him as much as I could. I did not have to face poverty, but I did abuse my body through hard work. I admit that.

"I went back to Japan for the first time after twenty-two years, with two of my children. When my oldest sister saw me, she could not believe that I was the same person because I had aged so much. I emigrated here in 1915, so it must have been 1937 when I went to visit Japan. Even if I had stayed in Japan and we hadn't seen each other for twenty years, I would have looked different. But I came to America and worked at all kinds of hard jobs to which I was not accustomed. These things caused my features to change, I suppose. My older sister asked, 'Do you have to work that much to make ends meet?'

"I replied, 'If I didn't work hard in America, we would not be able to live.' She said, 'Is that so. Then you'd better come back to Japan.' But I told her, 'My children are Americans, and I want to be where my children are.'"

Despite her insistence that the children remain Americans, Iyo wanted to educate them in Japanese values and customs. She explained a common practice. "I left my older daughter Kiyoko in Japan and took the younger one back to America. We had Kiyoko return before World War II. She had graduated from high school in June and returned before Christmas.

"God works in strange ways," Iyo continued. "We sailed to Japan on a ship called the *Tatsuta Maru*. Helen, my future daughter-in-law, was on the same ship, but we did not know each other then. Her mother had died, and her father was returning to Japan with four children. When Helen married into our family, she told us that she had gone back to Japan and lived there till she was twenty years old and then returned to America. I asked her the name of the ship, and she answered, '*Tatsuta Maru.*' She also said that she had spent Christmas on the ship. When she said that it was in 1937, I realized that we had been on the same ship. I asked her whether she knew Kiyoko-san from Watsonville, and she said she remembered her.

"One night, you see, Kiyoko-san [Iyo's daughter] was holding a young child and had come into our room. The child was fussy that night, so Kiyoko said, 'You'd better be a good kid. Your papa is really tired, so you better let him rest.' I asked her, 'Where is the child's mother?' She said, 'The mother died. That's why her father is going back to Japan with four children.' I said, 'Is that so. What a pity!' Well, you see, that little girl was Helen's sister.

"After coming back to Japan, Helen's father became his aunt's *yoshi*, because she didn't have a son. The aunt raised Helen until she came back to America after the war. Her father was in Watsonville, and she went there to live. Then she became my daughter-in-law and joined my household. I always tell her that it was not just a coincidence," Kiyo said, declaring her belief that some things are predetermined by fate. Obviously pleased with the turn of events that brought her daughter-in-law, Helen, into the family, Iyo had fortified herself with positive memories in order to continue another sad chapter in her life story.

MIDORI KIMURA

While Setsu Yoshihashi spent some of her first months in the United States living in a leaky tent, Kiyo Miyake hoed in the blazing heat of the Imperial Valley, and Iyo Tsutsui lived in what she described as something like a stable unfit for human habitation, Midori Kimura's life was secure and comfortable. Other issei brides faced the loneliness of a foreign land without the support of family or other women friends. But Midori had family and support. "My uncle and his family lived with us for about six months," she explained. "Then they bought the house next door, so I was never lonely," she added gratefully. "There were those women who were taken to work camps in remote places," she continued. "Those women were very homesick, and they cried a lot. I was fortunate to be able to live in a fine house."

Other issei brides would work grueling eighteen-hour days and tend babies as well. Midori's life was much less taxing, despite her large family. "I had seven children," she said. "One good thing about my husband's work as an insurance agent was that he was often free during the daytime and could watch the children for me, so I attended the church's women's association meetings during the day. My husband used to take my uncle's children and ours to various places. He was used to changing diapers, too.

"Because of my husband's job contacts,' Midori continued, "we knew a good doctor, Dr. Lincoln Corseland. When our child was sick, this doctor made house calls, even twice a day when the illness was very bad. He was a good man, and a friend.

"Once a friend of ours became sick with asthma. My husband brought the doctor to examine our friend. Because it was evening, I thought the doctor would charge a lot. But he said, 'I would not take money from that poor farmer.' He was that kind of a doctor," she emphasized, "and he was very good to Japanese people. You see, he had to give physical examinations [when clients bought insurance], so he knew the conditions under which most Japanese people lived."

Even in her relationships with Caucasians, Midori seemed particularly fortunate. While the Kimuras' cordial business relationship with Dr. Corseland was not unusual, the fact that their families had a social relationship was. "One time we were all invited to go to the doctor's house for dinner, and I ate a fine [American] dinner for the first time in my life. We also invited them over for a *sukiyaki* dinner. We trusted each other. He worked for the [insurance] company for over twenty years.

"The doctor used to tell my husband, 'If I die first, then you look after my family. If you die first, then I'll look after your family.' Dr. Corseland died in 1927. My husband escorted the family at the funeral. Even after the funeral, his wife consulted my husband instead of her relatives about banking and other matters."

Midori's reflections on her comfortable life were not based on hindsight. "I had heard about some issei women who ran away from their husbands," she commented. "But I was well taken care of compared to those women who had to work on farms," she added. "I heard of a young man who stole another's wife and ran away. There were stories like that in the [Japanese/English] newspaper, but I have forgotten the details.

"In those times," Midori continued, "all the Japanese shops, *ofuroya* [bathhouses], grocery stores, and pool halls were located on Fifth and Sixth Streets [in San Jose]. There were still gambling houses in the area on Sixth Street, and many Japanese used to gamble. I never heard of a woman going there, but there must have been some women who gambled in those days. I did not know anyone like that. Besides," Midori revealed, "I did not live in a Japanese neighborhood."

Because his days were free, Midori explained, her husband also worked for the *Nichibei Shimbun,* a Japanese/English newspaper. Later on, she continued, "My husband began working for another Japanese/English newspaper, the *Hokubei Asahi* [*North American Rising Sun*], when my uncle began to work there. Mr. Mineta, the Congressman's father, took my husband's place at the *Nichibei Shimbun.* My husband was with the *Hokubei* until we were evacuated.

"Our daily lives and raising children kept me so busy that I was completely absorbed, and I really didn't have a chance for much reflection. My children never suffered any harsh treatment at school. They never came home and complained about mean treatment by other children. They used to help the teachers. You see, Japanese children were very quiet and helpful. And I don't remember any cases of discrimination, though there must have been some.

"Even during the Depression, I did not suffer too much. We were able to give our children's hand-me-downs to needy families. My husband was a long-time president of the Japanese Association, which quietly helped those families who were in dire need. I suppose the association had information about each family. I don't know about those things in detail, because they tried to help discreetly so that others would not know about it," Midori explained. Because they were not eligible for citizenship, issei families did not qualify for relief; even if they did qualify, few if any would apply because of the public nature of the aid.

"According to the stories, some families did not have money to buy bread. Most Japanese families, however, had rice. When they could not afford bread, they made *onigiri* [rice balls] for their children's school lunches. Embarrassed to eat *onigiri* in front of other children, the poor students retreated to a corner of the school yard and ate quietly." Empathizing with those less fortunate, Midori, like other Meiji women, knew that fate might quickly change her circumstances.

SHIZU HAYAKAWA

Learning how to dress appropriately, how to use a toilet, how to walk in shoes, how to bathe, meeting a new husband, being introduced to a new religion, and then taking a job with still more to learn, must have been confusing and stressful for Shizu Hayakawa. Then with no time to make any secure adjustments to

her new life, Shizu's emotional connections to her past were sev-
ered by events totally out of her control.

"Only three months after I arrived," she said, "I received news
that my father had passed away. This made me sad and very lonely to think I was the only one left." But self-pity was not an option
for Meiji women. "My own brother was only eight and my stepmother had two children, seven and five, left to raise. My stepmother suffered from intestinal hemorrhaging, so it was
impossible for her to work. Recognizing her responsibility to help
the family, she added stoically, "I took a live-in job to help her out.

"Mr. Mizuno had a cleaning shop with several small rooms in
the back, and we lived in one of those rooms after we were married. At that time my husband worked cleaning windows. I had
come [to the United States] registered as a schoolgirl," which was
what a domestic worker was called in those days, Shizu explained,
"and earned twenty-five cents [an hour] washing dishes. They say
in those days American teachers only earned about one hundred
dollars [a month]. At that time labor was cheap in Japan, too.
Schoolteachers there only earned eight or nine yen." Yet Shizu
recalled questioning the low wages paid to immigrants. "In some
ways we felt that Caucasians used us, but this did not bother me
much," she stated and then explained how she relied on the
lessons of her Japanese background to manage her conflicts. "In
Japan we had been taught to work very hard; therefore, I was liked
and appreciated by many."

"When I started work as a housemaid, board and room was free.
My husband lived with me and went from there to his own job
every day. I made seventy-five dollars a month and sent fifty to my
stepmother to help her feed the family. My husband did not object
because this was his own sister we were helping," Shizu commented and then quietly added, "It took seventeen years to put the
children through school.

"The family I worked for was Italian. The husband was the vice-
president for the Bank of America. He had come from his country
to New York. This man began with a job hauling coal. He succeeded in business and finally was able to become vice-president
of the bank. This man's father-in-law also came to America from
Sicily and struggled to get a grocery business going. Since those
people were able to get through difficulties, I felt the hard times
we came through were quite natural."

Shizu never complained that her work was strenuous, but she
did reveal the details of a long work day. "I usually got up at seven
and made coffee and breakfast for the family. Then I washed dish-

es, cleaned the house, did the washing and ironing, made beds, and did whatever else there was to do.

"There were four adults and no children in the household," Shizu explained. The vice-president of the bank was the master of the house, and his wife and her parents completed the small family. Even without children, there must have been a great deal of work to do, because Shizu does not mention any other servants in the household.

"Lunch is the most important meal to Italians," Shizu continued. "The husband always came home for lunch and his wife cooked it. I watched and helped with whatever I could. As you know, Italians love to talk, so the old lady used to talk to me by the hour as we worked in the kitchen. She told me of all her experiences and the hard times she had come through. I learned what little English I know by listening to her talk.

"By the time we cleaned up after lunch and washed the dishes, it would be 2:30 P.M., and the elder couple would rest until supper time. I rested, too. For supper I helped and waited on the family. Since the master of the house was the vice-president of the bank, he always brought home guests. And on Sundays they would have a lot of their young Italian friends in, so it was hectic.

"I would finish work around nine in the evening, and then we [my husband and I] would have dinner. Around 11:00 P.M. the family would retire, I'd do whatever I wanted, and then go to bed. Monday was my day off and I was able to go to Japanese town.

Shizu's work day may not have been as arduous a those of other issei women, but she revealed that her days were long and lonely. "When you are work for a Caucasian family and there is no one to talk to, there is the chance of suffering a nervous breakdown. Well, you get up in the morning, make the coffee, and, like I did for ten years, do the same things every day. There is just no time to see and talk to other [Japanese] people. Then you become lonely and sad." Unlike Onatsu Akiyama and Kiyo Miyake, Shizu had no companion in her union. "There are some husbands who don't talk much, and when you do talk to them, they're not interested. They make no reply. When we were young," Shizu said regretfully, "this was something which made me sad.

"There were picture brides who came, met their new husbands, didn't like them, and returned to Japan. There were others who found other men they liked better and ran away. There were all these different tales."

Understanding the plight of other picture brides, Shizu commented with great empathy, "Some of the girls would say that no matter how much they tried, they could not bring themselves to like the man they were to marry." There would be attempts to maintain the same stringent codes of conduct as in Japan, and Shizu explained, "Then some of their friends would try to force them to marry and get along.

"The girls were very young. They came to America with the idea that they would have a good life, but were immediately expected to work very hard as servants. It was very difficult for women folk in the beginning. We had to clean coal stoves. If this was not done, the oven would not heat properly to bake, and in those days everyone baked their own bread. There wasn't any hot running water like there is today. We had to heat kettles of water on a coal stove.

These brides had no place to call a home and lived in very small quarters in strange, large houses. Lacking a working knowledge of English and often embarrassed to use what little English they knew, Shizu explained, "These young brides were left to themselves and weren't able to go anywhere. They wept from the extreme loneliness. Some had nervous breakdowns during their pregnancies and committed suicide."

It was obvious that Shizu experienced that same sense of isolation and depression and was not left unscarred by the experience. In an attempt to explain her ability to endure, she said, "From childhood on, in Japan we were taught that we would have to serve our husbands and look after them. I worked very diligently with this in mind. I guess I was one of the steadfast ones."

For nearly ten years the Hayakawas managed to exist on the limited income that they earned and, for Shizu, on whatever meager emotional resources were available to her. "In 1929," she continued, "just before Christmas, my husband developed a large growth on his neck. The lady of the house introduced us to her friend, who was a doctor. The doctor operated and cut the growth away. We thought that the wound would heal, but by husband developed a very high fever. I knew I would have to look after my husband and thought it would not be fair to stay on [at my employer's home]. I asked the lady of the house for time off until my husband recovered. I was not sure whether he would live or die, because every day he ran a fever of 104 degrees or more. We rented a house where I nursed him for six months, but he did not show any signs of improvement."

Mr. Hayakawa's illness was serious, and thoughts of the need to die and be buried in Japan must have surfaced. Since they had no children during their ten years in the United States together, there was little to bind them to this country. "I decided to take my husband back to Japan," Shizu said, "and admitted him to Kokura Hospital, where he had the operation repeated."

Ever mindful of their limited funds, Shizu related, "On our way to Japan, we stopped in Hawaii and learned that the American stock market had hit rock bottom. The Depression had hit America. It was during this difficult period that Mr. Hayakawa was ill. In spite of the hard times, I paid for my husband's hospital and medical expenses, and continued to provide money for the education of my father and stepmother's children in Japan.

"In Japan we stayed at my husband's family home. For the next four months my husband had to go back and forth to the hospital for treatments. I instructed the girl [niece] whom we had been supporting to come and look after my husband for a while. As soon as I had made these arrangements, I returned to America to continue my work." Though Shizu related this episode in her life story in a matter-of-fact manner, she admitted, "This was the most difficult experience of my life." Shizu took great care not to be critical of her husband, but the loneliness and responsibility of supporting him as in invalid, as well as his sister's children, must have left her dispirited at times.

"My husband stayed in Japan for about a year. He never fully recovered and never really worked again," Shizu said. "We really lived a poor life, but we didn't have any children," she added, partly to express relief and at the same time a suppressed longing for something missed.

As financial head of several family members, Shizu explained, it was extremely difficult to earn enough to support everyone. "During the Depression there was virtually no employment. What work I had paid thirty cents an hour, and unlike today, we did not receive any carfare. My husband was not able to work; even if he was well enough to work, there was simply no employment. We tried very hard to economize as much as possible."

Shizu explained that before the Depression, "My employer suggested that we buy stocks, and the Trans America Company seemed to be the best investment. I remember purchasing the stock bit by bit. The stock went down during the Depression, but my husband advised me not to sell. The stock nearly became worthless, but later the tide turned, and it gained in value and interest. It is because of this investment that I am able to live without working now."

During her years in the United States, Shizu's Japanese attitudes began to undergo a subtle change. She was a loyal employee, but she also began to consider her own needs in the decisions she made. "I worked for the Italian family until the master of the house passed away. I stayed there for seventeen years and then quit. It was sometime before the last war. The family asked me to come back and work for them many times, but," Shizu staunchly declared, "since I had come to America, I didn't want to always live like a servant. I wanted to live more like a human being."

Shizu decided to do housework just three hours a day for another family, and just before the war, she began working for a Japanese-owned catering business.

○ ○ ○ ○ ○ ○ ○ ○ ○ ○ ○ ○ ○ ○ ○

The Meiji picture bride was, more often than not, stunned by the harshness of her life in America. The daily grind of pulling one more weed when every bone ached for rest, of washing one more dish when loneliness seemed unbearable, or of ironing one more shirt at four in the morning, was compounded by needing to care for young children. Within a few years some of these brides who had been deceived into marrying men ten or fifteen years older, had to begin nursing their aging, ailing husbands. Many of these women became the primary economic support for their families.

The issei pioneer woman never saw herself in a traditional, Western, historical perspective, but her years of toil helped mark the direction of agriculture, commerce, and industry in the West. Her work helped establish a truck farming industry, develop new strains of crops, open new markets, provide new agricultural marketing techniques, and encourage small businesses. The issei woman struggled against enormous odds for the sake of her family, and her efforts eventually reaped rewards.

According to Meiji values, difficult times and difficult marriages were not considered acceptable reasons for divorce or desertion, though in some instances they occurred. Still, the issei woman did not consider *gaman* or endurance of difficult times a negative sacrifice. She had been trained to expect *kuro* as a lesson in life. Her endurance had a more positive end, that of upholding the spiritual values of the Meiji woman. Her reward was, again, not individual but the collective well-being of her family unit.

Although the issei pioneer woman would continue to cling tenaciously to those Meiji values which supported her family, transplanted to a society that allowed more freedom for women, she also began to take advantage of new opportunities. Ironically, the country that offered these opportunities was to retract many of them with the advent of World War II.

CHAPTER FOUR

The War Years

TEIKO TOMITA

Teiko Tomita recalled her surprise when a friend ran over to the Tomita nursery from the village and shouted, "'Stop working! Stop working! Japan and America have begun to fight! Japanese airplanes might come over Seattle and drop bombs."

"I was shocked at the news," Teiko said, "and turned on the radio. My friend said that she had heard on the radio that we Japanese would be taken away. We talked a lot about what might happen."

Channeling most of their energies into providing some measure of economic security for their families, few issei even considered the possibility of war despite deteriorating relations between Japan and the United States. The Japanese attack on Pearl Harbor was as much of a shock to the Japanese community as it was to the rest of the American public.

Nonetheless, blaming the issei and their American-born children became an acceptable outlet for American wartime hysteria and lent fuel to already existing prejudices. West Coast newspapers carried editorials supporting drastic measures. Fear for their personal safety and rumors that the Japanese population would be gathered and gunned down or starved added to the shock and confusion of the times. Many issei thought they would be imprisoned and then shot or starved.

Issei community leaders were quickly arrested and detained by the FBI. The arrests created a leadership vacuum in Japanese communities in those crucial weeks and months when the Roosevelt administration made the decision to imprison tens of thousands of persons of Japanese descent. The issei men remaining in

Japanese communities were often the ill and elderly. Although issei women would not fill the leadership vacuum in visible political terms, they took up much of the slack by tightening the bonds of family and community whenever possible in the difficult days that followed. Working in ways they had never before imagined, sometimes breaking one tradition to maintain other traditions, these women relied on their Meiji attitudes and strengths; at other times they consciously measured the risks of casting off some of their Meiji ways to maintain what they considered their most valuable assets.

"Even though our village was a small one with only twenty-five families," Teiko continued, "we had a *Nikkeijin Kai* [Japanese Association]. Leaders of the Japanese community like Mr. Kumasaka, president of the *Nikkeijin Kai,* were taken away. They were held in the immigration office for a few days and then were taken to other camps." Japanese community leaders suspected of collusion with the enemy were imprisoned in internment camps, along with German and Italian prisoners of war. "Mr. Heiji Okuda and all other prominent leaders were taken away," Teiko revealed. Then expressing the prevailing mood, she said, "Everybody was afraid.

"My husband was treasurer of the association. Since he was one of the officers, I was scared that he would be taken away, too. The children were young, and I didn't know anything about the outside world, so I worried. My husband worried, too, because the children were too young to face the world alone." The rumors about relocating Japanese communities to special camps continued to surface and added more stress. On February 19, 1942, President Franklin D. Roosevelt signed Executive Order No. 9066 authorizing the massive evacuation of persons of Japanese descent on the West Coast. "I was very anxious until we received the evacuation notice," Teiko said. For her the anxiety of separation was so great that she was almost grateful when the evacuation notices appeared. "When I learned we were all to be taken to a camp together, I was greatly relieved," she affirmed.

Still, the relief that Teiko felt for her family could not dispel the distress of other losses. "We tried to sell as many of our belongings as we could," she recounted, "but we had poured all our savings and all our energy into this nursery from 1929 until 1942. It took us thirteen hard years to get to the point where the nursery produced trees that could be sold every year. Some of the trees could be left alone for a year or two, but no longer because they would grow too tall."

In some areas on the West Coast, Japanese communities had only a few days to dispose of their property. The Tomitas were fortunate to have the time to make some financial arrangements. "Gardeners, both Japanese and white, used to buy our trees," Teiko explained. "There was an old, white gardener who came from Tacoma to buy from us. We knew him quite well and he paid his bills on time. He came over and said, 'You people have to be evacuated, and I'm very sorry about that. If you want me to take care of the nursery, I'll keep it going for you until you come back.' My husband was the kind of person who believed in everybody. Besides, at that time we felt like drowning people who would grab at any floating straw; so we agreed to have him manage the nursery for us.

"We consulted with lawyers and had them draw up a contract. The agreement was that this man would take care of the nursery, so that the place would not go wild. He would sell the trees, but he was supposed to send us one-third of the profit and pay the taxes out of his two-thirds of the profit. Unfortunately a year later, the lawyer sent us a letter saying the man had stopped paying the taxes and asked us what he should do. Well, we didn't know what to do."

Still, Teiko was fortunate that Mr. Tomita was present and able to help with the family's evacuation. In the days following the Pearl Harbor bombing, when several thousand issei men were arrested for questioning, the task of deciding what household items could be taken, what should be sold, and what might be safely stored was often left to the issei woman. The military restriction that evacuees could take only what they could carry meant they could take only the bare essentials. The evacuation notices appeared on telephone poles and buildings in West Coast Japanese communities. Those who were fortunate had two months' notice; others had only a few weeks; and some only a few days to make decisions about possessions so dearly earned with years of backbreaking work and sacrifice.

The evacuees were housed temporarily in assembly centers, often the stables of community fairgrounds, while more permanent relocation centers were being constructed. "We were evacuated in the middle of June, the hottest time of the year, to an assembly center near Fresno. I've forgotten the name of the place now," Teiko said, but remembered in detail how spare the accommodations were. "The barracks [where we lived] were very poorly constructed with tin roofs. It was hard when it got really hot in the assembly center, because there were no shade trees. The barracks were built on blacktop tar-paper, so when it got hot, the floor got soft. Then, the legs of the beds became imbedded in the tar.

"During that summer, my oldest son became sick with sunstroke. He had a temperature of 103, but there was nothing we could do for him except make him drink water. I put a blanket on the floor under the bed and laid him down there. I thought it might be a little cooler there than in the rest of the room. I really felt sorry for him. There must have been a doctor in the camp, but we didn't know how to find him. Fortunately my son recovered soon. But then," Teiko said, recalling what befell so many issei women whose husbands were ten or fifteen years older than their wives, "my husband became ill with a disease and could not move very well because his motor nerves were affected.

"We were there [in the assembly center] for a few months, and then in the fall we were moved to Tule Lake, where we spent the winter. We moved again in the spring to Heart Mountain, Wyoming," Teiko said. She never complained about the difficulties of moving with a sickly husband because she was so grateful that her family remained intact. In addition to the the Tule Lake Relocation Center in California and the Heart Mountain Center in Wyoming, the War Relocation Authority (WRA) administered eight other sites: Manzanar, also in California, Gila River and Poston in Arizona, Jerome and Rohwer in Arkansas, Granada (also called Amache) in Colorado, Minidoka in Idaho, and Topaz in Utah. The evacuees referred to these centers as "camps."

"Tule Lake," where the Tomitas were moved in the fall, Teiko explained, "was like a continuation of the assembly center. It was just bigger, and the facilities were prepared." At that time the population of Tule Lake was about 16,000. "It was so big that there were many, many Japanese from California. We wanted to be in a camp with people who were from Seattle," Teiko said, indicating the need for the support of friends, "but they had been sent to Minidoka. Those from our area–Tacoma, Deming, and Sunnydale-were sent to Tule Lake."

Functional but in shock, Teiko recalled, "We felt like we were delirious. We were totally confused. We were not allowed radios, or Japanese or English newspapers in camp," Teiko said, although newspapers were permitted later and the evacuees were allowed to publish their own papers. "All of us–issei, nisei [children of the issei born in the United States, second generation] and sansei [grandchildren of the issei, third generation]–were detained there.

Yet," Teiko added as an afterthought, "even if America was at war with Japan, I didn't think our lives were in danger." But other issei women continued to fear for the health and safety of their families and even dried bread crumbs in camp against the day when food might no longer be forthcoming.

Finding it difficult to express her mood and attitudes during that time, Teiko conveyed ambivalent feelings as she attempted to find the positive and hopeful aspects of her situation. "The American government took care of us, even though they put us in camps. We felt that we were thrown into prison, and the food was rather crude, but we were able to eat until we were full. Later on I heard that Japanese POW's in Russia were treated very badly. Then I was really impressed by the fact that the American government did treat us rather decently.

"I recall more of the pleasant memories than the frightful ones," Teiko said. "There were English classes for those who wanted to learn, and I attended a poetry class."

But Teiko also remembered that the relocation camps were far from ideal. "In the barracks where we were housed, we were placed at the end, where the biggest rooms were. We were assigned only one room with a double bed and three single beds. I remember that when you talked in a normal voice, everything could be heard by your neighbor. It was the first time in my life that I experienced that kind of living."

With all of the trauma sustained by issei women and the rest of the evacuees, it seemed almost impossible that they could sustain another major stress. But the loyalty issue appeared, and the debate and division that it provoked strained individuals and their families to the breaking point. It is to the credit of these people, and issei women in particuar, that they retained the core of their values and over the years adapted and rebuilt their communities with pride in their cultural heritage.

The swift and unprecedented actions by the United States government in uprooting and relocating Japenese Americans propelled the nisei, usually dutiful to their issei parents, to decide for themselves their own futures. Stirred by patriotism, duty, and the need to prove themselves loyal, many nisei volunteered for the armed services. Impressed by the dedication of the early volunteers, the War Department decided to form an all-Japanese-American combat team (442nd Regimental Combat Team) and prepared a loyalty questionnaire for all male evacuees. In the meantime, the WRA also needed a questionnaire. Ironically, as quickly as the relocation camps were established, evacuees found themselves in demand because of the need for wartime workers in fields and factories. In its haste, the WRA used the same loyalty questionnaire that the War Department had prepared. Unfortunately, the simple question of loyalty to which the vast majority could reply "yes," became confused with other issues and caused painful emotional struggles from which many families never recovered.

In particular, Questions 27 and 28 were the focus of the "yes-yes, no-no" controversy. Question 27 asked if the evacuee was willing to serve in combat. Most women and aged issei replied "no." Question 28 asked if the evacuee would relinquish allegiance to the Japanese emperor and nation. Because the issei were denied naturalized U.S. citizenship, many replied "no" for fear of being left stateless. Since the evacuees were to be segregated in different camps according to their replies, some nisei who were caring for aging parents felt compelled to answer "no" to keep their families together. Few evacuees arrived at their decision without difficult reflection and often heated family debate.

When loyalty questionnaires were distributed in the Tule Lake camp, all of the Tomitas indicated their loyalty to the United States and avoided any family conflict, but longtime friendships were lost. "Our neighbor in Sunnydale was an ardent Japanese loyalist, so our relationship was strained in the camp. He treated us as if he hardly knew us. When Tule Lake became a special camp for disloyal people, we were moved to Heart Mountain. He didn't even come to say goodbye when we left. I believe his stand was wrong. He belonged to the *katta gumi* [winners' group]. They didn't believe that Japan had lost the war even after it was over." According to the loyalty questionnaire, several thousand evacuees and their minor children were technically considered disloyal, but it is amazing how few of them, like the Tomitas' neighbor, affirmed any political loyalties to Japan.

The years in relocation camps gave Teiko time to attend poetry classes and time to make friends. Her pleasure in returning to intellectual and personally satisfying activities after years of difficult physical labor undoubtedly left her with some positive memories. "I attended *waka* [short poem] classes in camp. I still compose *waka* sometimes, but the members of the *Waka* Association are becoming fewer each year.

"I made a lot of friends in camp, and I learned a great many things from them. Those are the warm, happy memories. I don't have any bad memories from that period," Teiko insisted and then added a comment that revealed continued ambivalence and unresolved emotions. "If I forget the fact that Japan and America were at war against each other," she reflected, "I think I spent a very peaceful time there."

Iyo Tsutsui

As Iyo Tsutsui sat in her house on the farm purchased with so many years of sweat and pain, she recalled the events of World War II. "When Pearl Harbor was attacked, I was living on this land," she declared, emphasizing the roots she had established. "I was summoned to a police station," Iyo said. Considerate of his wife's apprehensions, which were understandable, Mr. Tsutsui tried to be humorous. "My husband jokingly said, 'See, it's because you always criticize the government. You're gonna be sent to Missouri.'

"It was odd that they should want me, because I was not a leader of any organization, and I thought it might be a case of mistaken identity. My husband was an officer of the Japanese Association in Stockton. If he were picked up, it would make sense. I was really worried. I took my daughter with me [to translate] and went to the police station.

"They asked me if I had been in Japan recently. I answered, 'Yes.' They asked why I went. I replied, 'I have parents and also brothers and sisters living in Japan. I went to see them.' They asked if I went alone. I said that I took two daughters. One had finished high school, so I wanted her to see Japan. I also wanted her to learn Japanese traditions and customs. My younger daughter, who was only four years old, could not be left alone at home. One daughter stayed in Japan for two years and another was there for three years. Before the international situation between Japan and the United States became tense, I brought them back."

The children apparently had never wanted to stay in Japan. "They were very homesick," Iyo recalled, "and wanted to come back." But having raised them as she was raised, it is not surprising that Iyo declared, "They always obeyed me."

After being questioned, Iyo was released, but she recalled her daughter's fear that her mother would be sent to an internment camp.

"It was unbelievable that Japan would fight against America after the attack on Pearl Harbor. I remembering telling Papa that

Japan would lose because America has such abundant materials. My husband felt the same way."

Despite their personal opinions, the events ruled the day and the Tsutsuis lived in fear and panic. "We had a picture of my husband's brother, who was an officer in the Japanese Imperial Navy. We burned all those pictures while preparing the *ofuro* [Japanese bath]. We also had shotguns, which we threw into the river. My husband's uncle in Los Angeles had sent us some Buddhist writings. We burned those, too. We were really afraid, and we had no idea what might happen to us.

"There were those who said that the government was going to gather us up and massacre us with gas. My husband said that America was not a barbaric country and the government would not do such a thing. He was not that concerned."

Despite her husband's reassurances, Iyo fretted. "I worried about my children. If we were evacuated to a camp, how were we to educate our children? When were we to be freed? These were the most pressing questions. I really felt like crying then," she admitted, recalling her despair and frustration at so many unknowns. "I didn't care so much about us, but our children were still young. Only one of them was married. Fortunately, it turned out all right in the camp and the rumors were unfounded.

"As for the evacuation, when the orders came, we went to the Stockton fairgrounds. It's still located at the same place on Charter Way. We entered on May 2, 1942, and we left for the camp at Rohwer, Arkansas on October 12, 1942.

"We asked the bank to take care of our land. Even though those of us who didn't have citizenship couldn't lease [or buy] land," Iyo explained, "an influential man in the Buddhist church by the name of Mr. Miyata was my husband's good friend. His nephew was a citizen of this country, and we arranged to pay this newphew some money, about $500, to use his name when we bought the land.

"My daughter used to baby-sit for the banker's children, and his bank did a good job of taking care of our land during the war.

"At that time most of the people around here were Italians. Japanese and Italian character is very similar. If you ask politely, humbly, as though you were subordinate, then they are very helpful; but if you go against someone, you are an enemy forever. Because Tsutsui was a calm person who never wanted to make enemies, he got along with everyone and people were good to him. Our children went to school with Italian children and made close friends in a very natural way. People begin to grow in *ninjo* [humanity, common kindness] as they associate with one another. Yes, they [Italian neighbors] were very good to us."

With a few months to prepare for the evacuation, Iyo said, "*Akiramete imashita* [we were resigned to it], so we didn't feel any pain by the time we had to leave, but it was sort of lonesome. We climbed up into the grandstand at the fairgrounds and looked in the direction of our house," she remembered and then added, "but it was not that bad," and focused once again on the positives. "Later on, we got used to it. When we went to Arkansas, they cooked Japanese-style food, so it was much better.

"Just tarpaper covered the outside walls of the living quarters," she said and added, "but we farmers were used to this kind of life. It was not that bad. We didn't speak up in the middle of a crowd and didn't indulge in gossip, so our life was very peaceful."

Before leaving the Stockton area for the Rohwer Relocation Camp, Iyo said, "I petitioned for *ohakamairi* [visiting a loved one's grave]. My son [who had drowned in the river] was buried at the cemetery in Oak Park. One of the Caucasian officials took me there in his own car. I never thought that the Caucasians were that bad. On the contrary, they could be very kind if the favor you needed was a small one.

"After we were transferred to the camp in Arkansas, they asked me to work in the kitchen, where I washed dishes. After a while, I quit working in the mess hall to work in the fields." By this time, the government needed farm workers, whether they were imprisoned evacuees or not, to help harvest food as the entire country mobilized for the war effort. "This was better because I didn't have to stay inside the barbed wire," Iyo said, recalling her relief. "They would take us out to the field in trucks, and I felt that my mind was liberated and I was happy." Indicating a depression she did not openly acknowledge, she admitted, "Then I regained my sense of well-being."

Once settled, the evacuees breathed a collective sigh of relief as they settled into camp life, only to struggle with another source of anxiety as the loyalty questionnaire was circulated. This controversy, which tore apart some families, was not a cause of concern for the Tomitas or the Tsutsuis. "As for the loyalty question," Iyo said, "we did not have a boy of draft age at that time, and I don't remember anything about the draft issue."

Although she never complained about her harsh life on the farm, like Teiko Tomita and other overtaxed issei women, Iyo found her life during the years in camp physically easier. Still, never one to be idle, Iyo recalled, "I did not waste my time. I learned English; I learned to weave and to arrange flowers, and I also learned how to make dolls. The time was spent very creatively."

Although Iyo voiced positive statements about some aspects of camp life, there was much in her own comments and actions to indicate a suppression of negative emotions. As the months wore on, she actively encouraged her family to leave the camp as soon as the opportunity arose. "All I recall about camp life is that I worked in the fields and learned many things; however, I don't think the camp itself was interesting or fun. I never thought about revisiting that place."

HISAYO HANATO

"On Sunday December 7, as I came out of church," Hisayo Hanato painfully recalled, "a friend's son came up to me and said, *'Obasan* [Aunty], war has broken out! Japan attacked Hawaii.' I was really shocked. My first and only thought was fear for my children. Even though we [issei] could not be helped, the children had to be protected.

"We continued to run our restaurant [in Long Beach] until we were evacuated, but we closed many days and there was no consistency," Hisayo said. Curfews, travel restrictions, and a freeze on bank accounts for persons of Japanese descent made it difficult to conduct business. "Our hearts were not in it," she dolefully remarked.

"We had moved our restaurant downtown in February, 1941. We had just bought completely new furnishings and were doing very well. We had paid cash for everything because I didn't like to be in debt. In December of the same year, war broke out."

When notices to evacuate to relocation camps were posted, Hisayo said, "We had to sell many things very cheap and also gave away many things. People would not buy from us because they knew that we had to evacuate. They asked us to sell our things for such a low price that we decided not to sell [most of the restaurant furnishings]. We stored a lot in our friend's garage; however, when we were in Jerome, we sold everything [through our friend], because my husband had a stroke and we thought that we would not be able to return to California." Many elderly issei husbands like Mr. Hanato, who were more susceptible to the stresses of evacuation than their younger wives, succumbed to illness. Continuing her commentary of that chaotic time, Hisayo said, "I didn't think we would be killed, though there were such rumors, but I felt just terrible. I don't know how to express these feelings," she added, as memories brought back the anguish of that painful experience.

"At first we were sent to Santa Anita [assembly center]." The place smelled awful because, you see," Hisayo recalled with distaste, "it was a race track. Beds were placed in the stables. It was a terrible place to sleep. We used hay for mattresses and made our beds. In the beginning the food was terrible but it got better later on."

As Hisayo remembered her reactions to one of the most difficult of her life experiences, she also recounted what sustained her. "We used to hold worship services in the race track stands. From there we could see Mount Wilson. As we looked at the beautiful mountain and worshipped together, we forgot that Japan was at war with America and that we were evacuated into an assembly center and sleeping in stables."

But Hisayo also recalled that the faith that was her mainstay had not been acquired easily. "Several years before the war, we had taken our young daughters back to Japan for their education. It was a very popular thing to do in those days," she explained. A Japanese education guaranteed instruction in all the cultural traits that the Japanese valued so highly. In addition, long-distance childcare also freed parents to work harder. "During my eight-month visit," Hisayo continued, "I made arrangements for them to attend Hiroshima Jogakuin [a girl's school] and left them in my mother's care. As I took my leave, my mother and I bowed to each other in a formal farewell in front of *butsudan* [a household Buddhist shrine], and she said, 'Hisayo, I have nothing more to say about your going back to America; however, there is one thing I would like to ask you. Please do not become a *Yaso* [Christian].'

"While living in Long Beach, I associated with many Christians, attended church, and was urged to be baptized on my return from Japan, but I just could not bring myself to do it. I always remembered my mother's posture, that she asked me not to become a Christian.

"My mother knew almost nothing about Christianity, and what she knew was bad. As a Buddhist, she believed that one achieved salvation through the power of Buddha. She had heard that, according to Christian beliefs, salvation was achieved through one's own power and ability. She saw this as a basic difference and did not believe that man could be saved by his own power. People in Japan used to call Christianity a heretical religion. It was believed that those whose funerals were held in Christian churches could not attain salvation and that they appeared as ghosts in Japan.

"I returned to Japan a second time to bring my daughters back and told my mother about my Christian beliefs. Finally, she said, 'Well, I trust that you know what you are doing. Follow your heart.' As soon as I returned to Long Beach," Hisayo said, "I was baptized." And then, affirming the importance of receiving her mother's blessing, she pointed out a propitious omen by simply stating, "It was on Mother's Day."

Continuing her commentary on the war years, Hisayo said, "From Santa Anita we went to Jerome [Arkansas Relocation Center] where we stayed for two years. While we were there, we had to answer the loyalty questions. There were a lot of problems which arose from this. You see, we were not American citizens." And according to the Naturalization Act of 1790, Asians were not eligible for naturalized citizenship either. "And so," she explained, "I leaned toward going back to Japan. When we first came to America, we intended to return to Japan in a few years. We were not able to accumulate enough money that soon, and then our children were born. I wanted them to be educated in Japan and sent them there for three years. They returned when they were thirteen and fifteen, just three months before the war started."

Although Hisayo had often been guided by her devotion to filial duty, her own daughters were directed more by their individual desires. Because they had spent only a few years in Japan, Hisayo explained, "Our children preferred to stay in the United States." Their insistence on remaining in the United States forced the Hanatos to reconsider their original plan to return to Japan after the war. "They were American citizens," she said, "and needed to be here." The Hanatos chose instead to keep the family intact and stay in the United States. "Of course, we had to stay with our children, and this was the reason we decided to live here until we died. We finally decided to answer 'yes' and 'yes' [to the loyalty questions]." This decision did not come easily to Hisayo, as her use of the emotionally laden phrase "to live here until we died" indicates.

As Hisayo continued her commentary, she expressed the attitude of most issei concerning the imprisonment. "Because we were enemy aliens, I can't complain about the treatment we received," she stated but separated the treatment of the issei from that of their children. "However, I felt very badly for my children who were American citizens. They were still too young to be separated from us, so they had to stay with us [in the camps]. And when I think back, we were probably safer to be in the camps. Ultimately everything worked out for us in spite of all the things that happened, but," she continued, "I felt that the government had dishonored Japanese Americans. The government was also inconsistent. They put the nisei in the camps, and yet took them away to fight for America. Even though I believe that because the nisei are citizens, it was natural for them to do their duty, and even if the result was a glorious end, I felt that the government acted irresponsibly. I had no sons, so I was spared a painful situation. If I had had a son, I might have voiced my opposition much more loudly," she declared.

The loyalty issue caused Hisayo much anxiety. "There were some educated people who decided to be loyal to Japan," she began. These "educated people" were *kibei*, American citizens by birth who had been educated in Japan and then returned to the United States before the outbreak of the war. Because of their Japanese education, their loyalties tended toward Japan. "They demonstrated daily and believed that if they returned to Japan, they would be treated royally. Sometimes they would say spiteful things behind our backs because we had declared our loyalty to America. There was a young neighbor in camp who angrily said to me one day, 'You are an American dog!'" For a people who valued consensus, these open breaches caused enormous tension in the relocation camps.

Although the United States government had officially determined that all persons of Japanese ancestry were potentially dangerous, individual Americans often saw reality from a different viewpoint and were moved by humanity and social conscience. Touched by the memory of one such individual, Hisayo Hanato spoke emotionally about the times.

"There was a woman, Janet Smith, who was very concerned about us [Japanese]. In years past she had worked at the Hokusei Jogakuin [a women's middle school in Japan] without pay for thirteen years. [After Pearl Harbor was bombed], people were very worried. We had no peace of mind because we were greatly troubled by the many rumors. Janet Smith told us not to worry. She said we wouldn't have to evacuate. Because of the many restric-

tions which were placed on us, she ran all kinds of errands for us."
A curfew, a five-mile travel limit, and frozen bank accounts were
the most cumbersome restrictions.

"When the orders to evacuate came, Janet Smith came over to
us and said, *'Sumimasen* [I'm very sorry]. I'll go wherever you
might be sent!' When we were moved to Jerome [one of two relocation centers in Arkansas], she came, too. She stayed in a nearby
town and commuted to the camp by bus because the camp officials refused to let her live in the camp. She would seek out families who were in need or in trouble. She comforted people, visited
the sick, and taught English classes.

"The memory of Janet Smith makes me realize that I am still a
very imperfect person. I am quick-tempered; she was not so. She
felt as if she were the one who had committed this crime of evac-
uating the entire Japanese population. She apologized to all of us,
helped us at the assembly center, and followed us to the Jerome
and Rohwer Relocation Centers. After the war was over, she
returned to Long Beach and got the community ready for our
return. Whenever I remember her words, 'I'll go with you wherever you might be sent,' I still cry with gratitude."

SETSU YOSHIHASHI

Setsu Yoshihashi described her great personal apprehension following the Pearl Harbor attack. "I was surprised to hear about the
attack. All I heard was people calling us 'Jap, Jap' all the time. The
newpapers called us Jap and the radio called us Jap. It didn't seem
real. I was very frightened. Both my husband and I came from military families and we had pictures of our relatives in military uni-
forms. My children were afraid, so we burned all the pictures in
case we might have to face the authorities.

"I was working for the Cramers at the time and went to work
the day after the attack as usual. Mrs. Cramer came down from
the second floor and said, 'Don't worry, Oriental, you did not personally start the war. There is nothing to worry about. Just continue to work.' As she was consoling me, it started to rain. I held
my breath because the rain sounded like planes; I thought they
had come from Japan. Mrs. Cramer kept telling me not to worry.
She advised me to get all my savings and investments and put
them in the name of the store. She also told me to gather all my
important papers and belongings and bring them to her house
because it was going to be a risky and dangerous time.

"I was very impressed by her concern," Setsu stated and then presented the ultimate compliment, "If she was a Japanese woman, I don't think she would have offered help and advice."

Mrs. Cramer also made a most generous offer, which was weighed against Setsu's continuing commitment to keep her family intact. "Mrs. Cramer told me that I could leave my daughter in her care if we had to leave for camp. She told me to bring my daughter, Eiko, to her." The advantages of living in the household of a wealthy and caring family could not have escaped Setsu, but she must also have recalled the anguish caused by the lack of parental love during her childhood and the years she spent being shunted from household to household. "Well, because of the uncertainties of war, I felt it was best to keep the entire family as a unit. All our family members went to camp together."

Faced with one of the greatest crises in her life, Setsu, like Teiko Tomita, Hisayo Hanato, Shizu Hayakawa, and so many other issei women, had an elderly, ailing husband to care for. "My husband was ill when the war started, and by the time we had to go to camp, he was bedridden and couldn't help with the packing and moving. With the help of my two sons, we took all our belongings to our next-door neighbor, who was also our landlord. He stored our belongings in his house and later sent our things to us. I worked until the very end, until the day before we left for camp."

Setsu Yoshihashi, who faced disappointment and drudgery from the day she arrived in America, who worked incredibly long hours laundering clothes to supplement her other jobs, who was the sole support for a family of seven, who tolerated the constant criticism of an opinionated and ailing husband, and who had not received a personal gift in years, summarized the evacuation process and its subsequent disappointments and heartaches in a few concluding remarks about the fate of a beloved sewing machine. "Since my elder son was now making eighteen dollars a week, he told me he wanted to buy a sewing machine for me." A younger son had taken the elder son's old job at a grocery store, and, Setsu said, "The two boys saved their money and bought me the machine. They were so proud of themselves and made me so very happy," Setsu declared of the gift that represented gratitude and, most important to her, the Meiji response of filial devotion.

"But then," Setsu said abruptly, "when the war started, we had to sell the machine. My children were very sad about that," she said pointedly but did not offer a comment about her own feelings. Instead, she repeated, "We sold the machine and went to camp."

Continuing her memories of that troubled time, she said, "We got on the train in Pasadena and went directly to Tsurabe for a while and then went to a camp in Gila, Arizona. It was a good place.

"Gila was a desert with sagebrush everywhere, a very hot place. When we first arrived, it was horrible, but we were all in the same boat. Camp life turned out to be very good." Camp life was curiously something of a relief for an overtaxed Setsu. "We all enjoyed ourselves. I learned flower arranging and made belts. There were plays and entertainment. Life was easy, and we had everything we wanted–soy sauce, rice, and other items. I was so afraid I wouldn't be able to have Japanese food once I was in camp that I smuggled in rice and soy sauce, but that wasn't necessary. We didn't go without for a single day. We were given clothes and even spending money. We had plenty. America treats people well. If this had happened in Japan, we would never have been treated this well."

Although camp life provided some issei women with a respite from difficult labor and economic responsibilities, new dilemmas that appeared posed such difficulties that the psychological fabric of their families was severely strained. In many instances, issei women openly asserted themselves against their husbands for the first time.

For the Yoshihashis, the loyalty issue was one of the most difficult problems to resolve. The nisei, American citizens by right of birth, tended to be staunchly loyal to the United States and were sometimes at odds with their parents, particularly their fathers. Issei women, who had carefully defended the strong role of the father in the Japanese family, now openly defied their husbands to defend the position of their American-born children. According to Setsu Yoshihashi, "The hardest thing in camp was to answer the 'yes-no' question." The Tule Lake Relocation Center was designated a center for those declaring loyalty to Japan, and, Setsu said, "My husband had said we would all go to the Tule Lake camp and then return to Japan.

"Our sons turned pale and started to cry. I felt sorry for them. I told them that just because Papa was saying those things, we weren't going to blindly follow him. We would consult our relatives and friends, and then we would take the action that was best for the whole family. I told them, 'You must do what is best for you. Be sure to decide now so you will not regret it later. Think carefully and ask your friends for advice. Then and only then make your decision. This problem cannot be solved solely by your father and there is no reason to follow him blindly.' My boys, therefore, went to talk with Jimmy Sakamoto and some other friends." The Yoshihashi sons were also torn because a married sister lived in Tokyo at the time. But Setsu said, "They finally decided to join the army and fight in the war. They joined the 442nd Infantry in 1944," Setsu added, knowing that mention of the 442nd elicits a community respect for bravery, courage, and commitment. The 442nd Regimental Combat Team, composed of Americans of Japanese descent, was the United States army's most decorated unit in World War II.

"Our youngest [daughter], Fumiko, told her father, 'Papa, we can't even read or write Japanese. How can we live in Japan? I'm not going to Japan.' My husband couldn't argue with that. When I told him that the children were old enough to decide for themselves, and that he did not control them, he was furious with me. He told me angrily that because I was the way I was, the children didn't listen to him.

"Papa was so angry," Setsu repeated, "but I told him that our children were born and raised in America, that they were fully grown and couldn't always do just what he wanted them to. I argued with him about this, and I'm very glad I did. If we had listened to Papa and had gone to Tule Lake and returned to Japan, I just can't imagine what would have happened to us. I was able to live after my husband died because my boys went into the [United States] army and sent money to us. That issue, whether to stay in America or to return to Japan, was the most difficult for us. The issue didn't affect just our family; everyone had difficulty making the decision. The issei father's idea of having total control over his children is an outmoded idea," Setsu declared. "When children are grown, they just can't obey their parents blindly. The 'yes-no' issue was indeed very difficult to resolve." Despite angry words and almost unspeakable defiance, the Yoshihashis and most other families remained together.

"The extremists were sent to the Tule Lake camp," she continued. "Of this group, many returned to Japan [after the war], and they had so many problems. The Japanese in Japan were unkind to them, and Japan was a desperate nation at that time in history. What would have happened to us? I'm so glad we didn't return to Japan. My sons returned [from the war] without any injuries, and the eldest son was able to go to college after he got out of the army. I was so grateful."

Setsu, who had never experienced any emotional nurturing from her natural parents, still maintained the ideal of filial compliance, though she consciously supported her children against her husband. She empathized with those families permanently torn by the loyalty issue.

"The saddest things I saw in camp," she said with deep emotion, "were the funerals of nisei boys who had gone to war in opposition to their parents' wishes. They weren't my own children, but to be at a funeral where the son went against the parents' wishes and died in action . . . oh, that was so sad. The bugle blew, so sad and lonely. I remember the funeral of Henry Kondo—that was the saddest funeral I have ever attended. It was so emotionally disturbing. Henry Kondo died in action in France without a parting word to his parents. It was," she repeated, "such a sad funeral. A very difficult funeral—we all cried hard. Wars . . . I never want to see another war."

KIYO MIYYAKE

Kiyo Miyake declared about the Pearl Harbor attack, "It was really terrible!" Despite threats against the Japanese in America, she added, "but I didn't think it would be dangerous for the Japanese here. I believed in America. I wasn't afraid, though I really felt that Americans were foolish. I don't understand how they could do something like that [put us in camp]. There were no spies among us. On top of that, when they created the 442nd Unit, there were hundreds of young nisei who were willing to sacrifice their lives for America. They possessed the Japanese spirit of *Yamato Damashii* [the soul of Japan] and they dedicated it to America. They really served America well."

Whatever Kiyo's personal opinions about the evacuation might have been, she found that events precipitated by the war meant difficult decisions requiring careful and forceful presentations on her part. "After [the evacuation order was issued], my husband wanted to sell the farm before going to camp," Kiyo explained. "The owner of a famous floral shop in San Francisco came to buy a piece of land, and my husband said he was interested in selling ours to him." Aware of the shattering disruptions that the evacuation might cause, a distressed Kiyo adamantly told her husband, 'When we are free to come back [to California], that little bit of money [from the sale of our land] is not what our children will need. What they need most through this difficult time is a place they can call home. That is more important than anything. We owe our children that much. If you think I'm wrong, then you go ahead and sell, but I must say what I believe.' So you see," Kiyo pronounced, "we did not sell this land after all. We leased it and went to the camp."

Kiyo Miyake, raised with all the strengths of a Meiji woman but with a Western vision of herself as a pioneer woman, was a force to be reckoned with. As a Meiji woman she would hold her family together, and as an issei pioneer woman she would tenaciously cling to the family "homestead." Speaking of her husband's independent nature but recognizing that it was a trait they shared, Kiyo continued, "Even though we had a small farm, we were independent because of my husband's nature. We had never joined the growers' association. [After the evacuation notices were posted], the manager of the co-op [growers' association] came to see my husband every night because we were about the only ones who had not signed up with the association. I told the manager, 'If you are the owner of a large piece of land, you might come out ahead, but we have only a very small farm. The expense of managing the land might be more than the profit we might realize from the farm.' I vigorously discouraged joining, because the manager and everybody else were going to be on the payroll.

"We knew that our neighbor was not that good a farmer, but he would keep the farm for us. They [he and his wife] had been good neighbors. I liked his wife very much," Kiyo continued and added a comment that certainly was applicable to herself. "Some people might not give much credit to women, but they can be a real force in a family. She was incapable of doing wrong." Secure in the knowledge that the family home was safe, Kiyo concluded, "That's how we left our farm.

"Well, we went to the Merced Assembly Center first. I believed that this would be temporary and was not that upset over the situation. We were used to meals which suited our [Japanese] tastes; therefore, the food was not satisfactory in the beginning. However, I did not let our children complain because we had to think about others who were on rationing. They didn't even have butter. No one should complain at times like that."

A short time later, the Miyakes were transported to the Amache Relocation Center. "The Amache camp was in a desert," Kiyo recalled. "Miraculously, within a short time it became a city of flowers. I was so impressed. The Japanese planted lovely flowers between the barracks and around their bedrooms, and it became a very beautiful place. This really shows something of their heart," she asserted, knowing how despondent so many had become.

"There were some even more exceptional people, of course. My daughter-in-law's mother learned how to sew in camp and sent all her children through school [with money she earned as a seamstress]. She is seventy-five years old now, but she still sews for actors in Hollywood. Those people [issei] who seized the opportunity and learned some skills in camp were very wise. There was no opportunity to learn anything up to that time."

Though not required to work, most able-bodied internees took jobs in the relocation camps. "My husband," Kiyo remembered, "cared for tuberculosis patients and enjoyed his work. I felt that this was a very good chance for me to study, so I went to an English class. I had to start with the ABC's.

"Meanwhile, people began to look for jobs. Soon everybody had a job except Mrs. Koda and me. I was asked to work in a dress shop, but I couldn't count money. Besides, I wasn't a good salesperson, so I decided not to take that job."

Though Kiyo remained buoyant and hopeful, life in relocation camps was emotionally stressful for all of the interned, and Kiyo, through what she modestly termed a case of mistaken identity, was asked to help in the camp social services office and finally took a job suited to her talents. "One day," she explained, "somebody came to see me. She was a huge white woman who stood at the door, and no one could get in or out. She said, 'I'm Miss Brown, head of the Welfare Department. I have been looking for an appropriate person to work with me, and I finally found you.' I was really surprised and didn't know where she had heard about me.

"I didn't have much confidence in my English, although I did understand what I was told and could also read and write. It was my conversational English that was not very good. I tried to refuse the job, but she insisted that I was the right person and wanted me to think about it for a few days. She said, 'This job requires strict confidentiality and you will be exposed to many different problems. I can't hire just anyone. Please consider this very seriously.'

"When my husband came home, I told him about the interview. I said that it might even be a case of mistaken identity. My husband said, 'It's okay. You won't need to write a research paper.'" A comment of this nature offered by an issei husband amounted to overwhelming approval, confidence, and support. Kiyo then mulled over other family considerations. "By that time, I had sent three daughters out of camp for schooling on the East Coast." Persons of Japanese ancestry were free to travel and seek employment in all areas of the United States but the Western Defense

Zone, which was roughly the area west of the Rocky Mountains. Apparently the United States government considered them a threat only in particular areas. Recognizing the advantage of employing this work force in the war effort, the government used the interned in everything from harvesting crops to, ironically, working in defense plants. "I also had two sons," Kiyo continued. "If they stayed in the camp, they could become lazy, so I sent one out to work on a farm. I thought the experience would be helpful if he decided to become a farmer. The other son was in high school." Realizing that she had attended to the needs of her children, Kiyo made her decision. "I decided to work while he [the younger son] was still at school."

Emulating her mother's successes in dealing with troubled people, Kiyo found enormous satisfaction comforting people despondent over property losses and shattered lives, helping widowed women obtain funding for their children's education, and attending to the entire range of social problems in camp. "This job was the best experience I've ever had in my whole life," she declared. "I really enjoyed it. I was consulted about all kinds of family and personal problems. In the beginning, I had only a few cases of my own. Everyone was deeply tormented, and people wanted someone to talk to. I also translated for some Japanese people who spoke little English. Soon people began to ask for me and I began to carry a larger number of cases. By the time I left camp, I was responsible for over seventy cases by myself.

"I had to write reports on each case. It was a difficult task, and I was really ashamed of my English. Miss Brown was remarkably helpful. She told me, 'Don't worry. I don't know a word of Japanese. You know two languages. If you can write this much, you are doing very well. If your grammar is wrong, I'll send out the reports.'

"I was very busy. The receptionist used to tell me, 'There are ten people waiting for you. Why don't you tell the person who is with you to leave?' But I could not ask a person to leave without finishing the discussion at hand." The Meiji etiquette learned as a child might have kept some waiting, but to the troubled person involved with Kiyo, it was a reassuring gesture in a time of upheaval.

"I never mentioned God in my discussions, but my attitude showed. Some would say, 'I swore to myself that I would never reveal this to anyone, but I would like to confide in you.' There was an old woman who said to me, 'Please let me consider you as my daughter, so that I can open my heart.' This old woman had suffered a stroke and could not walk well. When I went to visit her, she would try to walk to the cupboard, risking a fall, to get me some candy. She'd say, 'Please give these to my grandson.'

"I really appreciated her effort," Kiyo said. But, because Japanese etiquette requires that gifts must be of sufficient value so as not to insult a guest, "Someone once criticized her by saying, 'Don't offer such a little thing!' I said, 'No, it isn't cheap. It is more valuable than a diamond ring.' The old woman was really happy to hear me say that.

"Although there were four persons with master's degrees in social work in the office, they were white people who could not speak Japanese. They could do administrative work, but not the basic grass-roots casework."

As she continued to describe her work, Kiyo expressed her empathy, particularly with women. "When it came to dealing with individual problems and pains, they were felt, for the most part, by women. The women would not talk to the men in the office about their problems. They brought their problems to me."

Strict moral and ethical standards had always been evident in Kiyo's personal life, yet with others she was a good listener with an enormous capacity for compassion that was nonjudgmental. "People did get disoriented in the camp," she explained. "It could not be helped. We heard most often about male-female relationships which were not proper. People just had too much time on their hands. Still, those cases were small in number. High school students had the roughest time, I think. They just couldn't stay still, so they got into trouble with each other. Our family was very close. My daughters used to tell me about their romances, though they did not tell my husband. We talked about everything, but the youngest boy didn't confide in me.

"There was a young couple who got to know each other in an intimate way. The boy didn't want to keep his commitment and ran away. The girl gave the baby up for adoption. In another case, I advised a young woman not to sue the boy. If the case came to court, she and the boy could blame each other but neither would profit. I said to her, 'You should raise your baby quietly. You made a mistake once, but you are not solely responsible. Promise yourself that you won't make that kind of mistake again. There is no need for you to feel sorry for yourself, either. Your future is up to you.' At first, she didn't even come to eat meals in the dining room, but I recommended that she begin to live a normal life. This was needed for her baby, too. Later a young man from Japan proposed to her, and they were married."

In still another situation, Kiyo's intimate knowledge of Japanese etiquette and her sensitive manner were assets. "One day a man came in the office. He seemed to be yelling at us. A young nisei woman didn't know how to handle this situation, so she came to me, because she couldn't understand the man. After a while, I realized he was deaf. I didn't know sign language and decided to communicate through notes." Because there are three basic styles of lettering in Japanese, Kiyo realized, "The way I wrote depended on his education, which I knew nothing about. He was dressed like a farmer. On the other hand, his manner indicated he had quite a bit of education. I couldn't use simple student lettering; it might be rude on my part, but if I wrote in the running style, he might not understand too well.

"At first I wrote, 'What is your name?' and after his response, 'What is your occupation?' He wrote, 'I used to be a Buddhist priest. I should have stayed a priest, but I became greedy and began a business. You can't do anything wrong without being punished. I was attacked by a burglar and became deaf. Now I cannot talk to others except through writing.' This man knew a lot about Buddhism and also knew how to tell fortunes. His problem was getting to work, so I found somebody to take him," Kiyo said, pleased that she could solve his problem.

"There were many other cases. There were some issei who had saved up little by little and had bought small businesses–pool halls or stores–and finally were able to take a breath and say, 'Now, I can relax and eat easier!' But after the Pearl Harbor attack, they were forced to sell their property very cheap and they lost all their life savings.

"There were those who were extremely depressed because their land was confiscated, and there were many people who suffered huge economic losses and were very despondent about it. Those were the majority of cases," Kiyo explained. "There weren't very many husband-and-wife fights, because the feeling of oppression came from outside.

"Many women had lost husbands, but they wanted to send their sons to colleges and did not have enough money. I tried to open some doors for them. Mine was such satisfying work," she declared.

As Kiyo concluded her commentary on this segment of her life story, she articulated the questions the evacuation order raised and produced a litany of whys that have only begun to be addressed and resolved by the remaining generations of Japanese Americans. "It was strange, incomprehensible, that America would evacuate Japanese people into camps. There were so many wise government officials and politicians in the United States. They spent enormous amounts of money to transport and detain the masses of defenseless Japanese Americans. We had not committed any crimes, either. I just don't understand why we were evacuated and what motivated the government to do what they did. I don't know why America was so afraid of the Japanese. I still wonder about it to this day. There has never been a case like that with any other race in the history of America. Americans had to spend so much money to keep the Japanese in camps. If we were allowed to farm, for instance, we could have contributed so much to American society."

Always looking for the positive aspects in almost any situation, Kiyo said, "Perhaps there was a greater plan, God's guidance. If America didn't do what she did, then the nisei might still be in remoter areas of California and not have had opportunities to extend themselves. Because of the camp experience, they had a chance to go to the East and to other places."

On the other hand, dispelling the widespread belief that the issei tacitly sanctioned the evacuation, Kiyo delivered this damning pronouncement: "Americans lost the confidence and trust of minorities. On top of that, Americans disgraced themselves. That's how I look at it—that those shiny, dignified politicians would go along with this kind of wholesale evacuation of one people. It's the most disgraceful blunder by the American government against its own people in history."

KATSUNO FUJIMOTO

For Katsuno Fujimoto, the strain of all the difficulties she had faced over the years nearly broke her; had she been in the Amache Camp, a sympathetic Kiyo Miyake might have offered her good counsel. Fortunately her children, for whom she had sacrificed everything, helped to sustain her. Recalling that Katsuno more than once considered suicide rather than live with a man twenty-three years her senior, it is not surprising to find that she often disagreed with him.

"My husband worked alone to support us and it was very hard. During the Depression he had no regular job, and we did suffer. Once he said to me, 'Why don't you go back to Japan with the children for a while?' I answered, 'Just a minute. No matter how much we suffer, these children were born in the United States and I want to raise them here.' Then my husband's younger brother who was listening to all this, said, '*Niisan* [big brother], any child born here should be allowed to grow up here. If you want financial help, I will help you out.' We economized and somehow or other managed to get along. I never took my children back to Japan.

"I used to push my children for good grades in school. I surely am embarrassed about it now. I was also strict on manners. Whenever the children were involved in a fight, I used to tell them, '*makete katsu*,' or 'lose and win' because in fights no one is a winner. Actually, down in my heart I didn't want them to get hurt. Now, looking back on it, I should have said, 'Go ahead and fight.'

"My children did not complain much. The other kids used to push them off the school bus and sometimes they'd get hurt pretty badly. I used to wonder what kind of parents these children had."

Though her emotional comments are spare, evidence of mounting stress appears in Katsuno's reflections of how the war affected her family's life. "It was so sad! My daughter came home from school with tears in her eyes and said, 'I am a Jap!' They had called her a 'Jap.' My children said that America had been stabbed in the back by the Japanese. They thought that the Japanese were savages." With Meiji patience, Katsuno said, "I answered, 'Just wait, wait. There must be some reason for all this.' You have to listen to both sides before you can form an opinion." But as Katsuno cast around in her memory for her explanations, it is evident that none had ever satisfied her. This lack of resolution only added to the strain mounting within her.

"I thought, 'What a terrible predicament we are in!' I knew the Japanese militarists were capable of doing such a thing. But, you see, we had always been called 'Japs.' Americans wouldn't even sell us [emigrants] land. I guess Japan finally couldn't stand how their emigrants were treated," she naively commented. "Throughout this whole period of time, no matter what befell us, I concluded, '*shikataganai*' [It cannot be helped]." Although this seemingly fatalistic attitude was the most prevalent one among the issei, the continued belief that the rewards of hard work and diligence would eventually be accrued, perhaps by one's children, prompted the issei to make the best of their situation.

"Soon after the attack on Pearl Harbor, the [issei] men who were active in Japanese clubs were questioned by the FBI and interned. I was a member of the women's society of the Japanese

Association and had been president for several years; therefore I had a suitcase ready when the FBI came after me for questioning. They finally realized that I was not dangerous and sent me home.

"We obeyed the law and did exactly what we were told to do. They told us to shop between certain hours and within a radius of certain miles. They gave us a list to shop for unbreakable utensils in preparation for camp life." And according to evacuation regulations, Katsuno explained, "All we could take with us was contained in the luggage we carried in our two arms. We left as much as we could in the church basement, but we lost a lot and some nice things were stolen. For us to be the sufferers just couldn't be helped, *shikataganai*," she repeated. "My feeling was to just obey, obey, and obey.

"We were sent to the Tulare Assembly Center and then to the Gila River Relocation Camp in Arizona. It was hot during the day and cold, very cold at night. There was only cold water for showers in the beginning," she said, as she described the discomforts of camp life. "We were all so happy when we got hot water. The toilets were not private, so we made curtains. Each family had only one room to live in. There were big holes in the floor boards, and the planks were placed a quarter inch apart. Whenever there was a sandstorm, the dust would blow up through the cracks and holes in the floor. Sandstorms would hit us while we ate in the mess hall, and we'd have to eat sand with our food."

Katsuno affirmed that the difficulties of camp life were exacerbated when the loyalty questionnaires were distributed. "As president of the women's society, I made speeches frequently, especially when the boys were drafted into the army. I remember saying that the boys did not have to be loyal to Japan because they were born here in the United States. But I told them to remember that they had the blood of *Yamato Damashi* in them and to be good citizens of this country. One young man came to me and asked, '*Obasan* [aunty], what shall I answer regarding the loyalty question?' I answered, 'I am not a smart woman,' but I told him that I wanted my children to be good Americans and loyal to the United States. Still, I didn't want to push this youth into any decision, so I told him to think it over carefully. The next morning he came to me and said that he was so glad he had talked to me. He had decided to answer 'yes.'

"Lots of other people used to make speeches praising Japan, but not I. I found out what kind of people some of my friends really were. I was very upset by some people's attitude. Some had such filthy minds. I wanted to leave [camp] as soon as possible," Katsuno declared, as she recalled the toll of the mounting stress and anxiety. "When my youngest son went into the U.S. army, I suffered a mental breakdown."

ONATSU AKIYAMA

"'It's a lie! It's a lie!' I kept saying when I heard that Pearl Harbor had been attacked. I just couldn't believe it," Onatsu declared, as she offered her recollections of this most difficult time. "Before the attack," she continued, remembering an event that seemed to portend the disaster, "Papa had a dream. In it he saw thousands of airplanes lined up at the railroad station, which was, in fact, right next to our house. I recall saying to him, 'What a very strange dream.'"

Onatsu also described how she first heard news of the attack. "Well, our friend had gone fishing. He came home with the news, saying, 'It's terrible! It's terrible!' But no one believed him until we found out otherwise.

"We continued to operate the store, but it became more difficult," Onatsu stated, as she recalled the curfews, the freezing of bank accounts, and the travel restrictions that were imposed in the weeks following the attack.

As if the confusion of the times was not enough, Onatsu experienced a robbery. "Five young Filipinos drove up in a car one Saturday," she related. "One stayed in the car and the other four came into the store. They took avocados and started to eat them. I was cleaning fish and said to them, 'They taste better with salt,' and gave them some. Then two small children came to buy ice cream. When I went over to make up the cones, I saw those four grabbing money from the cash register. I was really mad, because here I was trusting them and trying to be kind. I went over to the cash register and only a little change was left. I called out, 'Hold it! I'm calling my husband.' He was taking a nap in the next room, but he didn't hear what had happened. While I called out for Papa, one of the men said, 'I'm sorry. I made a mistake.' As he spoke, they all went out the door.

"We notified the police and gave them a description of the car. The robbery was broadcast on the radio, and we were soon informed that the robbers were captured. The boys had borrowed the car, and the woman who owned it gave information about one of the boys to the police.

"When the police returned the money to me, I said that I didn't want it and told them to donate it to a church or the Salvation Army. They just stared at me in disbelief, but I didn't want that money back. Those boys were only sentenced to six months in jail because they had no weapons.

"The same robbers had held up four or five stores in Sacramento, but the police couldn't catch them. The news that I identified those boys appeared in the newspaper," Onatsu related with amusement. "Many people from Sacramento came to see me. They thought that I must be a devil-like woman. Well, they found out differently and wrote about me again in the newspaper. We had a good laugh over that." But the laughs came few and far between in the following days.

"Then the FBI came and took my husband around the end of April. I think it was because of his involvement with *kendo* [Japanese fencing]. He used to take kids to Fresno and Los Angeles and even to Seattle for *kendo* matches. The FBI also thought that Papa was in contact with the Japanese government because he used to entertain dignitaries from Japan. Once His Excellency Tsuruki Maruyama came, and Papa threw a party in his honor. When the FBI came, they asked about his connection with the Japanese government. The people of Florin wanted to welcome Maruyama, that's all," Onatsu explained, and, of course, the FBI did not understand that Japanese etiquette dictated a public reception for this dignitary. "The FBI also asked why my husband landed in Seattle the last time he returned from Japan. They pointed out that he had always docked in San Francisco before. Well," Onatsu said, providing a simple, logical explanation, "the ship was scheduled to land in Seattle; it wasn't his choice.

"The FBI search was upsetting and very unpleasant. This agent and two policemen searched the house for guns and swords. They even looked in the attic and the toilet. When Papa went to the bathroom, they went with him. Papa was a very gutsy person. He was not afraid and said to them, 'I need a shave before you take me in.'

"Our friend [and boarder] Hitoshi-san, brought whiskey and said, "Let's have a drink before you go.' The FBI excused themselves during this ritual, and we drank together for the last time.

"I asked the policemen in my broken English, 'I think my husband is the most wonderful man in the whole world. Why are you taking him away?' One of them said to me, 'That's why we are taking him to a nice place where there are lots of beautiful flowers.' I believed them because I didn't understand what was going on. Later I learned that my husband had to stay overnight in the Sacramento jail. Then he was moved to an internment camp, and we were separated for two years.

"I think the reason Papa was jailed was because all of our correspondence, books, and notes were in Japanese.

"The sixth day after Papa was arrested by the FBI, one of the robbers called me and asked, 'Are you Mrs. Akiyama?' I answered, 'Yes.' Then he asked again, 'Are you really Mrs. Akiyama?' I said that I was, and he threatened, 'I'm coming to kill you soon! You better watch out for me!' When he said that, my knees started shaking.

"I was so scared that I couldn't walk and dragged myself upstairs where Hitoshi-san was staying. He called the police and they patrolled the store for a whole week. I don't know whether or not the caller came. I suppose he threatened me because I identified them [the robbers] and had them put in jail."

That same month Onatsu recalled, "They posted notices for Japanese people on telephone poles." These were government notices informing persons of Japanese descent about the date, time, place, and rules concerning evacuation procedures. Onatsu admitted, "We were really afraid. We had run the grocery store for eighteen years, until the beginnning of the war and the evacuation. I have it written down that soldiers came and nailed the doors shut."

With Mr. Akiyama in an internment camp, Onatsu was left alone to care for their four children and make family decisions. She was careful to make no complaints, but she hinted at difficulties that would have been trying for any person alone.

"We went to the Fresno Assembly Center first. It was okay except that it was very hot there. When we lined up in front of the mess hall, many people fainted because of the extreme heat. I don't remember any trouble in the Assembly Center. I was only there for five months."

Although her words do not express any anger, Onatsu continued this next segment of commentary with terse phrases. "From there we went to the Denson Relocation camp.[1] It was very interesting," she said quietly, understating a stressful incident. "If you cleaned toilets, they gave you eight dollars and fifty cents per month. When a government officer asked people to volunteer for work duty, no one raised their hand." Apparently unaware of a group

[1] This reference is actually to the Jerome, Arkansas, Relocation Center. Denson is the closest town.

decision not to cooperate with camp authorities, Onatsu said,
"Then I raised my hand and became a toilet cleaner. [After I
started my job] some people said, 'I can't use the toilet and sit
down on the commode which Mrs. Akiyama has cleaned.' There
were those who went to the next block to go to the bathroom."
Obviously hurt by the community ostracism every Japanese
avoids at all costs, she asked indignantly, "Well, if they felt that
way, why did they not clean bathrooms themselves? When I left
that camp," she added with satisfaction, "some people asked me for
my job."

Added to that initial ostracism was some disheartening news,
news that was depressing even to one as spirited as Onatsu.
"While we were in camp, I received a letter from a white friend
that our house was burned down. She sent me a newspaper clip-
ping which said that by the time a fire engine arrived from
Sacramento, it was too late and the whole house was gone. I wrote
to Papa about it," Onatsu related and then added without explanation, "I was sure the letter hadn't reached him. The next time I
wrote, I said that someone got in the house, made a bonfire and
warmed himself up. Well, this letter got to him, and he understood that the house had been burned down. He expected something like that might happen."

Community ostracism, news of possible arson, and mail cen-
sorship were difficulties enough, but like other issei women separated from their husbands, Onatsu also faced the threat of a
crumbling family structure. "Our children had been in Japan for
five or six years. My first son lived in Japan from the time he was
fifteen until he was twenty-one. My second son was fourteen.
Both of them were educated in Japan, so they have the Japanese
spirit. It was a most impressionable time in our children's life,"
Onatsu explained.

"Because Papa was interned, I was responsible for the four children. One night the boys did not come home until very late. I
waited for them till 11:00 P.M. and hoped nothing had happened.
When the eldest returned, he said, 'I'm sorry,' and bowed very formally."

With great restraint, Onatsu wisely matched Japanese custom
with Japanese custom in her appeal to her eldest son. "I had
brought the *Akiyama kakucho* [record of the ancestors] with us to
camp," she explained. "It was the treasure of our house. According
to the *kakucho*, Papa was the thirteenth generation. I instructed
my son to take it out and so he did. Then I said, 'Ichiro, you know

what this is. You know you are the first son and Papa is not at home. You must take the place of Papa in his absence. I have three other children for whom you and I are responsible. I want you to be very careful about what you do. I just want to remind you not to get yourself in trouble carelessly.' He answered, 'I'll be home on time from now on.'"

With few exceptions, the nisei children of the issei were amazingly loyal to the American war effort despite their incarceration. As their commentaries reveal, some issei women had sent their American-born children to Japan for an education. Depending on their length of stay in Japan and their circumstances, these *kibei*, American-born but Japanese-educated children, tended to form the nucleus of the pro-Japan groups in the relocation camps.

"Some nisei," Onatsu related, "said that they were sorry that they were born Japanese. The *kibei* were angry and said, 'You can't talk like that! We'll bury you alive!' These *kibei* ganged up on some of the nisei. I was afraid that my son might have been involved in this trouble [because he was a *kibei*]. If he was, I wouldn't know how to explain myself to Papa for the actions of his children. Ichiro was the oldest son and was in a very responsible position. He understood me well. Every night after that he was back home before 11:00 P.M."

Though Onatsu obviously handled a difficult situation well and was never one to complain, she quietly commented, "Camp for two years was very difficult.

"Many young boys [in the camp] gambled and smoked. Even my sons' good friends used to sneak out at night and fool around. My boys did not.

"In the third year," Onatsu disclosed, "we joined Papa at his internment camp." In most instances, issei men separated from their families were eventually allowed to join them in relocation centers. Though Onatsu is careful to indicate that her sons were not involved in any dissension concerning the loyalty question, the Akiyamas were among the small minority of evacuees who chose to remain loyal to Japan. "I can't remember where it was," she continued. "I think it was called Crystal City. There were about 2,000 Germans and Japanese there. They said it was a camp for POW's, mostly officers, so the people were well-mannered. Because Papa was home–there was a dignity about him–I didn't have as many worries. Things were a lot easier," Onatsu said, remembering that she was comforted by the knowledge that her family was together again.

MIDORI KIMURA

Consumed by the details of daily living, Midori had seemed unaware of the international political climate. "When Pearl Harbor was attacked, I was at church. I had returned home and was getting ready for lunch when a telephone call came from Kozo Ishimatsu. He said that we should turn on the radio and listen because Hawaii had been attacked.

"My heart went, 'Thump.' I thought, 'There's going to be big trouble.' I was so upset and stunned that I could not talk. I still remember that feeling of shock to this day. We gathered our household and warned everyone. We wondered why Japan had to fight against the United States. I had not been aware of the mounting tension between the two countries at all and it was a real shock to me.

"When the war began, some people were picked up and placed in special detention camps," Midori said, as she explained the reasons for the incarceration of many leaders within the Japanese communities in the Western United States. "Some parents whose children were in *kendo* clubs were detained. There were very few of those cases in the San Jose area. Some owners of Japanese stores and the president of the Japanese Association of that year were detained. Even though my husband had been president of the Association for a long time, he was not arrested. It was because we had helpful members of the Council of Churches in San Jose.

"There was a teacher by the name of Miss Coolidge. My girls used to visit her often. In any case, she did a great many things for the Japanese people. There was also a minister and his wife, Reverend and Mrs. Peabody. These people were very close to the Japanese community, and the Japanese people did their share to keep up the good relationship. I think these factors had something to do with our not going through very harsh treatment when World War II broke out. In some other communities, almost all the men were taken away and only the women were left behind.

"I know a woman from another area whose husband was taken away and she had to give birth to a baby by herself. She was in such desperate need. I entered the relocation camp with all our family together in peace."

Seven children kept her very busy, but Midori had never suffered the severe physical and emotional deprivations of most issei women. A comfortable house with relatives nearby and a husband whose job allowed free daytime hours to spend with his family were a far cry from laboring in fields for fourteen hours a day with children to care for and being grateful that substandard housing replaced a blanket roll on the ground.

Though the Kimuras were fortunate enough to remain together during the relocation, events of the war foreshadowed a change in Midori's charmed life. As she continued, her comments became disjointed and random, as though she were reliving the distress of that tortured and confusing time.

"The only white friend we had was through business connections, so . . . before we evacuated, Dr. Cutrale came over and gave us shots for typhoid fever. We had to take care of so many details, but we were in a state of shock. Then a curfew was imposed and we had to stay within a certain distance from our houses. We also saw General DeWitt's notice of evacuation."[2] These notices were posted on telephone poles and buildings in areas where persons of Japanese descent tended to congregate.

"We had to buy suitcases, sacks, and many other things. We were completely occupied with the problems of packing and taking care of our possessions. I was in a state of distress. First of all, we didn't know where we were to be sent. We could not take too many things, heavy things." Evacuees were instructed to take only what they could carry. "We thought," she continued, "that we needed to take some food, too, like soup, in case we would be in the mountains. We had to be prepared to spend unsheltered nights in the open."

Disposing of property, a major task even in the best of times, added to the mountain of major decisions. "We owned our house," Midori explained. "I think my husband bought it in 1919, before we were married. He bought it by using the name of a person who fought in World War I. He was a Japanese person, a nisei who is now a physician," Midori stated, as she recalled that issei could not purchase property legally.

"The house was managed by an attorney," she explained. The agreement was that he should collect enough rent to pay the taxes. I realize now that we should have received some income from it as well.

"The house had a large basement, and we stored the household possessions of three other families there. The renters stole many things from the house."

[2]General John L. DeWitt, commanding general of the United States Western Defense Zone, was responsible for carrying out the evacuation.

Lamenting decisions that had to be made with little time for deliberation, Midori then continued, "We were to gather at the depot on Third Street. Members of the Council of Churches came out to the depot and served us tea. I would say this is one indication that people in San Jose were less prejudiced."

Continued support from Caucasian friends was welcome comfort, but no amount of friendship could stay the unwelcome move. "We were transported to the Santa Anita racetrack," Midori stated. The housing situation was difficult for a family as large as the Kimuras. "The youngest child was four years old; the next two were six and seven," Midori recalled. "The next daughter was five years older, in junior high school, and then a daughter who was in senior high. Then there was a son and a daughter who were in college.

"Fortunately, the place where we were assigned was a newly constructed barracks and not a part of the stables. It was still a terrible situation. All nine people in my family were placed in one room. Yet compared to the people who were placed in the stables, we were really fortunate. We went to visit one friend living in the stable, and it was smelly and humid. We could also see horses' teeth marks on the walls."

Because of the heat and dust and the public nature of their humiliating treatment that the mess lines represented, Midori echoed a common complaint among the evacuees. "I did not like to line up for meals," she said with disdain. "Meals were so bad in the beginning that I could not identify things which were on the plate, because everything was so mushy. The people who cooked and those who served seemed to know nothing about food. It was so terrible that we could not eat. We were so hungry at night that we heated the soup that we had packed. As we got used to camp life, the cooks got organized, and it became much more livable.

"Santa Anita was very hot at the end of May," Midori continued. "I recall a date, May 29 to be exact, because we celebrated my daughter's birthday there. My daughter's Caucasian friends had ordered a cake for her, organized this party, and got a permit to come into the camp. We borrowed an unoccupied room, and Miss Coolidge joined us, as well as our friends, Mr. and Mrs. Dubnek. It was one of the most memorable events in the camp," Midori recalled. "Yet," she added, "we could not shake hands because we were placed in separate rooms since we were classified as enemy aliens. It was very sad."

Taught from childhood to accommodate the self to the total society whenever possible, the issei, and in particular issei women, looked for the positive and applied their energies toward adaptation, even in relocation camps. Despite the incarceration, the poor living conditions, and the emotional toll, Midori also searched for ways to adapt. Midori Kimura, whose entire life seemed an exercise in deriving a balance between unusual personal circumstances and the intricate dictates of a highly structured Japanese social order, once again accommodated.

"The camp was very quiet as a whole," she said. "Most of the people were quiet, peace-loving farmers who were very gentle people. I might be criticized for saying this, but I think people who lived in cities were more aggressive.

"I recall one big disturbance–a demonstration in the camp. One boy who came from Los Angeles opposed certain treatment by the government. The demonstrators who supported him were arrested, along with another boy who was just standing around watching. I don't know what happened to them.

"We were in the assembly center [Santa Anita] about three months. By the time we were moved to Wyoming [Heart Mountain Relocation Center], it was the end of summer. The train ride was rather pleasant. There was no special place to sleep, so we just slept in our seats and were fed in a dining car. There were those who ate pure American-style food for the first time, no *shoyu* [soy sauce] and no *miso* [soybean paste]. We passed through Salt Lake City and Ogden [Utah] on the way. The whole trip took about four days."

Recalling her arrival at the Heart Mountain camp, Midori pronounced, "It was terrible. We were searched and admitted. They took our radios, cameras, and anything else that could be used as a weapon. Then we were escorted to our block." Each relocation camp housed the evacuees in barracks. Each block comprised groups of barracks and was separated from other blocks by firebreaks. Row upon row of poorly constructed barracks housing thousands of people could only look dismal at best to Midori. But, to make matters worse, Midori recalled, "The day after we arrived, there was a big snowstorm and it was very cold."

Despite the nearly overwhelming dejection experienced during those first few weeks, Midori reported that she, her family, and the other evacuees settled into a life of sorts. "I did not work in the camp," she said, resuming her commentary. "At first my husband did not work either. Later he became the Japanese [language] editor for the *Heart Mountain Centenary* [the camp newspaper]. It was printed in both languages. Sometimes he had to translate articles from English into Japanese. He received nineteen dollars a month for this job," Midori stated, as she recalled that adult internees were encouraged but not forced to work. Those who cleaned, cooked, and worked on maintenance crews were paid sixteen dollars a month. Supervisors of work crews, doctors, and other professionals were paid nineteen dollars a month. "I could not work because my children were still young," she added.

As Midori described camp life in more detail, her need to accommodate continued to surface. "It was very unfortunate that we were placed within barbed wire. However," she added, as she continued to search for the positive, "from the standpoint of food availability, we seemed to have it better than those who were outside because of the ration system. In this instance the American government provided for us very well."

Continuing on a positive note, Midori remembered, "Some learned calligraphy or flower arranging. I learned to knit and sew in my free time. I don't remember any confrontations," she said. Then the memory of an issue that created enormous tensions resurfaced with a jolt. "Oh . . . yes. There was something. It concerned the children [nisei] volunteering for the [United States] army. The other one was about the loyalty question. These two matters became problems in all the camps.

"I had been living in this country and had been taken care of by this country. My children are nisei and Americans; therefore, we decided to declare our loyalty to America. My son entered the army and was a member of the 442nd Regimental Combat Team. There were two boys, including my son, who went into the army from our block. Those people who came from the city areas talked behind my back," Midori stated, still sensitive to the social criticism that Japanese avoid at almost any cost. "They spoke ill of me in the laundry room or wherever they met. They even called us 'reds' [communists]. I was never told that directly to my face, but my friends heard them and reported to me. They called us 'inu' [dog] or 'aka' [red, communist]." Although the vast majority of evacuees were staunchly loyal to the United States politically, criticism was always considered a reflection upon the entire family and therefore was never taken lightly.

"Our oldest son was sent to Italy," Midori continued, "but he had to return because he had a severe sinus condition. He sent us letters describing the ship traveling in darkness. Later he was assigned to a veterans' hospital in Denver, where he worked as a medic."

As restrictions against the evacuees were eased, Midori went on, "Our children gradually left the camp. The oldest daughter was admitted to a university in New York. She transferred her records from San Jose State [where she was enrolled before the evacuation]. The next one went to Oberlin College. The next one went to a high school in Minnesota. Two boys and a girl were left with us, and the five of us together came back to California after the war ended."

SHIZU HAYAKAWA

"People [Japanese] who came from the East told us that they expected war," Shizu stated. "They told us not to worry because they would drop the bombs and the country would be taken over by the Japanese! I did not believe that kind of talk and was shocked to hear that Pearl Harbor was bombed."

For all persons of Japanese ancestry who lived in the United States before the outbreak of World War II, the bombing of Pearl Harbor is a significant marker in their lives. Hard-working, self-sacrificing, and not given to self-pity, Shizu shared the conflicts dividing the Japanese communities with a candor unmatched by any of the other issei women. Extreme discretion or simply attempting to avoid discussion of internal community strife is similar to a Japanese family hiding family problems. The discussion of these previously hidden conflicts is evidence of Shizu's confidence in her own opinion that the exposure was ultimately more helpful than silence.

"I felt dreadful when I heard we would be relocated. The nisei were ashamed of us [issei] when we were fingerprinted and numbered. We knew very little English, but the authorities tried to ask us many questions. The nisei became very angry and upset since they thought this unfortunate situation had befallen them because of their Japanese parents. They repeated over and over again that it was because of the issei that they had to go to relocation camps."

When it was time to leave for the camps, Shizu recalled, "There was a lot of strange talk and rumors. We thought we'd all be killed. We were all lined up and told where we could not go. Then we were told to pack up our belongings. The people I had worked for had a big house and they very kindly let us store all our goods there. How fortunate we were in this respect. They later sent us parcels of candy and other treats.

"All the Japanese men I had been working with, like Mr. Kimura, who owned the catering business, were taken away [for questioning by the FBI]. He was married to a Caucasian lady, and, of course, after her husband was taken away by force, she cried a great deal. She called me 'Suzie' and she said, 'Suzie, was your husband dragged away, too?' I said, 'No, my husband had nothing to do with the government. He wasn't involved in anything, so he's still here.' She had three children, and in those days they were called *happa* [half and half] and were looked down upon.

"The Japanese called them *keto keto* [hairy foreigner] and they had a very hard time. When her husband was taken away, she was left with three children to feed. The Japanese could no longer go out at night to work, because of the curfew," Shizu explained, "but since this lady was white, she could take a night job."

For the second time in her life, Shizu helped another woman left alone to care for children. It is a measure of Shizu's strength that she risked criticism to help this family, who were considered outcasts. "I felt sorry for her. I got a job working in a factory because I told them I was Chinese. It was difficult for anyone to tell the difference. I became Chinese and tried to do my best to help her out," Shizu explained, "because it was quite difficult for her to care for and feed her young children.

"Mrs. Kimura, my Caucasian friend, had one daughter, who was just about ready to graduate from high school. The mother thought that perhaps they would not have to go to camp, since she at least was Caucasian. But her daughters had Japanese boyfriends and preferred to go into the camps. I persuaded the mother to prepare to go with her children.

"On the very day we were to leave, the father was released by the authorities and came home. I was very thankful and relieved, because even though I had advised the mother to go with the girls to camp, down in my heart I was afraid they would be ridiculed and called bad names. Later we were all to meet again at Tanforan [Assembly Center].

"It was difficult for people in those circumstances because they would be misunderstood by both Caucasians and Japanese," Shizu added with compassion. "The daughters are still here in the [San Francisco] Bay Area. One is now Mrs. Morioka and the other Mrs. Ishida. They were called *keto keto* but now," Shizu declared, "they have every reason to be proud.

"When it came time for us to go into camp, I remember we received cards from our church to say we were members. The pastor of the church and some others thought that if we had those cards, the American government would have no reason to expel us. I did not express my thoughts then as I do now," she admitted, "but I remember thinking, 'Is it right for me to have this card and expect different treatment?' It seemed to me that it should not matter whether we were Buddhists or Christians. We were all Japanese. To reject the Buddhists, but treat us [Christians] like Americans was not the right attitude. I did not know how to speak up at church," Shizu said, still bearing the compliant demeanor she was taught as a child in Japan, "so I just took the card and went home. Yet I still remember that experience and feel it was wrong for us as Christians to have had such expectations." Although she was reluctant to be vocal in those days, Shizu gradually, almost imperceptibly, began to gain the momentum to express her views.

"We [my husband and I] went by train to the Pomona Assembly Center near Los Angeles and east of Santa Ana. It was a long trip, which took about two days. Whenever a train came from the opposite direction," she said, remembering the tedious journey, "our train had to wait until it passed. We were not allowed to see where we were going and did not know our destination until we arrived.

"Not all the Japanese people from San Francisco and the Bay Area went there, just those who had no children and single people. The rest of the people [like the Kimuras] were taken to Tanforan. There were a lot of orange trees at Pomona and it was a very nice area, but the housing was just barracks.

"The kitchen workers at the Pomona camp were unrefined folk and didn't know how to cook. Those who were supposed to serve food were inexperienced as well," Shizu stated and recalled that, like most institutionalized people, "the rest of us complained a lot about the food. The food was portioned so that everyone could have a fair share. But those who ate first were selfish and took what belonged to others!" Distressed with this kind of behavior, Shizu commented, "It seemed like people didn't use their common sense, and this really troubled me." Thousands of miles from Japan, and more than twenty years distant from traditional Japanese society, Shizu still believed, as did most issei, that the bad conduct of one was an indictment of the whole. She had spent her adult life in sacrifice for others and found the conduct of some evacuees wanting.

After additional, but still temporary, quarters were built at Tanforan, the Hayakawas were transferred there, and once again they met the Kimuras. Though her stay at Tanforan was brief, Shizu described an incident that reflected how so many Japanese customs had survived over the years. Shizu had previously shared her experiences as an immigrant on Angel Island and had explained the Japanese method of bathing. Most immigrants who lived on farms built *furo* or Japanese-style tubs to accommodate their taste for bathing. Shizu related, "There was a farm family from San Jose who had never seen or used a shower before. At the camp they had a shower set up for us, and the young children were intrigued with this strange, new gadget. They were caught doing many mischievous things in the showers.

"Later we were moved to the Heart Mountain Relocation Camp [in Wyoming]. As I traveled through the desert, I wondered why the Japanese were rejected and denied a place in this vast expanse of America," Shizu commented. Like most other issei, Shizu was committed to the United States, yet she understandably expressed her dismay that they were treated so badly. "There was surely no need to have war and rejection of the Japanese! We couldn't wear our national costume, nor could we go to the movies. Why did we have to be treated like this? These thoughts went through my mind as we rode the train.

"There were twenty thousand people in the [Heart Mountain] camp, so it was like a town.[3] The camp was situated in the desert, and when the wind blew, it was very dusty. In the winter it snowed." Neither weather situation would have been particularly bothersome except for the fact that the barracks in which the internees were housed were poorly built. Dust seeped through inch-wide cracks in the walls and floorboards, and cold easily penetrated the thin walls.

Reacting the way anyone else would when imprisoned without provocation, the interned reacted with minor infractions of the rules to irritate the authorities. "We were told," Shizu related, "that we must stop when a soldier called out to us. There was a fence around the compound and we would often go past a certain boundary and not heed the warning call. Then the Caucasian soldiers would aim guns from the tower at us.

"The only furniture in our rooms was two beds," Shizu continued. "We wanted to make shelves, so we'd sneak out at night in search of boards, and often someone would get caught and be severely reprimanded by the guards.

"One of the most irritating things was that after we were in bed, nisei policemen would do a bed check. No matter how often they came around, their count was always wrong! When it was hot, we'd put blankets on the floor to sleep, since it was much cooler

[3]Government figures indicate the population of Heart Mountain was approximately 10,000.

that way, but the young people would go outside to sleep. We would be awakened several times a night with people trying to tally their count! I remember thinking, 'Will they ever get it right?'

"The food [at the Heart Mountain Camp] was not good," Shizu stated, and the Japanese hated eating in mess halls. "Everyone had to line up for their food and everything had to be carefully divided among the people. Eggs were almost impossible to get; when we were fortunate enough to get some, those with children were anxious that they should have some to eat. They would complain about having only one egg and then go after another.

"Parents were worried about their children not getting enough to eat and would send their kids out of line, past others, to get fed first," Shizu said and then, she recalled people would become quarrelsome. "I recall thinking what a miserable and pitiful group of people we Japanese had become. It was a sad sight for the Americans to see the Japanese quarreling amongst themselves. They [the men] drank a lot and made fools of themselves. After a year in camp," Shizu said, expressing relief, "we settled down pretty well."

Besides the problems of difficult living conditions, Shizu explained, she felt anxiety about the small, but vocal, group of internees who supported the Japanese government. "I lived in America and I took it for granted that I should be loyal to this country. But in the camp there were many lectures [by Japanese] to impress us that we should honor our own country. However, even in camp I had the *San Francisco Examiner* sent to me; and although I could not read or understand English, people who did helped me to understand the content.

"The Japanese loyalists complained to me about my stand. When we were in San Francisco getting ready to leave for the camps, I was severely criticized by a Japanese loyalist because I had worked for Americans and took the American side."

In the early stages of relocation, the dissension among the internees over which country should claim their loyalty gained momentum. Group pressure in the form of ostracism, name calling, and in some camps even violence was used by groups loyal to Japan. Shizu reported, "I was never beaten or mistreated because of my loyalty. I did have some friends who stuck up for me. While I was still in camp but towards the end of the war, my Caucasian friends sent me a message stating that they would like me to work for them again, and this disturbed the Japanese loyalists."[4]

Explaining how the issei and nisei could maintain strong emotional ties to Japan, yet be politically loyal to the United

States, Shizu said, "In Japanese history it is recorded that during a civil war, one must fight for his master; therefore, if you have come to America and have become a citizen, then you should be loyal to your country. My friends' children all became instructors in the [United States] military even before the war began, and they were totally misunderstood by the American army personnel. 'How is it that these Japs can offer themselves for military service?' they'd ask."

Shizu shared the pain and anger evoked by the callous attitude of many Americans. "One younger [Japanese] person said to me, '*Obasan* [elderly lady], the Americans know we are Americans, too, but even so we are called "Jap" and are rejected; some day perhaps they will not ostracize us any more and they will call us "Japanese."' This person spoke repeatedly to me about this and it always made him angry. The nisei thought they were Americans, but the Caucasians did not see it that way."

Though Shizu sympathized with the nisei, she stated, "I did not think it too strange that we [issei] had to go into the relocation camps because, after all, we were foreigners, and it is understandable and natural that the Americans take those precautions. Of course," she added, "later some thought differently."

Like so many other evacuees imprisoned during the war, Shizu has never resolved her feelings of loyalty to the United States and her belief that the detention was unjust; but justice is not a concept prominent in the Japanese worldview. Shizu relied on the Meiji attitude that someday the misunderstanding would be rectified and that the future would provide the means. Until then, diligence and patience were basic requirements. Most of the few issei still alive today support the current Japanese American redress movement. Redress efforts included a request for an apology by the American government to those detained, a token monetary compensation, and a review of several Supreme Court cases on constitutional issues raised because of the evacuation. It would seem that the issei viewed the redress movement as the timely means to rectify the wrong.

KO HAJI

Earlier in her commentary Ko Haji explained that both her father and grandfather were *yoshi* or adopted sons-in-law, whose

---

[4]This incident probably occurred earlier than Shizu recalled. By the end of the war, the loyalists had been segregated and were housed in the Tule Lake camp.

special charge it was to carry on the family name in a family without a natural-born son. The importance of a son was especially ingrained in Ko's mind because of her family circumstance. With this in mind, her wartime commentary carries added poignancy.

"I had one son and two adult daughters. My daughters and my husband had left camp earlier, but I stayed with my son until he finished his high school courses." Ko then joined her husband in Monroe, Washington, and said, "We were thinking of buying a home for him, my son, Tom. He had attended one year of college and was drafted into the service. They were short of soldiers then, and boys were sent overseas after only four weeks of training." The details of his last visit remain etched in her memory. "I said that I wished he could stay just a day longer with me. He replied, 'Mother, don't you think I should go as soon as possible to relieve those who are already there?' I also remember that he told me not to work because my health was not good at the time. My son's words, I cannot forget.

"In four days he was sent to the front. His last letter to us was written on Easter Sunday, April 2, and he died on April 9. He was eighteen years old. Losing my only son was a great sadness to me." This was the son who was to carry on the family name. "But I don't regret coming to America," Ko quickly added. "People are sympathetic that I lost my only son, but I am proud of him because he served his country and he is remembered for that. Every Memorial Day he is honored." Then Ko added her voice to chorus of parents who had lost sons in the war, "But I think the ones that served in the war, came back, and are still working for their country are performing a greater service."

o o o o o o o o o o o o o o

Less than seven months after uprooting entire communities, causing enormous financial losses, flagrantly violating the civil rights of thousands of American citizens, and subjecting an entire segment of the populace to extreme mental anguish, the War Relocation Authority had an already operational work/leave program and began to outline a resettlement plan allowing evacuees to relocate anywhere in the United States except the West Coast. Once again the individual and collective spiritual resources of the issei pioneer woman were in demand.

CHAPTER FIVE

Pioneering Again

However reluctant the Japanese evacuees were to enter the WRA camps, and no matter how difficult the move may have been, the decision to leave was rife with complicated considerations. Rumors of continued prejudice against returning Japanese were more than just a passing concern. Physical assaults and harassment were common in many West Coast communities. Still, the United States government began actively encouraging internees to leave before they had spent their first year in the camps. Many of the interned were released on work permits to harvest crops in surrounding areas because of labor shortages created by the war. Others were allowed to leave if they settled east of the Rocky Mountains and had a sponsor. Young men and women seized the opportunity to leave and continue their educations in the Midwest and on the East Coast, and large numbers of young men left to join the service. It was the young and strong who departed the camps, leaving the issei, who by that time were well into their fifties and sixties. The age disparity between issei husband and wife continued to take its toll, and more issei women whose elderly husbands had died or were ailing found themselves the heads of households.

HISAYO HANATO

"It was in the camp that my husband had a stroke. He was in the hospital a long time. He was not paralyzed, but he moved very slowly and could no longer work." Although she had been compelled to assume financial responsibility for her family, Hisayo said, "It wasn't a great hardship, because our children were no longer young."

As the Japanese evacuees left the camps, the WRA began to close some centers to consolidate the interned. "Toward the end of the war we moved from [the] Jerome [camp] to Rohwer, and then we left [the camps] for Chicago, where one of my daughters lived with her husband. Although she did not consider her husband's ill health a great hardship, whatever Hisayo earned was their only income. "I found some work sewing," she said. "We lived on this income though we could not live extravagantly. We stayed in Chicago for two years before we finally returned to Long Beach. Then I got a job at a fish cannery where most of our friends worked. I worked at the cannery for a long time . . . about fifteen years.

"I usually did not work on Saturdays; but one Saturday I was called to work, and while I was away from home, my husband had a stroke and died." With Meiji demeanor, in a simple, unobtrusive comment that reflected deep feelings, Hisayo said, "I really regret that I was away from home when he died."

TEIKO TOMITA

"People were asking, 'When is this war going to end?' The young and ambitious ones were leaving camp to study or to work. As for my children, the oldest daughter graduated from a university in Minnesota. Then she left for New York. She worked part-time and put herself through school. The oldest son was seventeen or eighteen years old, and he wanted to work and go to school, too, so he also left camp. There was a high school in the camp, but it didn't compare to regular schools. The second daughter left camp after the oldest daughter. The youngest son was still with us.

"Gradually even the older issei felt that they couldn't stay. We could leave the camp as long as the government knew where we were going. Many people had already left."

Leaving the relocation camps became a domestic issue between many issei husbands and wives. As in the case of the Tomitas, it was usually the wife who wanted to leave. "I, too, felt that we should go out and start working, and I tried to encourage my husband to leave. In the beginning he said no, but because his friends were leaving one by one, he decided to leave camp, too. We left," Teiko added ironically, "on the Fourth of July.

"With a recommendation from Reverend Kitagawa, we got jobs at a large nursery near Minneapolis. I felt rather insecure when we left the camp, but upon arriving at the Johnsons' ranch, we found they were such nice people that there was no need to worry about anything. They say that people in Minnesota received Japanese people kindly. We were really fortunate.

"Mr. Johnson took us to see many places by car. As he drove, the radio was playing. They were broadcasting from the battlefields. He was very sensitive about our feelings and turned off the radio. We were treated like guests.

"Mr. Johnson had 300 acres of nursery plants and vegetables. Besides us there were about ten white workers. There was a yard as big as a park, which my husband took care of. They already had a lady who came each week to clean the house and a laundress who came once a week, too. The only thing I did was to dust here and there, cook, and clean up the table. That's really all I had to do. I had to cook for just the two of them and us, and we all ate the same things. I enjoyed my time there."

"We had arrived at the Johnsons' in July," Teiko continued. "The war ended two months later [*sic*] on August 15. Both of us cried all that night in our room," she said. "We could not bear to come out." Declaring political loyalty to the United States had been easy for the Tomitas, but their spiritual attachment to Japan remained. "People were sensitive about our feelings, but the Johnsons' neighbors celebrated. They drank and sang songs until early in the morning. I suppose the Japanese would have done the same if they had won the war, so I cannot blame them for that. The Johnsons were more than generous to us the next morning. Mr. Johnson said, 'Even though Japan lost the war, America will not treat Japan cruelly, so don't worry about it. Please stay here as long as you can.'"

Three years in relocation camps, though tense and anxious at times, had offered Teiko respite from years of arduous labor and being haunted by *kuro*. In view of her statement that she had enjoyed her stay at the Johnson ranch, it is difficult to imagine that she would choose to return to Seattle and a life of hard work, but life without her family brought no fulfillment. Returning to the ranch, the family homestead, was unfinished business, and the children considered the ranch home.

"A few Japanese-language newspapers began publishing, and we subscribed to one. It was a rather simple paper with various news items from Japanese people," Teiko explained. It printed, 'So and so went back to where they came from. Such and such apartment opened up for Japanese returnees.' I said to my husband, 'Let's go back to our house in Seattle. I didn't know that people were returning to their homes when we left the camp. Because many of our friends are going back to Seattle, I would like to go back there, too.'"

Obviously aggressive in pushing her point of view, Teiko admitted, "I repeated this all the time until my husband got mad at me. He had gotten used to his job and was doing very well. His ability was recognized and he was trusted. He just didn't feel he wanted to go back then." He angrily reminded Teiko that it was her idea to leave camp. "'I came here because you wanted to come,' he said. He was very angry." Undaunted by her husband's resistance, Teiko persisted with a singularity of purpose and the staunch determination that she had exhibited as a young, highly successful student so many years before in Japan. "A move like this couldn't be delayed, because we weren't planning to stay there forever," she said. "I insisted that we go back. We had a lot of work to do at the nursery.

"I finally talked my husband into returning. We arrived by train on Thanksgiving Day."

After eleven years of labor marked by eighteen-hour work days, and despite harrowing experiences, which included the tragic disappearance of a young daughter, the Tomitas had worked fallow land into a productive nursery. Then the war had forced the Tomitas to leave the fruits of their labor in the hands of a caretaker who unfortunately had abandoned the land.

"Right from the beginning we had to earn some money from that abandoned nursery. We had to start from scratch again, for we had no other place to go. The fields were in such bad shape that we couldn't even begin working without spending some money. My husband worked for a gardener and generated some income. He did that for about a year, but he couldn't do that the rest of his life. He fixed his old truck, which had been stored somewhere, and began to work in our fields. He planted some vegetables because the trees were now too big to sell. We had to begin again from scratch.

"We worked hard and had to pay off the back taxes. The government let us pay in ten year installments. We did not want our land to be confiscated, so we paid off the debts." Even to contemplate beginning again was overwhelming, but the Tomitas, with Teiko's singular determination, tackled this work. In explanation, she could say only, "Well, in our lifetime we've experienced all kinds of things which cannot even be shared with others.

"In the meantime, our children were becoming adults. The oldest son had been drafted and was sent to Fort Snelling, where they taught Japanese. He had attended Japanese school back home for eight years and could speak quite well. He was trained [at Fort Snelling] to be a translator to help communicate between white officers and Japanese people. He ended up not going overseas. Fortunately he did not have to fight. After the war he went to college and graduated with a degree in chemical engineering. He graduated with honors and had a chance to go to Europe to study on a full scholarship. However, he was the first son, and we didn't want him to go far away from home." An echo of Teiko's earlier need to abort plans to attend teachers' college sounded as she said of her own son's acquiescence to filial duty, "He gave up getting an advanced degree.

"The oldest daughter," Teiko continued, "graduated from the University of Minnesota in psychology. Then she went to graduate school in New York, where she got a good job. She is head of a human resources agency and travels all around the world.

"The third child graduated in journalism. I didn't encourage her to become a journalist, but she knew that I liked to write. I was afraid that if she left home she would get married [and live far away], but she returned home and married here.

"The youngest one is a mathematician. He got a job at Boeing as soon as he graduated from high school. He worked for a couple of years, saved his money, and then went to a university. It took him a while to graduate. He still had a part-time job, even when he attended classes. After he graduated, he got a better job at Boeing."

Content with the success of her children, as well as her success as a parent, Teiko added before continuing her commentary, "I have no worries [about the children]. If I died now, I have nothing left undone.

"Some seven years after the war, my sons said that we had lived long enough in that dilapidated old house and began building us a new one. About that time we were allowed to submit compensation claims for losses from the evacuation. We consulted a lawyer and submitted a claim. We had to wait for a long time. Finally a notice came which said that the government was sorry for the damages; however, we received a little less than half of what we claimed. It had been quite a while since the end of the war, and we felt that we had to accept whatever they would give us without complaint. The lawyer said that as soon as we signed the papers, we would receive the money.

"My sons had started to build the house and had already put in the foundation. They were very happy because we could use the money to build the house, even though the money had decreased in value by then."

With enormous pride Teiko described the details of the construction. "Our sons built the house by themselves. They hired a contractor to do the electrical wiring, plumbing and heating, but they did all the rest.

"We lived in that house for some time--until all our children had gone and just we two were left. The second son built a house very close to us and could come over in a few minutes if I called him by phone. We depended on him a lot. He took us shopping every week because my husband couldn't drive any more."

With pride and contentment, Teiko underscored the mutual satisfaction she and her husband shared at this point in their lives with the simple statement, "We decided that both of us would die there."

But circumstances did not recognize the Tomitas' great attachment to this specific house, built with the labor of devoted children, or to this particular piece of land built after years of work into a productive nursery business, abandoned because of the relocation, and then reclaimed with even more years of toil. "The airport," Teiko explained, "needed to expand their runway and wanted to buy our land. We fought against it, but we had to move. It was so very disappointing. My husband said, 'Oh, I spent forty years of my life on this land and wanted to be buried here. This is the home which our children built for us. But now we have to move again.' They gave us some money and we moved three miles away to Beacon Hill.

"We still thought about the old farm," Teiko said, acknowledging the sentimental feeling that lingered and the bond that the years and unforeseen changes could not break. "Whenever we were in the area, we'd pass that street and look at our property. We'd see the foundation of our house and the trees we had planted, willows and pines. They had grown tall. We were really touched by this. My husband was still alive then," Teiko added.

"When we passed the area recently, I found that the place was completely changed. They had leveled the hill and made a sports center for young people. It's the flow of time, the changes of time. We have experienced a great deal."

SETSU YOSHIHASHI

"One day before we left for camp, my husband said, 'I may die in camp.' True to his words, he died there. The camp authorities took care of the funeral and the burial expenses. I was very grateful for that. I took care of the funeral arrangements and then prepared to leave for Ohio. We had entered the camp in 1942, my husband died in 1944, and I left in 1945 before the end of the war. With money from an insurance policy, I was able to buy some furniture."

Her words are spare with no expressions of loss or regret about her husband's death. Because Setsu had been the economic head of the Yoshihashi household for years, as her husband's health continued to deteriorate, she had no difficulty making any of the major family decisions by herself. She did, in fact, breathe a sigh of relief to be free from the constant criticism of a most difficult and demanding husband.

Although Setsu had quickly decided to leave the camp as soon as her husband died, she admitted, "I was frightened to leave camp. We had lived with all those Japanese people for so long in such safe conditions that to go out into white society was quite difficult. We had made many friends in camp and I felt safe there." Engulfed by the emotions generated by the memories, Setsu continued, "When I went out to find a job, I felt . . . I can't put it into words," she said haltingly, ". . . like a beggar." Steadying herself again, she recalled, "But I gave myself a pep talk and went to work for a white family.

"I moved to Ohio and rented a nice, large house. When the boys returned [from the war] and saw our home, they were very happy. Their friends all stopped at our house, ate Japanese food, rested, and then returned to California. My sons were very happy to live in a nice house. My boys never talked about the war after they came home.

"After my sons enlisted in the army, they said, 'Because elder sister is in Tokyo, we don't want to fight against Japan. We've decided to fight in Italy and France. It's dangerous there now, but it's better than fighting Japan.'

"My eldest daughter had gone to Japan as a bride and was living in Tokyo at that time," Setsu explained. "She returned to America after the war and died from an illness. If she was alive now, she'd be sixty years old. I lost two daughters, so I only have three children living now.

"The saddest thing that happened while I was living in Ohio was when the war ended. I had some anxious thoughts on my mind and had decided to go to the movies. The theater was crowded, but I was the only Japanese. I sat in the back and watched the news of the Japanese general signing surrender papers for MacArthur. It was so painful to watch. I just cried and cried. I had no intention of seeing such news, but unfortunately, I went on the day they were showing film of the Japanese surrender. I felt so sad that I went home crying.

"Many of us, including my husband, didn't believe Japan would lose. Friends told me that Yoshihashi died at a good time because had he lived to see Japan defeated, he would be the type of person to commit suicide. It was fortunate for him to have died before Japan lost the war."

Although Setsu continued to express her gratitude to the United States for her well-being, her pride in being Japanese was bound to Japan's successes and failures. Her feelings about the country of her birth were as complex as her attitude about Caucasian Americans.

"I had many difficult times [after the war]. Ohio is the home of the devil. It is true that some whites were nice to the Japanese after the war, but I saw that they were two-faced in their kindness. But there are both good and bad white people.

"While I was in Ohio, the YWCA decided to have a Japan Day and the profits were to go for YWCA expenses. They had us [Japanese] make cherry tree props, sell tickets, make sushi and salad, and perform Japanese dances. We were told to make sushi and salad for 100 people. Imagine, we had just gotten out of the camps. We entered with just two suitcases and came out with the same. We were like beggars; we had nothing. And they expected us to sell tickets, make food, perform Japanese dances. We were just like merchandise on display," Setsu declared and continued in short, clipped sentences. "I was very, very angry. I refused to participate. I just wouldn't do it. So there were complications. I was branded as an enemy and a woman came to my house and yelled at me. She was a white lady, the wife of a professor. They were not good people. I was very troubled by this.

"On the other hand, I met people like Mr. Blackman and Mrs. Dacon, who were professors at Ohio State. They were honest, sincere people who were very kind to us. I spoke to them about everything in my broken English.

"White people had always treated me with kindness, even though my English was not good, and they trusted me. Because I didn't speak English very well, the trust was not transmitted by words but by my character.

"Well, I had wanted at least for my eldest son to go to college, no matter how poor we were, but then the war started. When he got out of the service, we were living near Ohio State University, where he got a degree. The government paid for his education. Oh, that was a lifesaver. I really wanted at least for my eldest son to go to college. That was my goal.

The Japanese were not ostracized at Ohio State the way they were in California. My son was able to mingle freely with other students. He went to his friends' houses and invited them to ours. My son still tells me that he had the best time of his life at Ohio State."

Finding the fulfillment promised by her Meiji way of life in the achievement of her children, Setsu added, "It's been twenty-five years since I returned to California. My eldest son is a very good man, so I have no worries."

KIYO MIYAKE

Kiyo Miyake's satisfying social service work came to an end as internees were processed out of the relocation camps to begin their lives again. But relocating the evacuees posed its own problems. She recalled, "We had a lot of work to do when the camp was to be closed. There were many people who didn't know where to go. They didn't have a place they could call home. And, too, everyone was afraid." Threats against returning Japanese were common. In California there were thirty-six authenticated acts of violence in 1945, and many went unreported. Mr. Miyake, like many other heads of households, returned to California in search of a job and housing, which was very scarce, before moving his family.

Returning families shared houses, and Japanese churches became temporary shelters. Other families split temporarily and individuals took jobs as live-in domestics in order to find shelter.

"My husband," Kiyo continued, "came back [to California] by himself, but no one came to greet him. The Japanese farms here were managed by an association that leased parcels of land to Mexican people with a share arrangement. This association made lots of money, and they didn't want the Japanese to come back. Some people even threatened us by saying they would shoot us!

"When Mr. Kishi came back, someone shot a bullet through his window. When my husband came back–he was one of the earliest–no one would give him a ride from the depot. Finally, Joe, a white man who used to work for us, came by and gave him a ride. Joe was a good man. He had brought his wife along because he knew that people would not harm them if his wife was with them.

"Joe and his wife had been living in our house, but before my husband returned, they had already moved back into their tent where they used to live. We had no trouble with them. We didn't have any valuable things in our house, so we weren't worried about losing anything. Besides, our house was only a small shack. There were some people who lost their tools and equipment. We had rented ours to our neighbor, so we had no such troubles.

"I wanted to go home, too. But before I could leave the camp, I had to find places for the others. I had to write letters for them in my broken English. I really felt how little English I knew, how limited I was," Kiyo modestly lamented. But she was gratified to know that, like her mother who counseled others in Japan, she had been helpful to many in need.

"When I left the camp, so many people came to see me off that there was no place for me to stand," she recalled. Although Kiyo measured her successes according to the traditional standards for a Meiji woman, her life circumstances offered her a new dimension for fulfillment. "I haven't accomplished too many good things in my life," she said, "but this job was a wonderful experience for me. I enjoyed helping people, and I would have continued this work longer if I had a choice." The first choice for a Meiji woman would always be the welfare of her family.

There had been many changes in the Miyake family since the war began, and Kiyo needed to assure herself that her family was well. "My children had left camp to study in the East. We had sent them to Cleveland through the YWCA. My girls studied in business colleges. The oldest daughter became a secretary; the second became an accountant. They were good students. [Eastern] companies never had a chance to see Japanese faces before. Even so, they were hired with rather high salaries. Those who went east were the cream of the crop. Anyway, I had never been east and I wanted to visit them and see with my own eyes how they were doing."

Upon her return to California, Kiyo was gratified to learn that the property decisions she and Mr. Miyake had made stood them in good stead. "Those people who let the association take care of their farms lost most of their equipment. Their tools and equipment were passed around to the farms under the management of the association, and finally it all disappeared. I was really glad that we didn't join the association. No one received income from their land, either. The only thing the association did was pay the taxes and mortgages; that's all. Those who made money were the sharecroppers and also the managers of the association. They made a huge sum of money.

"We had leased our land to our good neighbors–honest, very kind people–and they paid us well. We received about five thousand dollars a year, though we only owned twenty acres. Others had hundreds of acres, but they did not reap any profits."

MIDORI KIMURA

"Mr. Kawakami and Mr. Kogura had returned to San Jose to see how things were," Midori recalled, as she spoke of how individuals scouted their communities to report back about housing, job opportunities, and the general atmosphere. "They sent word that it would be okay for us to return to San Jose. When we arrived, Mr. Kogura and my daughter's friend were waiting for us. They had made tea and brought us two hot dishes. The women from the Council of Churches also came to greet us. We were really surprised and overwhelmed."

The Kimuras were also fortunate to have a house to return to, even though it needed work. "The family that had rented our house were not good people," Midori had said. Earlier she had remarked that some of the items stored in the basement were missing and "the house was very dirty."

"My husband cleaned up the house and trimmed the trees, Midori reported of her husband. But, like many issei men who were considerably older than their wives, he had developed a heart condition during the internment, so he could not do strenuous work. "He died," she said, "of a stroke, a month and a half after we returned. He was sixty-two years old." And Midori, who had never had a job in her life, became the head of a household.

"Well," Midori paused slightly, as though gathering strength to relive the next segment of her life story. "The hardships began at this point. Until then," she acknowledged, "my life had gone easily. This was the most difficult time in my life. I didn't know how I was going to make ends meet. There were others in my situation who cried and grieved. But I could not keep crying forever. I had to do something to finish raising seven children. I had to be tenacious and strong," she said with Meiji fortitude. "I didn't understand people who just cried and cried. Well, I suppose it's all up to the individual.

"My husband didn't have very much in savings," Midori explained. "He had helped other people who could not pay their premiums and had very little left in his own life insurance. I was told some of his insurance was terminated because of the war. Later on when we requested reparation money from the government, I did not take this into account. I was so ignorant. I just submitted small items and did not receive much.

"The insurance company gave us his salary for the first six months, but the company did not pay for any social security benefits. We had to begin from scratch.

"Fortunately my daughter got a job with the WRA (War Relocation Authority) because she was taking a course in social work, and my other children worked part-time to send themselves through school.

"I began to do housework. Housework is a maid's job in Japan," this proud and privileged Meiji woman explained. "I had never done such work before. If I worked full time, I'd have to be away from home for a long time and the children would not be happy. With housework, I could work four hours a day, so it was very convenient." And despite Midori's college education, it was probably difficult for her to find any other job.

"My uncle, who lived next door, and his wife looked after my children when they came back from school. My youngest child was only eight years old then.

"It was very difficult to work as a housemaid," she said. "I tried hard to please the employer, and I was never fired from a job. Even though there were many unpleasant things that happened to me, I endured them. Some [employers] would bring out many more things to do saying, 'Would you do this?' or, "Would you do that?' even though I only had a few hours to do it all.

"Sometimes," Midori admitted, "I used to sit in the car and cry. I couldn't cry when I got back to the house because my children would be watching me. However," she added with characteristic grace, "those women who had worked and had various experiences were very sympathetic and kind.

"I also worked in a celery packing house. It was a very difficult job. There were times when my hands were so sore that they throbbed with pain. My friends used to say, 'Because you had such an easy life before, all the hardships are catching up with you.' I don't believe that. I accepted it as something that I had to endure. Complaining would not help. It was such a situation, *shikataganai* (it cannot be helped). I accepted this as the life which had been given me." This acceptance and the subsequent accommodation, though harsh, difficult, and demanding of all her energies, became a positive force in her life and provided her the means to continue.

Each of Midori's children matched her strength and persistence, and with their own energy they generated another source of affirmative support. "All of my children," she stated proudly, "worked their way through college. They could do it because this is America and not Japan. They could make it as long as they worked and as long as they had the desire to go to school. I was very happy that all of them wanted to go to college."

Like their mother, the children worked at menial and physically taxing jobs to save as much as possible for their education. "One of my boys had a job picking prunes. He used to say that the work was not for human beings. You see, the pickers had to crawl under the trees to pick up the fruit. It was backbreaking work. Another son worked in a cannery. The other children picked pears. Every child worked and graduated from college.

"It was very difficult," Midori repeated, "but there wasn't any point in worrying or complaining. In those days my faith really helped me, but I realize that one's interpretation of things is also important. If labor is considered sacred," she declared, "then a person can endure any kind of work." She then added, "I still work."

SHIZU HAYAKAWA

"We were in camp about two years," Shizu recalled. "I came out around April and returned [to the West Coast]. The newspapers were filled with names of the men killed in action," and that made her fearful about returning. "But," she reported, "there was not as much trouble as we had expected when the Japanese returned. Little by little, the people [Japanese] came back [to the West Coast].

"After the war I went to work for an English couple. The wife was ill in bed and needed someone to look after her. When I first had to go out to the market to shop, I was somewhat reluctant," Shizu admitted, because she didn't know how she'd be treated. "I summoned my courage and went by bus downtown to the market and back again, and nothing happened to me. Then I started going out more often. Perhaps they thought I was Chinese. My husband said it might be more dangerous if a Japanese man were to go out, but for women it would be safer.

"My employer had a sister in Atherton [California] who needed someone to do a little work, so my husband went there. Well, according to Japanese custom, it was improper to leave husbands alone. But my employer's husband was now an invalid so I stayed and nursed the paralyzed man for two years until he died.

After the man passed away, the wife cried and begged me to stay on with her, saying that when she died, she would leave all her wealth to me!" Money was never as important to Shizu as her need for an independent life. "I did not want to work like a servant forever," she stated adamantly. "I felt there would be a better place where I could find work. I almost had to fight with the woman to let me go. Even now, this woman phones and asks me to come back, but I know it would be very difficult, so I say 'no.'

"When I started to work again, I was hired by Mr. Kimura. Remember, I mentioned earlier that he was married to a Caucasian and had started a catering business. I helped in this business and it was most interesting because it involved going to exciting parties. Isn't it terrific to think that one Japanese had the bright idea of starting a catering business because so many Caucasians liked having parties! I thought it was just marvelous that in spite of some anti-Japanese feelings, Mr. Kimura had opened this business." Shizu obviously preferred this job to the years she spent doing housework. "The business was successful and I was kept busy until my husband passed away. It was just ten years ago. I worked for a long time, and I am still working now. I am seventy-five years old."

IYO TSUTSUI

"I had two children who had left camp and were living in Chicago," Iyo reported. "My husband, my son who was in high school, and I went to Chicago to see how they were doing. They were fine, so we came back to the camp."

Taking advantage of government resettlement regulations, the Tsutsuis made arrangements to leave camp permanently well before the end of the war. "A month after we returned from Chicago," Iyo said, "we went out to Colorado. We farmed near Denver for a year and a half and grew tomatoes, onions, and beans.

"My oldest daughter, Kiyoko, was in the Manzanar camp. She had returned from Japan, got married, and was living in Los Angeles when the war broke out. She had already given birth to one child in camp and had got pregnant again." Recalling the exact date, Iyo continued, "On January 18, I received a telegram which said that Kiyoko had given birth to a baby boy, but that she had died. I lost one girl," Iyo said giving way to her grief. Recalling the pain of losing her young son in a drowning accident, she tallied, "Now I have two boys and two girls.

"One week before she died," Iyo continued, "I had a dream. I saw a valley and high mountains on both sides. I was walking along a gravel road with Fusako, another daughter who lives in Richmond [California] now. We came by a bridge and there was a small boy playing there. I looked up on the other side of the stream and there I saw a coffin. I thought to myself, "Did anyone die recently?" I went over, peeked into the coffin and saw my daughter resting there very peacefully. I thought, 'My, my, there must be other places to sleep. She doesn't have to sleep in a coffin!' I thought about waking her up but changed my mind, because I remembered that in one of her letters she had said that she was extremely tired. The baby was very heavy and she was very close to her due date. Kiyoko's mother-in-law was very ill, so my daughter carried food to her three times a day. She was also busy teaching Sunday School. I remembered this, so in my dream I let her sleep.

"The next morning I told Fusako, 'I had a very strange dream last night. I dreamt Kiyoko was sleeping in a coffin. I hope she is not dead.' 'Well,' she replied, 'Mama, you once told me that if you dream of a person dying, he is going to live a long time.' I said that she must be right.

"I got a permit to visit Manzanar. When I arrived, I was really surprised. The camp was in a valley surrounded by high mountains. It was exactly the way I saw it in my dream. When I got off the bus, I walked on a gravel road like the one I saw in the dream. And then I saw the same bridge, too. It was exactly the same as I saw in the dream. When I attended the funeral, the coffin was same color as in the dream. It was dark green with a whitish pattern on it. I was shocked.

"My son-in-law took me to the nursery. He said that a white nurse told him that Kiyoko drew her last breath at the same time the baby cried for the first time. This baby boy had received Kiyoko's life and came into the world. Well, at least it was our consolation that we had this boy with us.

"There were many young girls in Manzanar. Two girls became nurses. They said that the doctor had ordered them to give an injection to try to revive her; however, it had no effect. The doctor asked the nurse about the drug, so she showed it to him. The doctor said, 'You made a grave mistake. It was the wrong drug!' The nurse answered, 'But you told us to give it to her.' It became a useless argument. It was a very busy day, and there was another woman who received an injection and gave birth to a baby. Because she got the correct drug, she was all right. The drug my daughter received was one that they use for dogs and cats. It was really tragic.

"But we were enemy aliens and couldn't do anything about it," Iyo said, recognizing the realities of her position at the time. Echoing the opinion of most issei women about their children, Iyo did add, "She was a citizen though. We could have sued the doctors, but even if we won, the dead person would not come back. And I had already received a message from God [through the dream]. Because it would not help my deceased daughter," Iyo said with the resignation that would help her accept the death and continue her own life, "we had to bear the burden." And Iyo once again experienced the tragic loss of a child.

"This is man's fate," she said with the Meiji resolve that would give her the ability to gather her resources to move ahead. "The only thing we can do is to *akirameru* [accept one's fate]."

During this period of time, Iyo was not physically well, but *kuro* served to strengthen this issei pioneer and she didn't give in to the years of labor and the loss of her two children. "I was going through the change of life then and needed hormone shots," Iyo continued. "I went to Denver, stayed in an apartment and recuperated there." During her convalescence, Iyo decided that she and her family needed to get on with their lives. "After I recovered, I didn't want to go back to the farm again, because I felt that I would be going back to the same environment. My husband moved to Denver with me, and we found work in a children's hospital." Iyo's intent was to continue her caretaking of the Tsutsui children.

"In the meantime, my married daughter in Chicago had a baby, so I went to Chicago. I got a job in a plastics company and worked for two years there.

"My two sons had been drafted. One went to Italy and the other to Germany. They came home safely," she said conveying her relief. The return of her sons gave Iyo a new direction in life. "They decided to farm in California, and I wanted to help them. But my husband didn't want to come back to the West Coast. He liked where he was," Iyo said, but like Teiko Tomita, she tenaciously asserted herself and said, "I insisted that we help our children even though it would be a sacrifice on our part. So," she added, "we all came back.

"We leased 1,000 acres on Venice Island[1] and grew corn and barley." It is difficult to imagine that this favored and somewhat pam-

[1]Venice Island is one of the many river islands that mark the farming area in the Sacramento-San Joaquin River delta.

pered daughter would, after years of toiling in the fields, choose to return to that life. But the life also offered her that singular reward for a Meiji woman, filial piety, the proximity and devotion of her two sons.

"When we came back to the Stockton area," Iyo continued her commentary, "my husband had to take charge of the farm [which we had left before the war]. We still had some payments left and cleared that debt in two years.

"We had left everything on the farm, but when we returned, everything was gone. All the heavy equipment–discs and every-thing–had been stolen. We applied [to the government] for com-pensation of damages. Well, my husband was a very honest man. He listed fifty cents for a hoe. I told him that he couldn't even buy a hoe for that and to list at least two dollars for it. Then he said, 'Mama, you want to buy a used hoe, which ours was, for a new price?' I reminded him, 'You know, if we buy a new one, we must pay at least that much.' However, he insisted that he had to list the old price. He was almost a fool when it came to things like that. So, we only received three hundred and fifty dollars.

"I think it's all right to be honest," Iyo said recalling her exas-peration, "but this was beyond my imagination." Then this woman who managed to coax her husband across half a continent said, "I couldn't do anything about it because I was only a woman. We had to spend a great deal of money to replace our equipment.

"We tracked down a Chinese man who had leased the land from us in the beginning. We asked him about the equipment, and he said that he had left everything when he left the farm. An Italian man had leased it next. When we asked him, he told us that when he took over, there was nothing left on our land. There was noth-ing we could do to get any of it back!"

The wartime difficulties imposed upon these issei pioneers by the American government did little to dissuade them from becoming citizens. They had spent decades of living with few if any legal rights, because they were not eligible for naturalized cit-izenship until special legislation was passed in 1952. "I received my citizenship in the 1950s," Iyo recalled. I had been taking lessons in English but learned that if we took the [citizenship] test as a group, we could take it in Japanese. I switched to the class which was conducted in Japanese." Realizing the legal benefits of citizenship was part of Iyo's efforts, but it was more a spiritual dedication that led her to declare, "I had decided to have my bones buried here a long time ago, so," she said, "I really wanted to get my citizenship."

Onatsu Akiyama

When the United States government announced the closing of the relocation camps, Onatsu Akiyama and her husband chose a different path than most issei who had been confined. "The war ended on August 15," Onatsu stated, "and we voluntarily decided to go back to Japan. You see," she explained, "we didn't know how my mother and my other son were [he was in Japan during the war], so we wanted to see them." The Akiyamas were among the 1,659 aliens who returned to Japan after the war.

Onatsu related the following incident to illustrate the seriousness of their decision to leave the United States: "Although we had petitioned to return to Japan and had completed the necessary papers, a white man came to see us. He entered our room and cautiously locked the door. He said that even though we had petitioned to go to Japan, we could still change our minds, that we just had to shake our heads sideways." The gesture would show that the family had understood and would stay. "We did not take his advice," she said.

Although others returned for political reasons, foremost in Onatsu's mind was the welfare of her son who was still in Japan. The youthful son was also concerned about his parents but could not join them in the United States because he had been trained in the Japanese army. Onatsu related an incident that her son told her after their reunion. "A teacher had asked my son's class how many would volunteer for the Japanese army. A lot of students raised their hands, including my son. Other students asked him why he wanted to serve in the Japanese army [because they knew he had been born in the United States]." Matching his mother's concern, he replied, 'I'm going to fly over America and save my parents first.' He completed pilot training on the day the war came to an end.

"We had to go back to Japan to see if he was all right. Besides," she added, "our house in Florin had been burned to the ground and we had no home to return to.

"From the camp, we were moved to Seattle [by train]. There was a guard who watched us. All the blinds on the windows were drawn as we traveled, so we could not see outside. When we thought we were near Sacramento, I tried to look outside, but the guard said it wasn't permitted. Sometimes we were allowed to get off on salt plains and exercise, but when the train passed through towns, we were not permitted to look out though the war was over by then.

"There were over one thousand people who went back to Japan," Onatsu recalled. Despite the radio reports and film clips of the Japanese surrender, Onatsu said, "Those people did not believe that Japan had lost the war." For Onatsu and others whose Japanese cultural identities were still strong, a loss of face for Japan was tantamount to a loss of face for the individual. The only way to circumvent the loss was to deny it had happened. Like the other issei who chose to return to Japan, Onatsu declared, "Even though the emperor spoke of defeat, I could not believe it." The United States government later recognized that these complicated loyalties would never be translated into political subversion and were based as much on cultural factors as on political beliefs. Onatsu neither criticized nor supported those whose political loyalties remained with Japan, and she may never have made a distinction between political and cultural loyalties, but she indicated that her family's reasons for returning were based on family concerns. "We had never planned to stay in Japan permanently," she declared, but because those who left for Japan were labeled hardcore disloyals, there was some criticism from the Japanese American community after the Akiyamas' return to the United States many years later. "People tell us it's strange that we returned to America again," she explained; chafed by the implied slight, she added, "Well, I just ignore those people."

"We left for Japan in December," Onatsu recalled, as she continued her narrative. "I believe it was December 24 when we arrived at Uraga Harbor. The shock when we arrived in Japan . . . . It cannot be expressed in words. We saw Japanese people gathering up plastic garbage bags floating in the bay. They were stuffed with table scraps discarded by the American GI's. Then I finally realized that Japan had lost the war." Distraught and anxious, Onatsu remembered, "That night we couldn't sleep.

"Still on board ship the next day, I looked at my friends' faces. They had changed so much overnight that I didn't recognize them any more. They had lost the will to live. Even Papa and my children made up their minds to commit suicide," she said, separating herself from them with characteristic independence.

From birth to grave, admissions of guilt and apologies were avoided because they constituted the individual's failure to contribute positively to family or society. If the individual lost face, to avoid condemnation of family or society because of individual failure, the person gave up his/her life by committing *sepuku* [riual suicide]. *Sepuku* actually bound the individual to society in a positive way by erasing the individual who caused the failure and once again placing the good of the whole above the concerns of the individual.

After the initial shock, the Akiyamas weighed their priorities. "Then Papa remembered that the reason we came back was to see our parents and our second son. He changed his mind when he realized that it was our responsibility to continue."

Adding to their already distressed state of mind, Onatsu disclosed, was a betrayal of trust. "Just before we went to Japan," she explained, "we bought whatever we thought we might need and took all the cash we were allowed. On board ship a white man said, 'If you are carrying cash, I will keep it for you; otherwise someone might steal it.' We entrusted this person with our money without finding out who he was and received no receipt. Well, when we arrived at Uraga, this man just disappeared."

Once again reminding themselves that their fortune was in their family's well-being, Onatsu recollected, "Papa said, 'Think of it this way. Our children are big and healthy in body, and they are good boys. We should be thankful. Don't think about the money as a loss.' I felt that as long as we were healthy, we could endure the cruelty of other human beings.

"[After we landed], we made our way to the train station. It was just mass confusion. There were so many people on the platform that we could hardly reach the train. People even tried crawling though broken windows to board. Others had lost their will to live and were walking around like sick persons. Finally we got back to our hometown.

"Our son, who was in Japan during the war, had returned to my mother's house. When we arrived at the railroad station near my village, he came to meet us. It was only five *cho* [blocks] from the house to the station." Filled with the emotion of that time, Onatsu related, "I can still picture the way he walked up to us."

Onatsu's relief at finding her son and family alive was replaced with the need to keep them fed well enough to survive. "When we arrived at Uraga," Onatsu recalled, "all they gave us to eat was *muji gohan nigiri* [rice balls made of rice and wheat] and *daikon* [Japanese radish]. That's why my children can't eat *daikon* to this day, because they recall how it was after the war. We sold whatever we could to buy food, but sometimes there was no food to buy. We ate *okayu* [rice gruel] or pumpkin, wheat or potatoes. After a while my boys, even though they were young and in their prime, could not lift heavy things. They had lost all their strength. It was almost like a beggar's existence.

"Everyone [those from the United States] knew Papa because he had the store and was also a cook in the [internment] camp. Many people wrote to him for help in getting a job." But the Akiyamas' existence was tenuous at best with all their money stolen and only a few possessions left. Having devoted herself to upholding Japanese family values, Onatsu now turned to her family for support. "I borrowed money from all my relatives," Onatsu said. "We opened a coal mine with only three of us to work it in the beginning. The previous owner had worked the mine quite a bit and only found lignite, but they say a mine produces lignite before coal. We were lucky and hit coal in a week."

Unable to find an outlet for her latent aggressiveness in Japan, Onatsu had sharpened her business acumen during her years in the United States. The freer social climate had nurtured her talents over the years. Taking advantage of the shifts in power and confusion of social roles immediately after the war, Onatsu assumed a role that normally only men claimed in Japan. She recalled with veiled pride and humor, "For the first week, I traveled three hours a day from the mine to relatives and banks in order to ask for financial help. Bank officials were surprised by my stubbornness and finally let me borrow 500,000 yen to start that mine business, but I needed a co-signer. It so happened that the local bank manager's in-laws were my distant relatives, so I convinced this manager to co-sign the loan. When they asked me how I wanted the money, I replied, 'Oh, I'll take the cash with me.' They exclaimed with surprise, 'You are a very brave person!'" The fact that Japanese businessmen would even consider dealing with Onatsu is to her enormous credit.

"Our business did very well. We constructed all the necessary supports and put in a road. We began with a small crew which grew to number forty-seven workers, but the men were rough and became difficult to handle as their numbers increased.

"Sometimes the workers fought among themselves. Once," Onatsu recalled with distress, "there was a violent fight over a woman. One of the mine workers slit another's throat and blood gushed out. I saw that with my own eyes! It was terrifying.

"They would steal anything, even one another's wives, and then run away. People like that move quickly from one place to another. That's why they were called *tori* [bird], because they flew from here to there.

"One day one of the workers wanted to borrow some money. If we let him have it, he would just disappear. My husband told the worker, 'I haven't gone to the bank, so I don't have any money right now.' The man replied, 'What? you can't give me the money? Come outside right now!' I knew he wanted to fight Papa.

"As the situation became more dangerous, Papa talked to me and said, 'This work is not for ordinary people. Let's quit. I'll be happy to give the mine back to the government without compensation. Somebody had to do it [shape up the mine]. No matter who did the work, the government would benefit. It's all there just ready to be taken out of the ground.'

"So Papa gave the mine back to the government and came home with a teapot and three bowls. Well, Papa was that kind of person. Others talk about owning land or a house or a business, but I say to myself, 'There are other things to be grateful for.' We never accumulated much of anything, because Papa was not such a person, but we were always rewarded in one way or another. For one thing, I am very healthy." Onatsu reflected a bit more and then articulated a common Japanese saying, "Our deeds always come back to us."

Undaunted by their initial problems in the mining business, the Akiyamas tried mining tungsten in Yakushima. "But," Onatsu related, "we had to give that up, too. The ore was not rich enough. You know," she continued, "I think we were taken." Apparently no one had told the Akiyamas about the living conditions or the odd geographical location of the mine. "The mine was at the summit of a mountain, which would have been difficult enough to reach," Onatsu explained, "but on the way up to the mine, we also had to skirt a big waterfall. It was several miles and took us a long time to get there each day. The native people used to make a ladder of vines and climb the hills, but we had to walk the long way. After the walk back each day, I had to cook for fourteen people."

Cooking was difficult because the land was not fertile, and very few vegetables and grains were grown in the region. "People used to eat sweet potatoes and mackerel or carp. Not very many people of the island could afford to eat rice. I was thankful that at least I could eat rice every day."

With characteristic optimism, Onatsu commented, "All things considered, I have no complaints. At least I was able to see many different places. When we left Yakushima, we also left everything we had there—quilts, clocks, and all kinds of things made in America. We were bankrupt and came back to Papa's hometown. From there we went to my hometown and opened a restaurant with a six million-yen loan.

"Our restaurant was called Mama Shokudo [Mama's Restaurant] and it still continues today," Onatsu affirmed. When we began the business, we had to scrounge for materials and it was hard. Years before, when I first left for America, my father had planted a hardwood tree in his backyard. He enjoyed looking at it when he was still well. He used to say, 'As long as the tree keeps growing, I feel it is a sign that Onatsu is healthy and doing well.'" Sad that necessity had to take precedence over fond memories, Onatsu said, "Well, we cut this tree down to make 100 bundles of firewood. We split the wood with my nephew, and used our share for the restaurant.

"We began as a noodle shop at a crossroad where there was a bus stop. On the fifth day of business, there was a joint festival of five nearby villages. The celebration lasted five days, and we made lots of money during that time. We managed the business well, and by the time we returned to America, the restaurant was worth quite a bit. We sold the business to my brother before we left. My sister-in-law wrote to say that they had expanded and to praise us for our keen foresight in this matter. The family business has since become a corporation with more than twenty restaurants.

"Although we didn't make any money during the six years that we had the restaurant, we repaid all our debts completely. By that time we had been in Japan for thirteen years.

"Our third son, Ryozo, was the first to return to America. Our second son came back with us, and our first son came back one year after we did. Because our children were U.S. citizens, they could return easily.

"While Ryozo was in Japan, he went to the Gorichi Shrine of the Gedatsu sect. There they say that if you circle the statue of Buddha as you pray one hundred times, your wish will be heard. Well, Ryozo prayed two hundred times each day, and his wish to return to America was granted.

"By the time we opened our restaurant, our third son had left Japan, attended school for a while, and joined the U.S. army. He used to sent us 20,000 yen every month from his army pay. We were able to return to America because our third son sent us this money to buy tickets for our passage back.

"But our case was very complicated. By that time we had been granted permanent residency in Japan. We had to confer with the American consulate in Kobe many times. The trip took two hours from Fukuyama [where we lived]. Whenever we went to Kobe, we had to stay overnight at an inn, and it became very costly.

"Our restaurant was closed during the New Year holidays, and it was then that we got the good news. We had relaxed and gone to a movie. We were paged in the theater and told that we had a phone call from Tokyo. The message was that we would be able to return to America in February. In actuality we did not leave Japan until June 20, 1959."

Recognizing that their circumstances were extremely unusual and required a great deal of bureaucratic untangling, Onatsu wished to elaborate, but continually checked her comments because of the undercurrent of criticism that surrounded her family's return to Japan after the war. "Our boy went through a lot of trouble for us," she said. "When we finally boarded the ship to return, people said that we were not supposed to be able to go back. You know, we had not done anything wrong to be treated like that," she commented defensively, "but that is the way it went.

"On our return trip, the immigration officer in Hawaii said it was very strange that our family was allowed to return. And then when we arrived in San Francisco, another immigration officer said that we were not supposed to be allowed to return. In any case, he told us to stay in the area because we would have to return for an interview in a week.

"They provided an interpreter and questioned us for four hours. All the proceedings were taped. Papa and I were questioned separately. When Papa forgot something and I tried to help him, they said, 'Keep your mouth shut!' Our third son was with us, and when he was asked later if the interpreter was good enough, our son said that he was not." After being patient and persistent, the Akiyamas were granted permission to stay.

"After we returned to America, we filed a petition to reclaim our property. Papa gathered all the necessary documents, and we took them to a lawyer, Henry Taketa, who worked on the case for three years. He finally said that there was [legally] nothing that could be done. We then took our case to Mr. Miyamoto [a leader in the Sacramento chapter of the Japanese American Citizens' League]. He said that he couldn't help either. He said that it might be possible to regain something if this kind of situation was publicized and a special case was made for it.

"We just continue to hold the documents. I suppose that it's because we went back to Japan that they confiscated all our property.

"It was very fortunate that the United States government allowed us to return," Onatsu reflected in her closing comments. "You see, Papa had a slight stroke in Japan, and he could not work anymore because he had lost his coordination." Assuming that her husband would share her feelings, Onatsu mused, "He must have been relieved to return and be close to his sons once again. He died three years later. That was fourteen years ago."

○ ○ ○ ○ ○ ○ ○ ○ ○ ○ ○ ○ ○ ○ ○

During the war many issei women became heads of households because husbands had been taken away, became ill, or died. Their difficulties were compounded when they were uprooted from their communities, stripped of whatever economic security they might have had, and then had to rebuild their lives in their declining years while facing hostility and prejudice. In effect they were forced to pioneer again. Using their Meiji strengths but adding the independence and aggressiveness developed after emigrating to a less restrictive society, many had gained the confidence to express their own opinions and to recognize and develop new skills. The restructuring of their lives was marked by their absolute refusal to doubt their ability to survive if the family welfare was at stake.

CHAPTER SIX

Coming Full Circle

Hisayo Hanato

The filial devotion so important to Hisayo, who had emigrated in part to assuage her mother's concern about a sickly sibling, had been passed on to Hisayo's daughter and brought Hisayo's life to full circle a generation later. "We had a house on Pacific Avenue [in Long Beach, California], which I sold to buy this house," she said and added, "because my daughter lives nearby." Hisayo assumed that the implied meaning, that her daughter would care for her, would be understood.

"It is interesting that I have forgotten all the bad experiences," she said, as she appraised her reminiscences. "I seem to remember only the joyous and pleasant events.

"I now have eight grandchildren," she said contentedly, "and I am grateful that every one of my grandchildren is straight and good. Although sometimes I feel that young people are lacking in perseverance," she added, "I realize that they also have some knowledge that I do not have."

Hisayo concluded her life story with an example of her philosophy of life that once again reflected her Meiji attitudes. "Years ago when I was passing through a park in Chicago, I noticed first the big trees, then I saw small trees and finally even the grass. This was nature in balance. We need everything in nature," she said. Confirming her belief in a natural hierarchy learned in a distant time and place, she concluded, "So I think that even though I might not be an important person, I do have a part in my church and in this world, and I appreciate a chance to play my small part in it."

SETSU YOSHIHASHI

Despite her now fragile health, Setsu staunchly declared, "I like America because I hate living in a two-faced society. It's against my character. America doesn't have that–America is a straightforward society," she said, acknowledging the country that nurtured the same character traits that were smothered in Japan. "A person can live honestly and equally here. You can be a house cleaner, grocer, laundry woman, or anything, and no one will make fun of you or look down on you. Even Mrs. Cramer patted me on the back and said, 'You did a good job,' and would encourage me. No one makes you feel stupid. When I took my children to do housework for half a day, Mrs. Cramer would let my children play on her beautiful back lawn. I'd work inside and be paid for the day. Then I realized what a fabulous place America is.

"When the war started, I went to her house, and she said, 'You didn't start the war, so don't worry. Calm yourself and do your work. Bring your valuables and store them in my house.' A millionaire's wife for whom I worked offered to do those things for me. She comforted me with her kind words, too. Such things would never happen in Japan.

"When I think about all this, I realize how democratic America is. I myself looked down on maids and butlers in Japan. It was only after I had to work at different jobs in America that I fully understood the pains and hardships of working as a servant. I earned only fifteen dollars a week, and five children and I lived in one room. What I experienced was *kuro*, the true pains of hardship. I had never known what it was like when I lived in Japan.

"It took me eighteen years to realize that I was a very conceited person, a snob. I was so proud that I came from a high-class military family. My aunt and uncle would tell me we were high class, and I believed them fully. If we needed a car, we would have had a chauffeured car.

"I didn't have any values until I studied Zen. Zen texts say to put your hand on your heart and meditate on your own self-conceit and ask yourself, 'Do you have value as a human being?' When I did this, I felt like I was being poked with needles, and I confessed my faults. It took me eighteen years to reach this point in my life. Then I realized that my sufferings and hardships were caused by my own self-conceited snobbishness," she said, musing over the emotional energy she had expended. "I was thirty-eight years old by then. There is nothing worse than one's own conceit."

Despite her self-criticism, Setsu savors the filial devotion lavished on her by her children. "I am rewarded now," she declared, with the satisfaction of knowing that *gaman*, or endurance, has its rewards. "My eldest son takes such good care of me. He says to me, 'You have really worked hard in your life.'" Then she added, with the satisfaction of a Meiji woman who has successfully imparted the value of filial devotion to her children, "He does everything for me."

Setsu Yoshihashi's goals in life were to educate her children and give them the loving, supportive family life that she lacked as a child. Her goals were not "modern" in that they were goals unmarked by individual, personal achievement, but ones that were realized through the success and devotion of her children. Assessing her life according to her own criteria, Setsu Yoshihashi obviously attained her goals. She concluded her interview with gratitude and praise for a free society that allowed her to achieve those goals. The theme of her life story is not only survival but success.

Ko Haji

Ko Haji had found peace and contentment in the last years of her life and valued the successes of her children and grandchild as her own. "I have only one grandchild," Ko offered. "She is married to a Caucasian. He is a lawyer, and she is also studying law. When they came to visit me, he asked if he could have something [Japanese] as a keepsake. Both are interested in a Japanese heritage. I think he is proud that he is married to a Japanese sansei," she said, relishing the limited connection she had to her granddaughter. But she also addressed the melancholy of having lived a long life.

"As an issei, there is a lonely feeling," she confessed. "It is not the fault of anyone. Times have changed so drastically. It is something hard for us [the issei] to understand, but we have to accept it."

Midori Kimura

As she began her concluding statements, Midori considered her grandchildren and left them with some parting thoughts. "I have four grandchildren. I might be very old-fashioned, but I would like them to learn Japanese manners. It's really important for Japanese. I would like them to also learn to respect older people. In this country aunts and uncles are treated as friends by using their first names. It's good in that everyone feels closer to one another, but I'm not satisfied with that. There must also be respect for older people.

"Even though they are Americans," Midori continued, "the younger generation needs to keep alive the good elements of their Japanese heritage. Yet," she cautioned, still exhibiting the Japanese concern for balance in society as a whole, "if they congregate among themselves too much, that creates its own problems. They need to live as Americans, but they should not forget about their good traditions. This is very important," Midori declared, as she intuitively recognized that it was her Japanese character traits that steadied her and moved her through her most difficult years.

As a victim of prejudice, Midori recognized that "here in America all races must learn to get along with one another. I see that some sansei are still very exclusive. They keep other people from their circles. They reject black people, for instance." Yet Midori also recognized her own problem with prejudice. "I live next door to a Chicano family. My daughter reminded me that we all need to learn to live with one another, so I try not to be prejudiced. If we can wipe out prejudice," she declared optimistically, "we will be able to live peacefully.

"I have interracial marriages in my own family. One of my granddaughters is married to a man of Chinese ancestry. He is a very gentle person. I was worried about his health, so I tried to voice my objections. Then my daughter and son-in-law said that I was prejudiced. I was just concerned because the man did not look very healthy and vigorous. Well, when young people love one another, you can't do much about it.

"My oldest daughter married a Japanese, a bright man. One son, a bachelor for a long time, recently married a white woman. She is a very fine person.

"I am grateful that all of my children graduated from college," Midori stated and then added, "I feel my job is accomplished.

"People ask me, 'Are you still working?'" I answer, 'Money doesn't come from heaven.'" Though she could not use her education in her work, Midori had found satisfaction in the independence that working gave her. She echoed a sentiment that one might expect of a feminist granddaughter. "As long as I work, I don't need to depend on others. There are people who say, 'Give me! Give me!' They receive welfare from the government. I don't want to become like that. It is good to work," she declared. "As long as I'm healthy, I want to work." Midori Kimura was seventy-seven at the time of her interview and she was still working.

Midori Kimura is perhaps the most enigmatic of the issei women whose interviews appear in this collection. After emigrating from Japan, she lived in relative comfort and ease until later in life, when her husband, fourteen years her senior, died leaving her to support and educate seven children. Gathering strength from her Meiji training, Midori exhibited a relentless will to work, survive, and educate her children. She emerged from her ordeal without bitterness and with confidence that she had accomplished her life's work.

SHIZU HAYAKAWA

"It's funny to say that I'm free since my husband died, but for a long time I was burdened and I wondered why God sent so many trials, one after another. But because I came to America, I was able to send my brothers to school. If I had been in Japan," she paused briefly in thought and then quickly added, "a Japanese woman would never be allowed to do this."

Shizu had never lived an easy life. She recalled delivering milk on mountain roads in Japan from dawn until dark. Her mother had died, leaving her father, ill with cancer, to care for nine children. Like all Japanese girls, she could view her future only in terms of eventual marriage. For Shizu the union meant an exciting but anxious trip to a new home in the United States.

Without the support of any immediate family, Shizu led a lonely life with a husband who, after ten years of marriage, became an invalid. Though her relationship with her husband lacked warmth and romantic love, Shizu stoically maintained her adherence to traditional Japanese views of duty and obligation. She never shirked her responsibilities to Mr. Hayakawa and nursed and supported him for over thirty years. During their more than forty years of marriage, Shizu first helped to support her stepmother and younger children and later lent support to a friend and her children. She concluded her life story with statements affirming an energetic commitment to life and the belief that her patience and duty had been rewarded.

"Because I am able to do things for other people and make them happy, I have the strength to live every day. I am told by other issei, 'Woman, you do not have to do so many extra things.' I've been told this many times, but I have the habit of liking work, so I have the energy to live, and," she added emphatically, "I'm very grateful."

A quick perusal of Shizu Hayakawa's commentary may lead to the conclusion that hers is a "little" story; but a closer scrutiny of her life story reveals that it reflects the lives of so many immigrant women whose constancy of effort fed, clothed, nurtured, educated, and inspired a nation's continued growth and development. Without these daily efforts, often performed courageously, the more public feats of individual creativity would have had limited success. Perhaps it is time to reassess our nation's definition of "heroic."

IYO TSUTSUI

"My husband died exactly twenty-one years ago," Iyo Tsutsui said, as her commentary drew to a close. "It was in 1954." Still responding to challenges, Iyo declared, "I was over sixty years old at the time. Well, there is a Japanese saying, 'At sixty begin again to learn how to write.'[1] Even though I had been a tomboy as a child, I thought, 'I'll never learn how to drive.' But after my husband died, I needed to drive. As the saying goes, 'If you need it, you'll do it.'

"I went to a driving school, and on the eighth day the instructor asked me if I would like to take the test. I said, 'I'm afraid.' He reassured me and said, 'There is nothing to be afraid of.' Well," Iyo said with satisfaction, "I passed the test on the first try. Then one of my boys bought me a new car. It was a present," Iyo said with pleasure. Instead of using the car for leisure in her declining years, Iyo said, "With this car I could get work picking grapes and harvesting potatoes and asparagus on Bacon Island. I worked so hard that when I took off my shirt, I could see white salt deposits of perspiration on the cloth."

After all the years of working for her family, Iyo's hard work was now for herself. Ever practical, she said, "I thought that if I worked, I'd be eligible for Social Security.

"I lived here alone at the time and felt there was nothing to worry about because I had my faith in God. There is no way to measure it, but I think my faith helped. When you have faith, you are not afraid. Otherwise," Iyo added, "no woman could stay out here alone.

[1]The Japanese believe that life is cyclical and that at age sixty (five times twelve, a lucky number combination), a person's life begins again.

"My son had planned a trip to Mexico, but before he left, he bought me a pistol. He thought an old woman like me needed to be able to defend herself. He said, 'If you must defend yourself and there is no other way out, use this.' He took me to the river and taught me how to shoot.

"One night I was asleep, and I heard the dog barking about 4:00 A.M. I got up and peeked out the window. I saw a man in a white shirt coming toward me. I had not locked the door because there had never been any reason to. Well," she continued, "the prowler came around to the back door and knocked. I didn't answer because if he found that an old woman was the only one here, there was no telling what he might do.

"He just gave up and walked away. My car was in the shed and he was walking in that direction. Then I remembered that I had left my keys in the ignition. I saw the car lights go on and thought he was going to run off with my car.

"I went out the front door and fired a couple of shots toward the river. Then I ran back into the house and phoned a boy who worked for us on the ranch. Finally, he answered the call in a sleepy voice. I said, 'There is someone prowling around; please come over quickly!' Then he woke up and said, 'Okay!' and ran over, but the man had gone.

"I asked the boy if he had met someone on the way. He hadn't, but he had seen a pickup truck abandoned in a ditch. I called the sheriff, and they found footprints. The truck in the ditch had been stolen from the government. Someone had tried to hide the government decal on the door by painting over it.

"I must be a very dense person because I wasn't afraid at all. In the daytime people have come and vandalized the place, but they took only very small things. I wasn't lonesome either," Iyo declared. "Now," Iyo added, "Helen, her husband, and three children have moved in.

"In Japan, I was scared to be alone. Even if it got a little dark, I had to have someone go out with me," Iyo recalled. I have changed a great deal. I've become very strong. It's just as my father said, 'If you haven't done anything wrong, you don't have to be afraid.' I believe that."

Realizing that her strength developed as a result of leaving Japan and living in the United States, Iyo reflected upon the differences between herself and her sister. "When I visited Japan in 1969, my older sister, who was a wise person," Iyo carefully added, "told me that I talked too much. Once spoken, words can never be taken back. Though my sister adopted one child from her husband's side of the family and one through an agency, her family is very peaceful, because she never does anything to ruffle feathers. She's never suffered much materially or otherwise.

"I'll be eighty years old next month," Iyo declared, but the conflict between an ingrained image of a mature, refined, Japanese woman and her active, actual self continued to concern Iyo. "I have a friend," she said, "Mrs. Muraki, who is about seventy. I asked her what she had been doing since she retired. 'Are you ready to die?'" Iyo bluntly asked. "She said to me, 'Mrs. Tsutsui, I've got no time to die. I'm so busy, I don't have enough time to do all that I want to do.' Then I asked, 'What are you doing?' She said, 'Well, we take turns visiting the *Keiro* [a convalescent home for the elderly Japanese] and help those who cannot eat by themselves.'

"I do have a desire to do such work," Iyo said, "and I am very envious of Mrs. Muraki. But I live in the country. I used to drive, but my doctor made me give it up after I had an operation on my leg. Instead," she said with relish, "I go fishing a lot. There is a river in front of our house where I catch perch, catfish, or striped bass. Sometimes my daughter takes me up to the High Sierra. I like to go there. I have to hike down to the fishing hole and climb up and down the road to the water. I just cannot sit still. I have to be moving all the time or reading books. I work in the backyard or fish. That's why I'm very healthy. If your muscles shrivel up, that's the end of you," she declared. But then she added with old, nagging doubts, "Sometimes I don't know whether I'm doing the right thing. I, too, want to help someone.

"There are things I would like to teach the sansei," Iyo stated. "I would like them [the sansei] not to act like they are superior. People don't like to be looked down upon. And everyone should always try to help others. Even in a household each person should try to help the other." Then Iyo reiterated the Meiji lessons that had stood her in good stead these many years. "One must also learn not to be careless or wasteful with things. Everything costs someone something. Someone took the time to make each thing, so one needs to be thankful about the things he has. That's what I say to children all the time.

"Children should also know how to say, 'Thank you.' When I went to Japan in 1969, I was surprised to find that children there used their parents just like servants. They'd say, 'Mother, I need this.' Before the war, it wasn't like that. After the war, people forgot to train their children. Parents seemed to act like children. Even after they finished dinner, they would say, *Gochiso sama*,

[The food was well-prepared and I am finished.] and go to their rooms. No one stayed and helped their parents. Most of the children here would at least take their dishes to the sink. I was disgusted with the lack of family education and manners. Japan needs to relearn order and manners. In the old days, they taught *shushin* [moral lessons] at school and at home. Children must learn good habits when they are very young.

"One must also experience hardships and learn to overcome obstacles," Iyo added, recalling how she managed the *kuro* in her own life. "This spiritual [lesson] is very valuable. Then a real human being is born. I don't think there is a future for people who have not experienced hardships." And then she added this assessment of her own life, "I don't think I suffered in terms of not having material things."

Iyo was over eighty years old when she was interviewed. Her son's family had come to live with her on her farm, but she had lived alone until she was well into her sixties, enjoying her independence, and was never fearful or lonely. And though she worked hard for her family, Iyo, unlike most issei women, did not measure her happiness only in terms of the successes of her children.

"I think a lot about the past. If I were young again, I wouldn't be farming. I think that I would run a hotel or some other kind of business.

"I think I've been happy because I came to the United States," Iyo stated with assurance, because she recognized that her own sense of independence would never have been allowed to grow in Japan. "When I think about Japan," she explained, "particularly the fact that Japanese people are too formal, I am happy that I came to this country. I prefer a more relaxed way of life. If I were in Japan," she speculated, "I would have created many enemies because I speak my mind too much.

"Americans are very broad-minded in many ways. This is the national character, I think. They don't really care what others do. If you were in Japan, you must do exactly what your neighbors do. I don't like that. I was lucky that I was sent to America," Iyo said with assurance, and added, "but I'm very proud of the fact that I'm Japanese."

TEIKO TOMITA

As a young girl, Teiko Tomita saw her dream of becoming a high school teacher thwarted. Rather than succumb to disappointment, Teiko became an elementary school teacher. When immigration brought a life of manual labor and the tragic loss of a child, Teiko still endured. Her life had been a lesson in *gaman*. Then, after toiling for thirteen years to build a nursery business from nothing, Teiko and her husband saw the small measure of success they had crushed by the events of World War II. Undaunted by the task of rebuilding from scratch, Teiko convinced her husband to leave a pleasant and secure job in Minnesota and try once again. Some years later, a new house, built by the devotion of their sons, seemed to be a sign that their fortunes had finally changed, until an airport expansion condemned their home.

"We were getting older by then and felt insecure about living by ourselves. My daughter lived in an apartment with her two children and husband, and they were looking for a house to buy. 'This might be a good chance for us to find a place to live with Kay and her family,' my husband said after much thought. 'I would like that,' I said, 'but nowadays young people have their own ideas. We need to find out how they feel about it.

"Papa asked Kay, and she said it was fine with her. We said that she should consult her husband since he is really *tanin* [outsider].[2] We didn't want him to feel awkward, and there was also their future to consider. A few days later they gave us their answer. They would welcome us. They said that Papa was such a nice person that they wouldn't have any trouble living with him.

"We looked for a house together. It had to satisfy all our needs–two old people and a young couple with children. My husband wanted to have two separate households. If we had enough time to build a house, then it would have been easier, but we had to vacate our house quickly.

"Fortunately, a woman realtor, a Japanese, told us about a new construction site. One house already had a foundation laid, but it was early enough to make changes in the original plan.

"It was a two-story house with three bedrooms, a nice-looking house with a large basement, half of which was above street level. We changed the basement into an apartment with a large bathroom, kitchen, and parlor. It was made in such a way that we could live independently. It was only a two-block walk to a bus stop, though it was a little distance to a store.

"After we moved in, Kay and her husband said, 'We live together, so why don't we eat dinner together?' We agreed that it would be very nice. Sometimes I made a small dish for them, too.

[2]In this case the Tomitas' son-in-law is considered an outsider because he is not blood related.

"After we moved over here, Papa didn't have to work in the fields anymore. He said that he wanted to visit our first son, who lived in Minnesota. It was the first time he had ever talked about it. Papa said that he didn't want to take a plane because he got motion sickness. If he let that stop him, he'd never visit anyone. Finally we decided to go anyway. The plane ride took only two and a half hours and was so pleasant that he was encouraged and began to talk about visiting Japan. I said, 'Oh, you've been saying for years that you didn't want to go to Japan.' 'It's not so much that I changed my mind,' he said, 'but if I don't go, you won't go. You have been in this country for over fifty years but have had no chance to visit Japan. Let's go next year.'

"He didn't think most of his relatives would be alive, but when we went, his nieces and nephews came out to welcome him. They were in their sixties and seventies. I had my sisters, their children, and grandchildren. We were welcomed by everyone. When we returned, he was content and said, 'Oh, it was such a good visit. I can die anytime now.'

"Little by little my husband's legs got weak and finally he could not climb the stairs anymore. He became weaker and died very peacefully. He even ate very well until the end. After everything settled down from the funeral, I rejoined my daughter's family for dinner meals.

Reflecting on the memories dredged up by her commentary, Teiko said, "I suppose people think that I still carry pain when I talk about my lost child. Every anniversary of that tragic day, I visit her grave and make an offering to the church and offer a prayer myself. I don't know how I survived those days. That's when I joined the church."

In explanation of that tragic event, Teiko offered, "Without hardships, I would never have known gratitude. Life is a long, long journey with lots and lots of problems. One of my joys now is that I have no more worries about my children or my grandchildren.

"Well, this concludes the story of his long life. It was full of troubles and tragedies. However, most of us went through similar experiences. We never knew what would happen on the next day.

"Now it's my turn. I don't know how my life will end. I only wish not to trouble my children too much. My life is very good now with nothing to complain about. There is no worry, no illness. When I am lonesome, my children comfort me. I feel very happy. One day I laughed and said, 'Even if I die today, there is no one to be troubled by my death. I can die anytime now.' Everyone said, 'You mustn't talk like that. We want you to live until you are a hundred years old.' It has been a long, long life with lots of twists and turns; however, I feel I've come to the last place of my pilgrimage."

Teiko concluded her interview indicating that this was "the story of *his* [italics mine] long life," identifying that whatever was his, was also hers; yet there seemed to be no sense of subservience, only one of sharing. The Tomitas began their lives together with the tradition of a wife's subservience to her husband, but in a less restrictive society this was modified. They also shared years of grueling work in which they were at least equal partners. Then came another modification when the years in relocation camps offered time for reflection and an equal weighing of two individual opinions. Finally, they shared in the rich benefits of a warm and caring family life. Teiko Tomita's concluding remarks are full of pride in her children and such contentment and inner peace that it seems appropriate to celebrate quietly the recounting of her life story.

KIYO MIYAKE

As the years progressed and the Miyakes resumed their lives after the war, Kiyo's comments about that time reflected the ability of the issei to continue to learn and commit themselves as citizens despite their advancing years. "We studied for citizenship later on," she explained." The Immigration and Nationalization Act of 1952 finally allowed persons of any race to apply for citizenship. "At first we studied in Japanese, but later on we switched to English because we thought we should be able to understand in English as well. After all, we had been in this country for over fifty years.

"My second son worked [our land] with my husband. In 1954, eight years after we returned [from the relocation camp], my husband died of a diabetic condition. Towards the end, he lost the sight in one of his eyes, but he worked until the last two months before his death." And with continued regard for her husband, Kiyo added, "Even in failing health, he worked twice as hard as anyone else."

Sitting in her home in Livingston, California, on the same parcel of land purchased more than fifty years earlier, Kiyo Miyake observed of her generation, "One handicap the issei have is that they cannot communicate with the young Japanese. They [the young] don't speak Japanese, their interests are different, and they live in a different world. Yet I feel I have lots of things to say to them," she said and presented this assessment: "The issei have endured many trials. The nisei are doing very well now; however, it was the issei who built a foundation for them. This was our most important accomplishment."

Recalling her dream of living Millet's *Angelus*, wondering how she processed those tons of raisins, remembering those energetic discussions with her husband each evening, and expressing her satisfaction with what she accomplished as a social worker in the relocation camp, Kiyo concluded her life story with some final observations.

"Without going through hardships," she said referring to the Meiji concept of *kuro*, "a man cannot understand much. Japanese old people knew more than modern philosophers. Their understanding was deep. I used to argue with my grandmother, but I understand her now. They [the old ones] did not go to school and study many subjects, but they knew a lot about living. They could estimate time by the sun and learn many things by watching worms. Even modern medicine can learn something from ancient herb medicine.

"When we say, 'I'm a Japanese,' I understand the good qualities that Japanese have. That's how we begin to build pride. But everyone still needs to keep growing. I always say to my grandchildren that sincerity, knowledge, and health, these three things, are the most important things in life.

"Japanese young people who can live in white society and deal with whites with dignity are those who have some feeling that they are Japanese. Without this strong sense of identity, they would be afraid. I have noticed that there are those Japanese Americans who have a tendency toward self-abasement. It is because they don't have something solid inside to help them stand up for themselves. Because of their historical handicap, Japanese Americans felt they needed to be more capable and more self-assured than the average white American."

o o o o o o o o o o o o o

Issei women never became prominent political figures, stars of the stage and screen, renowned philosophers, or giants of business; yet their contribution to the fabric of American life is enormous. they leave us not a legacy of self-effacement, but with another perspective on what constitutes success. Their lives are a testimony to excellence without a need for personal glorification, and they find contentment in having constructed a firm foundation for future generations.

Like the gardener in Etsu Inagaki's comment who "voluntarily undid half a day's work to change the position of a single stepping stone," issei women often gave up what was safe in their lives because they never lost their hold "on the best."

Their words echo through the generations that have followed. "I've never said this to anyone before," Kiyo Miyake said, as she ended her life story with a confession spoken hesitantly so as not to be construed as a personal compliment, "but I am very impressed with issei women."

List of Interviews

AKIYAMA, ONATSU, No. 176, Sacramento, California,
June 29, 1977.

FUJIMOTO, KATSUNO, No. 79, Los Angeles, California,
June 23, 1972.

HAJI, KO, No. 74, Seattle, Washington,
May 21, 1974.

HANATO, HISAYO, No. 95, Long Beach, California,
November 22,1974.

HAYAKAWA, SHIZU, No. 47, San Francisco, California,
November 26, 1973.

HIRONAKA, SATSUYO, No. 83, Sacramento, California,
July 26, 1974.

KIMURA, MIDORI, No. 98, San Jose, California,
December 12, 1974.

MIYAKE, KIYO, No. 142, Livingston, California,
July 30, 1975.

TOMITA, TEIKO, No. 76, Seattle, Washington,
May 21, 1974.

Tsutsui, Iyo, No. 13, Stockton, California,
February 9, 1978.

Yoshihashi, Setsu, No. 184, San Gabriel, California,
February 9, 1978.

All of the interviews above are located in a closed collection maintained by the Sacramento Museum and History Commission. By direction of the Issei Oral History Project, Inc., the collection will be available for public use after the year 2000.

Glossary

aka (red; communist)
akirameru (accept one's fate)
akiramete imashita (we were resigned to it)
amaeru (exhibit affectionate behavior)
arigato gozaimasu (thank you very much)
azuki (red beans)

banshaku (light evening drink)
betto (military aide)
botamochi (rice cake dumpling covered with sweetened bean paste)
bunke (loss of the right to inherit family property)
butsudan (household Buddhist shrine)

chawan (rice bowl)
cho (blocks--distance)
chochin (paper lanterns)
choshi (sake bottle)

daikon (Japanese radish)

engawa (veranda)

furo (Japanese-style tubs)
futon (japanese comforter)

gaman (endurance)
geta (wooden slippers elevated on two horizontal slats)
gochiso (party food)
gochiso sama (the food was well prepared and I am finished)
goza (a thin straw mat)

haiku (a 17-syllable verse form)
happa (half and half)
hosuka (finishing school)
hotokesama (miniature Buddhist altar kept in individual households)

inu (dog)

jinjoka (elementary school)
jogakko (girls' high school)

kakucho (record of the ancestors)
kagezen (meal for an absent person)
karuta (a card game)
katta gumi (winners' group)

keiro (convalescent home for
    elderly Japanese)
Keiyo (Seoul)
*ke*n (prefecture)
kendo (Japanese fencing)
kengaku ryoko (field trips)
kesa (formal priest's attire)
keto keto (hairy foreigner)
kibei (American citizens by birth
    educated in Japan who
    returned to the United
    States before World War II)
kiheitei (cavalry)
koseki (family register)
*koto*ka (equivalent of junior high
    school)
koto shihan (higher normal or
    teachers' college)
koto shogako (eighth grade)
kuro (severe physical or emotional
    hardship)

makete katsu (lose and win)
mino (straw raincoat)
mise gane (money to show that
    the immigrant was not
    indigent)
miso (soybean paste)
mochi (rice dumplings)
mushiro (thick straw mat used to
    dry grains)
mugi gohan nigiri (rice balls made
    of rice and wheat)

nakodo (go-between, matchmaker)
nata (hatchet)
naijo no ko (a wife is supposed to
    assist her husband)
Neisan (older sister)
Niisan (big brother)
ninjo (humanity, common kindness)

nisei (children of the issei born in
    the United States; second
    generation)

Obasan (elderly lady)
ofuro (Japanese bath)
ofuroya (bathhouses)
ohakamgiri (visiting a loved one's
    grave)
ojiisan (grandfather)
okasan (mother)
okayu (rice gruel)
omiyai (meeting of prospective
    spouses)
on (favors or acts of kindness)
onigiri (rice balls)
oyakoko (filial piety)
oyakoko seinin (young man who
    loved his father)
oyakudo mairi (saying one
    hundred prayers)
ozen (small dining table)

rekidai bako (family crypt)
ryoriya (Japanese restaurant)

saitako (Japanese emigrants to the
    United States who returned
    to Japan to visit and then
    returned to the United
    States)
sakajuki (wine cup)
sakaya (sake maker)
sake (rice wine)
sansei (grandchildren of the issei;
    third generation)
sashimi (raw fish)
sen (about half a cent)
seppuku (ritual suicide)
shan shan (walking with pride)
shichiya (pawnshop)

shikataganai (it cannot be helped)

shin heimin (lowest class of people in Japanese society)

shinpoteki (a progressive, modern person)

shinsu (moral lessons)

shinteo (free samples)

shoppaina (salty)

shoyu (soy sauce)

shushin (moral lessons)

somen (thin noodles)

soroban (abacus)

sushi (cold rice specialty)

sumimasen (I'm very sorry)

taiko (Japanese drum)

tako (octopus)

tanin (outsider)

taru (wooden containers)

tasuki (sash to tuck up kimono sleeves)

tentori mushi (a greasy grind)

tofu (soybean curd)

tokuhon (reading)

tori (bird)

waka (a 31-syllable verse form)

warabi (young, edible bracken)

waraji (straw sandals)

Yamato Damashii (the soul of Japan)

Yaso (Christian)

yojyo (adopted daughter)

yoshi (adopted sons-in-law)

zori (thonged sandal)

Index